WHAT PEOPLE ARE SA

NATURAL BORN SHAMANS

What a gift Imelda Almqvist's work is for our global community! Rarely have I met someone with such a spiritual and creative force. Imelda brings a freshness into her shamanic teaching and sacred art courses. Her Time Traveller's workshops with children are so needed and are unsurpassed in their power and healing. Imelda is a brilliant shamanic teacher with so much to offer.
Sandra Ingerman, author of *Soul Retrieval* and *Medicine for the Earth*

No one who has helped create a funeral for a deceased family pet doubts that children have an inherent spirituality, but it's a restless and unpredictable force. A rabbit in the garden, clouds across the moon, prophetic dreams about grandparents...small incidents of profound wonder and startling insights, but nothing that fits easily inside formal religion. Too often, for lack of a clear context to engage with this wonder, we try to tame it, discourage it, or simply ignore it. But what if we could meet a child's spiritual capacity where it lives and fan the flame? Imelda Almqvist's shamanic work with children dives straight into the heart of that place of wonder, and supports the rich experiential connections that children already have with nature's spiritual heartbeat. This is work that can help each young being learn to trust himself or herself, and to better step into the world at large, with imagination, creativity and self-worth intact. This is the empowered, wisdom-nurturing future I wish for every child!
Renna Shesso, author of *Planets for Pagans: Sacred Sites, Ancient Lore* and *Magical Stargazing and Math for Mystics*

Almqvist has written and devised a powerful shamanic tool for children (and their parents) whose lives will be blessed and beautifully touched by an exploration of her words and guidance. As a mother of young children I am extremely excited by this offering and the potential it offers to the spirit and lives of my young girls. *Natural Born Shamans* is a truly enchanting gift to future generations, in a time when it is sorely needed! Thank you Imelda for sharing your path, your insight and its power, magic and soulful joy with our little ones.
Alice Grist, spiritual author of *The High Heeled Guide to Enlightenment/Spiritual Living* and publisher (Soul Rocks Books)

I first came to the TT group as part of my research on Celtic shamanism for an independent project at school. I'd been fascinated by Celtic myths and culture as far as I can remember and was curious about any associated spirituality. I know Imelda's group is about broader shamanic practices, but this is how I came across the group.

Within the group, we have explored divination, spirit journeying and connecting with our spirit animals. We also discuss many topical issues that concern us, either personally or wider social ones. It gives us young people (our ages are seven to 15) a supportive space to share, learn and reflect. By going to the TT group, I realised I'd always had spirit animals, but now I'm more focused and conscious about them. I've also been able to bring more specifically shamanic practices (such as drumming) into my everyday life. I feel a lot more confident and centred about my spirituality.

Imelda is very patient and understanding, allowing us to really develop our own responses and we generally share them in a positive way. The games we play, that are always linked, are really enjoyable and encourage a deep level of connection to nature.
Ruby Van Alphen Gilburt, aged 14.

Imelda Almqvist is not only a brilliant shamanic practitioner and teacher she is a phenomenal artist and writer! Be assured when Imelda says something it has been well researched – not only with her helping spirits, but also with all available resources on Earth! I am honoured to call her a friend and colleague and look forward to the stunning success of this latest book.
Dory Cote, shamanic practitioner and teacher, The Center for Earth Light Healing, Brunswick, ME, USA

My 10-year-old son has been going the Imelda's Time Travellers group since it began over three years ago. The spiritual toolbox which he's cultivated in that time cannot be overestimated. He has a close relationship with his power animals, brilliant journeying skills and a firm grasp on several healing modalities among other shamanic talents. His sense of the sacredness of all beings and the spirit in all things is a joy to see. Not only does he have enormous fun in each session, but he also has an ever-growing confidence in his own spiritual connection and authority. I feel strongly that these shamanic teachings give him the best platform from which he can go out into the world with confidence and compassion. He has learned and is learning his own sacred place in the world. Our children truly are natural shamans and Imelda is such a brilliant teacher because she not only sees this so well, but she also allows them to trust their own relationship with spirit, their connection to the universe and their absolute right to be who they are. I wish I'd had such a group as a child. Children are Natural Born Shamans and I'm thrilled this important book has been written as a spiritual toolkit for our young people. Imelda is a true seer and weaves her magic from the heart of spirit!
Marie Lloyd, Mother of a Time Traveller

Imelda has written a blueprint for parents, grandparents, teachers, healers, practitioners and, indeed, our children so that

we may support our young people and future generations in a meaningful, holistic and compassionate way of living. By sharing her life experiences and the experiences of her healing work with our children, Imelda gives insights into supporting them in assisting not only in their own healing, but also healing our nucleic families, our communities, and our planet. This book will empower young people to dream a powerful and loving dream for their own lives and for the future. This book should be required reading.
Janet Elizabeth Gale, shamanic practitioner, teacher, and author of *The Rush Hour Shaman: Shamanic Practices for Urban Living*

Have you noticed how wise and sensitive your children are? In a way that may isolate them or expose them to abuse such as bullying by their peers? Imelda Almqvist, herself mother to three wise young people, presents us with a manual of practical magic for children: for how to encourage them to shine their inner light and allow the flowering of their gifts while facilitating growing up safely in a world that may not (yet) appreciate these gifts. Teaching our children how to use their spiritual gifts wisely is a new training ground in our Western society – and yet a very old one. *Natural Born Shamans* fills in the gap that opened up when we forgot our ancestral ways of preparing for the greatest Initiation of all – growing up. May this book travel to places near and far and serve the well-being of all children.

Thank you Imelda for showing the way, I'm grateful and honoured to share the journey.
Judith Bogner, TV presenter, corporate event facilitator, speaker, actress and shamanic practitioner

I want to say how deeply pleased it makes me to think of such a beautiful, important, elegant and personal book being available to young people and adults. Imelda, you write with care, humour and honesty, drawing us back to key points with gentle persistence

and allowing us to enjoy your experiences alongside with you. The guide for offering shamanic training for young people is so necessary and so joyous to see, and is both complete and very clear to understand. Imelda, I raise a mint-coke bomb to you and all the future ancestors whose lives will be enriched by this book.
Nick Taylor, author of *The Parable of His-Story*

Natural Born Shamans – A Spiritual Toolkit for Life

Using Shamanism Creatively with Young People of all Ages

Natural Born Shamans – A Spiritual Toolkit for Life

Using Shamanism Creatively with Young People of all Ages

Imelda Almqvist

Foreword by Sandra Ingerman

MOON BOOKS

Winchester, UK
Washington, USA

First published by Moon Books, 2016
Moon Books is an imprint of John Hunt Publishing Ltd., Laurel House, Station Approach, Alresford, Hants, SO24 9JH, UK
office1@jhpbooks.net
www.johnhuntpublishing.com
www.moon-books.net

For distributor details and how to order please visit the 'Ordering' section on our website.

ISBN: 978 1 78535 368 0
Library of Congress Control Number: 2016931744

A CIP catalogue record for this book is available from the British Library.

Design: Stuart Davies

Printed and bound by CPI Group (UK) Ltd, Croydon, CR0 4YY, UK

CONTENTS

To Quinn, Elliott and Brendan, our own three Natural Born Shamans and my greatest teachers. To all Time Travellers of the Present, Past and Future in my group. To my helping spirits who insisted I do this work. To my mother Nel Berendsen-Oud and in honour of my late father Herman Berendsen. To the Spirit of our house, for hosting and holding all that needs to unfold in safe sacred space. Last but not least to my husband, Ulric Almqvist.

Foreword by Sandra Ingerman

Giving birth to a child is such a precious gift, for life on this Earth is precious. We have hopes and dreams for our children that they will blossom into individuals who will manifest a life that reflects their dreams and desires. We wish the best for our children and hope they will contribute to the health of their communities and to the world.

In shamanic cultures when a child is born they are recognized for the gifts and talents they came into the world with and how they will contribute to the health of the community. Children are raised to embrace their true creative nature. They are taught that they are part of nature and how to honor all of life on this Earth. In community everyone learns how they are part of a larger whole and how to support each child in encouraging strength in each other. The work of empowering children starts from when they are in utero and continues to when they are welcomed into the world and throughout their lives.

In our modern day world we have broken many of the laws of nature. And unfortunately, despite some of the gifts available to us that come from living in a modern world, we no longer support a healthy life for our children, teens, and young adults. Nor do we give them the tools needed to navigate through life, inspire them to be the most creative beings they can be, and teach them how to live in harmony with nature and with their own peer group.

To re-introduce our children, teens, and young adults to how to live a healthy way of life on all levels is a desire for many parents and also our responsibility as a community. Many parents have lost their way and due to the breakdown in behavioral issues of how children bond together new tools are needed to heal the overwhelming issues that our children face today. We need to re-introduce children to spiritual principles that will help to empower them and lead them into living a fulfilled life that contributes to the whole.

Imelda Almqvist is so passionate about providing tools for parents and teachers who are seeking ways to heal many of the issues that our children face today. Imelda has courageously been willing 'to step out of the box' and explore spiritual practices that can be bridged into helping children find a good roadmap in a world going through such challenging transitions on all levels.

Natural Born Shamans – A Spiritual Toolkit for Life covers all aspects of doing spiritual or shamanic work with children and young people. The book is written for anyone who has an interest in young people and providing them with a good spiritual foundation. Imelda covers group and individual work from 'in utero' until age 18-plus. She describes the guiding principles behind shamanic parenting.

In *Natural Born Shamans* Imelda maps the challenges of doing spiritual work with children. For in a modern-day culture there are still prejudices and fears created by beliefs in society. She teaches how to dance with these issues and respect the boundaries of other belief systems. The book discusses the most pressing concerns for all age groups. And it addresses the unique challenges that children and young people face at this present time. These types of challenges might include self-harming, violence, addiction to video games, and so on. There is a spiritual perspective that Imelda opens us up to on what issues really seek healing through these destructive behaviors.

We are also given guidance for nurturing the natural and inborn gifts that these bright souls offer to our communities and lives today. This will serve a brighter future for our planet.

There is such a wealth of information that Imelda covers in this book. She even opens a powerful doorway to describe ways of doing spiritual healing work with both unborn babies and spirit children after a devastating miscarriage has occurred, an abortion or early death. Imelda shares how doing shamanic work with young children differs from working with adults or teenagers. *Natural Born Shamans* covers a lot of ground.

Natural Born Shamans also provides 32 'tried and tested' session plans for people looking for inspiration and 'where to start'. It ends with a section about rites of passage and initiation for young people today. It gives examples of highly innovative work being done right now in accordance with the spirit of our times and the needs of young people being born at a critical time of great global upheaval and paradigm shift.

This is such an important book for the times we live in!

To address the deep need of the times Imelda started a Time Travellers Group that has been running for at least four years. This group was born out of her experience of doing individual shamanic work with children over a period of many years. During this period she received an abundance of emails from parents, teachers, grandparents and others involved with young people in manifold capacities from all over the world. These correspondences were filled with requests asking Imelda to put her own experiences in writing, allowing others to use material she had arrived at through her dedication to her work and through trial and error.

There is a true lack of information in this field that *Natural Born Shamans* meets. There is a burning need for a book that discusses all possible aspects of using shamanism in fun and innovative ways with children of all age groups. Questions that parents and grandparents have asked Imelda through their correspondence with her became seed chapters for some of the information provided in the book.

I think this book is important at this time because it shows how to use shamanism creatively with young people, opening safe sacred space where they themselves communicate with helping spirits and receive a viable toolkit. The young people themselves have put forward many themes and pressing concerns over the years such as bullying, public speaking, communicating with pets and healing animals, conflict resolution, building resilience, doing dream work, coping with nightmares, creative writing, and so on. Imelda has made a point of acting as a 'scribe and organizer' so the voices of children and teenagers themselves are heard and their own wisdom shines through, showing all of us the shamanism of the future taking shape. Young people whose innate spirituality is fed and stays intact make life choices that promote wholeness, balance and respect for all sentient beings.

I have had the wonderful opportunity to train Imelda Almqvist to be a teacher of shamanic work. In the process she has become a peer and a leader who has a wealth of information, guidance, love, and compassion to share. I have always been awestruck by Imelda's creativity and how she is willing to take on the most challenging topics that deal with how to help children and adults work through issues we are all being faced with to thrive during these changing times.

This book is brilliantly written and is a must read for all of you who are interested in how we can lead our children into a healthier way of life and a bright future.

Sandra Ingerman, author of 10 books on shamanism
Santa Fe, New Mexico
December 2015

Preface

One night the spirits came and demanded I became a shamanic practitioner. It was the last thing I had in mind but, with great trepidation, I answered the call. One day several years later the spirits came again and demanded I start a shamanic group for young people. The notion of teaching shamanism to young children and teenagers seemed overwhelming (where to start?!), but I created The Time Travellers programme in London, UK, and it is still running four years later.

My name is Imelda Almqvist. I am a Dutch shamanic painter, practitioner and teacher, based in London, UK, at the time of writing this book. I have three sons (born in 2000, 2001 and 2004) with my Swedish husband. As a child I grew up in a Roman Catholic family in the Netherlands. I was a voracious reader and had an exceptional vocabulary for a girl my age, but I would not have known the word shaman. It was never mentioned in our house for all of the 18 years I lived with my parents.

I often had premonitions and a sense of deep inner knowing about things. I realised that I knew things without being told. I spooked people by knowing things about them that they had not shared with me. I quickly realised that I had better develop a cast-iron memory (helped by good genes on my father's side of the family!) In my mind I created a filing system where I kept 'voice recordings' of all conversations I had with people. While talking to people I would be scanning those files to avoid making a faux pas. I became very good at this over the years. I made it a rule to never mention anything I knew or saw on a psychic level, unless the person themselves raised an issue or indicated they wanted to hear. I soon discovered that the word *dream* is very useful in this context. Even today I will often say to people: 'I had a powerful dream about you, would you like to know what happened?' By saying yes, people give permission for the material to be shared in a non-threatening way.

As a very young child the spirits often called me at night to help newly dead people move between worlds. Today I know that the word for this is psychopomp work (also known as soul conducting or death walking. They would say: 'This person just does not seem to realise he is dead. We can't seem to get through to him at all. If a little girl appears, this might just be more familiar for the person. So could you please go and have a word?'

Today I do *not* recommend that young children do this work, because it can be very risky. However, I remain grateful for my own experience. As a shamanic practitioner today I can talk to children who have these abilities and understand what they see at night. I can give their parents advice on how to manage this issue, keep their children safe and create the right circumstances for uninterrupted sleep at night.

By means of a very quick introduction to other realms, in shamanism we make a distinction between *everyday reality* (life on Earth in material form, the things we can see and touch, consensual reality where you and other people agree on what is going on, like meeting for tea at 2pm today) and *non-ordinary reality* (this phrase was coined by Michael Harner), meaning the energetic parallel world, the Other World, the spirit world, the non-material eternal world. And in many ways the Other World has always been more real to me than the material world. I have always felt safe, loved and at home in the spirit world. I have known from birth that compassionate beings watch over me and guide me.

As a child I grew up wanting to be a medical doctor (the closest I could come to understanding my innate desire to help others and heal). I chose Latin and all sciences for my exam subjects to prepare for studying medicine, but then decided to switch to studying fine art and art history instead. At the age of 18 I moved to Amsterdam, in the Netherlands, to attend art school. In the decades that followed, those happy years, I very literally painted my way into shamanism. For me painting has always been about making unseen worlds visible and accessible to others.

Around my 40th birthday the spirits came and kept me up all night, saying it was time to become a shaman (and in the Western world we say shamanic practitioner out of respect for indigenous shamans, but I did not know that yet). This was not remotely what my waking egoic mind wanted for myself. By then I had been reading many books about anthropology and indigenous cultures. I had also made many paintings inspired by shamanic cultures, myths and dreams. And I knew one thing: if the spirits call you to become a shaman, you don't mess around. You answer the call and face the initiations and blessings of this path. The spirits have this way of always asking you to do things that strike fear in your heart. My shamanic practitioner training involved digging my own grave and undergoing a life burial. I had barely recovered from the rigours of the practitioner training before the spirits demanded that I start teaching my own courses in sacred art and shamanism.

Once I got all that up and running they came again one night and said: 'You need to start a shamanic group for young people now! You have seen a lot of children for individual healings sessions in your shamanic practice, but these children need to meet others who struggle with the same issues. They need community and a spiritual toolkit! And you are the person in the right position to provide this!'

In truth I thought: 'Not again! Not another impossible demand please! I would like to have a quiet and stress-free life!' But, as before, I knew that the spirits were asking for very good reasons. The Time Travellers group was born on the day of the Venus Transit, June 5th 2012. I have learned some astrology since. I think it was an auspicious day.

Introduction: Why am I Writing this Book?

When my children were younger, they would entertain themselves during car journeys by calling a race. All cars around us were 'in the race', if completely unaware of it. Our children would get very upset if any car overtook us because *they might now win the race.* In reality all these cars had different starting points and destinations. Some were big fancy cars and others were old bangers. They were never in any race, they were just on their individual journeys – but try convincing three young children of that! Today this memory returned and it seemed like a metaphor for the way we live. We treat Life as a race or competition (with all the aggression and fear of losing the race inherent in that), when actually there are only many journeys all unfolding at the same time...

There are so many books out there. For years now people have been asking me: 'When will you write that book about your shamanic work with children?' My answer has always been: 'I am not going to write a book just to have a book to my name. I will only write a book if I truly feel I have material to share that is fresh and of benefit to others.'

Over the past three years I have slowly arrived at this point. I have received many emails from colleagues asking about my shamanic work with children and teenagers. They have referred many people based all over the world to me: parents, grandparents, teachers and professionals in other fields. People tell me that they need pointers, ideas, tried and tested session plans. I gradually realised that I perhaps I was sitting on material and experiences that could be helpful for others. Putting my own experiences, and my own learning journey, in book form also means that hopefully others can avoid inventing the wheel all over again, because they can learn from the mistakes I made.

The Thirst for Magic

The Harry Potter books and movies have been a runaway success. What this tells me is that in our very linear society, where the dominant worldview is scientific and evidence-based, a great Thirst for Magic remains. This phrase was coined by my colleague Stuart Dole and I thank him for permission to use it. Children crave magic. Even adults crave magic. This book addresses this need and gives very practical pointers (even detailed session plans) for creating the right circumstances for magic to occur. And let me be very explicit here: magic is *real*! This book is about the kind of magic that transforms and heals lives. *Not* magic as in the meaning of *only in my imagination* or the escapism of a good book or film. This book is about *the nuts and bolts of magic,* you could say.

Doing shamanic work with children is magical and luminous, even miraculous. Children have not yet acquired the barriers and prejudices that maintain the dominant perception in our society, but those same prejudices and fears make this work more difficult than it needs to be. In this book I will address what those fears and prejudices are and answer some questions I am asked all the time by people from all over the world. Having said that, most of this book is about what works well, what children are capable of, what difference shamanism can make to children growing up in the 21st century. One of my core beliefs is that children need a spiritual toolkit if they are dance with the challenges of living in today's global village.

Part I:

Chapters 0-15

Chapter 0 or Surface Zero: The Shaman Mother's Spiritual Survival Kit for Kids

This chapter is based on a blog I wrote in January 2014 because my eldest son had received a death threat while standing in the dinner queue at school and our youngest son was experiencing issues with bullying and humiliating power games in the school playground.

Recently someone told me that so-called survival bags are now being handed out to homeless people. When we go camping most of us bring an insane amount of equipment. Imagine you were camping out every night, in all weathers, on mean city streets. What would you like to carry with you? Those are the items that make up a survival bag (emergency snacks, anti-bacterial lotion, a torch, baby wipes, change for payphones and washroom facilities...the list goes on.)

Native American people of course have medicine bundles and consider those their most precious possessions. Those bundles represent a person's spiritual life and are considered to have protective and healing powers. When people died their medicine bundle was either buried with them or passed along to a family member or friend who became its sacred guardian. Medicine bundles are also created and looked after for a whole tribe or community.

What do our children need to have with them before we send them out in the streets on their own, and into the shark-infested waters of primary and secondary schools?

Shaman Mum Puts Together Spiritual Survival Kit for Kids

- A fold-up Invisibility Cloak
- A pocket-sized magic wand
- A small pouch full of fairy dust to sprinkle wherever you go and whenever needed

- Some flying ointment (but please note that not all schools have adequate parking facilities for broomsticks)
- Your Power Animal (picture or figurine or small toy)
- Your Body Protector
- A feather to remind you to grow wings and to take yourself lightly!
- A small mirror plus a piece of paper with the following personal mantra:
  'I am perfect just the way I am, I am loved. I am not responsible for the feelings and actions of others, I am only responsible for my own response to the actions/feelings/ moods and decisions of others. This is my so-called response-ability!'
- A sky rope, to climb between worlds any time and to make a quick exit from dangerous situations
- A first aid kit and small sewing kit to repairs any small rips and tears you discover in your Invisibility Cloak
- A notepad and pen or pencil to write down the brilliant ideas that pass through any young human mind in the course of a day. (This can also be used to write a quick love note to someone whose love levels need topping up)
- One small musical instrument (a magic flute is perfect)
- A box of matches to remember we can choose to shine light in dark corners and we can 'set the world on fire' (but please don't literally set anything on fire unless instructed and supervised by an adult, that is called arson, not shamanism!)
- A whistle to blow the whistle on bullies and other *contemporary demons*
- A handful of change to give to the homeless people you see on your way to school or to people who forgot their dinner money
- A fold-up rubbish bag to fill with all unwanted energy we come across in a day – to be emptied ceremonially at the

end of the day by shaking it out on a hilltop while joyfully singing songs of transmutation to transform the energy into blessings for your city/village/forest/field and school playground

Next let's give some thought to creating a medicine bundle for our whole tribe, i.e. the world population and global community...

Enjoy the special gift of another day on Earth!

Fly safely!

Chapter 1

What is Shamanic Parenting?

It takes a village to raise a child and a community to keep the parents sane
African saying

What is Parenting?

Before answering what shamanic parenting is, maybe we first need to ask a far more basic question:

What is parenting?

The concept of parenting as a very conscious and active (possibly full-time) activity for a parent of either gender, grandparent, or foster parent/other carer, and is relatively new. In earlier times in Europe (the continent where I grew up) people had children, often large numbers of them, because safe birth control was not easily available and the Church looked upon birth control as a sin, thus putting people under pressure to have large families. Did all those children receive a lot of individual attention, a good education and music lessons? Of course not! I only need to go back two generations to see the reality of this in my own family.

My maternal Dutch grandmother, Oma Oud, was sent out to work at the age of 14. This took pressure off her parents, meaning that it reduced the number of mouths to feed at home, and allowed her to acquire skills. Even in those days in the Netherlands this was illegal. My great grandmother pinned up my grandmother Martina's hair so she would look like a 16-year-old. She was a servant in a house belonging to a posh family. She spent a lot of time down on her knees lighting fires and scrubbing floors. She actually spent so much time on her knees that they were damaged for life. In old age I never saw her walk without a walking stick and her knees creaked alarmingly whenever she sat down or stood up. Other problems occurred, like the father of the family groping her as her child's body developed the curves of a young woman. Can you imagine packing off your 14-year-old daughter to such a destiny today? Not many European families do, but globally speaking, child labour under inhumane conditions remains a cruel reality on our planet.

The word parenting entered the Oxford English Dictionary[1] in 1918, but it didn't become a common verb until the 1970s: *to parent,* as an action word. These words reflect a second half of the 20th century fixation. Before then people had children, but they would not have reflected too much on either their parenting style or their parenting competence. However, Pandora's box has opened and today many parents agonise over this. This reflects a shift in consciousness and it is a good thing.

The Good Enough Parent

Dr Donald Winnicott was a paediatrician who introduced the concept of the *good enough mother* in 1953.[2] He recognised the need for children to realise that:

> *...a mother is neither good nor bad nor the product of illusion, but is a separate and independent entity: The good-enough mother...starts off with an almost complete adaptation to her infant's needs, and as time proceeds she adapts less and less completely, gradually, according to the infant's growing ability to deal with her failure. Her failure to adapt to every need of the child helps them adapt to external realities.*[3]

His teachings boiled down to the fact that a good enough mother was better than the perfect mother. I remain grateful to Dr Winnicott. We don't need to be perfect parents, only good enough. (And yes, just that is hard enough!) Obviously children need a *good enough father* just as much as a *good enough mother*.

This book is about the spiritual dimension of parenting. It asks questions about the spiritual toolkit a child needs to express their true selves and reach their full potential in the world. It also asks the following question: who are the true experts when it comes to parenting? As you will see my answer is *not* psychologists or even the parents, but the children's own spirit allies and compassionate ancestors. We operate in a larger field. No family is an island in either space or time. Ultimately the children themselves must find the inner resources to express their soul gifts in the world and they themselves must become shapers of the world and leading voices in it.

We also need to bear in mind that it was only last century (roughly a hundred years ago) that Freud and Jung were doing their ground-breaking work. I am not asking you to choose sides or to agree with their very different conclusions. I just wish to acknowledge that the concept of either a personal *Unconscious* or *Collective Unconscious* did not exist before then. The work of these pioneers still shapes our vocabulary and thinking in the 21st century. The word archetypes (as cosmic blueprints wired into the human psyche) is another good example of this.

Tribal Parenting and Community

Along a larger historical timeline we can observe a picture of children being treated as mini adults for a very long time (think of my grandmother), then our Western concept splitting into *parents and children*, parents actively *parenting* and children *needing good parenting* if they are to do well in life. I would like to contrast this with tribal parenting, for lack of a better word. In tribal or indigenous societies all over the world parenting has always been approached in ways significantly different from the standards we live by today. Tribal people, living in a close relationship with spirits of the land, have always perceived themselves as part of a larger Web of Life where they have a duty to the ancestors as much as to the children. And not only that, they also feel a keen sense of responsibility for the future generations, the unborn, the children of the children of their children

Seven Generations

The concept of Seven Generations and sustainability comes from the Iroquois people. It is a concept often used in the context of ecology. It refers to the need of the current generation of humans (the people alive today) to work for the benefit of the seventh generation into the future. This originated with the Iroquois people, Native American tribes that lived around the area that today is New York State. The Great Law of the Iroquois states that it is appropriate to think Seven Generations ahead (about 140 years into the future) and decide whether decisions made today would benefit the children of their children, and so forth, Seven Generations into the future.

For tribal people community values are paramount. You might be familiar with the African saying: *'It takes a village to raise a child,'* but there is a less often cited second half: *'...and a community to keep the parents sane.'* Everyone is actively involved in child rearing; this not left to isolated overworked mothers in city apartments without much of a support system. Another thing that is vastly different about tribal peoples is that their relationship with Spirit is at the heart of all they do. They live in close partnership with the Spirits of Place. They honour the ancestors and consult them about decisions that affect the whole community. Children are taught from birth about being Earthkeepers: guardians for the Earth and all sentient beings. Teenagers are offered proper Rites of Passage and young people are expected to shoulder their age-appropriate responsibilities in the community. Part III of this book explores ways of returning this ancient art to contemporary Western society. Tribal societies do not have eternal students or 37-year-old adolescents. The cycles and progression of life are honoured.

One important comment I do wish to make here is that *we cannot go back* to living the way some tribal people still live today or earlier societies lived on our land long before modern inventions and technology arrived. I do not advocate this. Even first nations (tribal, indigenous) peoples had their issues: famines, prisoners-of-war, cannibalism, raiding neighbouring settlements, to mention but a few obvious things. It would be an illusion to think those ways of life were perfect. But I still feel that our society today can retrieve precious things we have lost over the centuries, by studying these peoples and communicating with tribal Elders today.

Kahlil Gibran[4] described parenting perfectly:

On Children
Kahlil Gibran

Your children are not your children
They are the sons and daughters of Life's longing for itself.
They come through you but not from you,
And though they are with you yet they belong not to you

You may give them your love but not your thoughts,
For they have their own thoughts.
You may house their bodies but not their souls,
For their souls dwell in the house of tomorrow
which you cannot visit, even in your dreams.
You may strive to be like them
but seek not to make them like you
For Life goes not backward nor tarries with yesterday.

You are the bows from which your children
as living arrows are sent forth.
The archer sees the mark upon the path of the infinite,

and He bends you with His might
that His arrows may go swift and far.
Let your bending in the archer's hand be for gladness,
For even as He loves the arrow that flies,
So He loves also the bow that is stable

Shamanic Parenting

So what is shamanic parenting? Shamanic parenting is about realising that our children are ultimately a gift from Spirit and that every child arrives with a unique soul path, a special contribution to make here on Earth. Even disabled or autistic children have a unique contribution to make and it is our sacred responsibility to receive and fully contemplate that gift. (See Chapter 9 in this book about shamanism and children with special needs.) The world misses out and we wound their souls, and ourselves, if we do not engage with this challenge. Marginalising people always means a loss for the larger community, as well as soul loss for those who do not feel they belong.

Shamanic parenting means raising our children in the awareness that children are luminous beings in their own right. They are divine beings in origin, as we all are, and often they are great teachers to us (their so-called parents or teachers). It means putting respect for the Earth, Life and all sentient beings (All That Is, the whole cosmos) at the very heart of our lives and existence. It means being willing to offer our children proper rites of passage when and where this is called for, so they are not forced to create transcendental experiences for themselves in risky and unsupervised ways. It also means listening very closely to them: do they need rites of passage, or do they perhaps need something else? It means releasing our fears of old age and the lack of respect shown to old people and allowing old people to be Elders again, sharing their wisdom with the younger ones. Children need Elders and grandparents as much as parents, because these people can give them many things parents cannot provide.

Shamanic parenting means parenting from a place of honesty and vulnerability, so children grow up honouring and allowing vulnerability in themselves and others. It means giving our children the freedom to make minor mistakes and misjudgements so hopefully they have a well-developed moral compass before the life-and-death issues, or big mistakes, kick in.

Shamanic parenting means dying with dignity and grace – so our children can feel at peace about the prospect of dying one day. Not spend all of their lives in denial of death and then viewing death as a personal injustice when the moment does arrive.

If any of this resonates with you. If you are willing to explore ways of offering young people a spiritual toolkit, this book is for you. If not, please give this book to another parent or teacher who may find it interesting. Thank you!

Notes

1. *The Oxford English Dictionary (OED)*, OUP Oxford, 3rd edition, 2010
2. *The Piggle: An Account of the Psychoanalytic Treatment of a Little Girl* by Donald Winnicott, London: Hogarth Press, 1971
3. You can Google the Alliance for Childhood to find their two websites: the first one is the UK-based one and the second on is the international site
4. *The Prophet* by Kahlil Gibran, Pan, Reprints edition, 1991

Chapter 2

The Shaman's Map

What is Shamanism?

So now we have some idea what shamanic parenting is. Before venturing deeper into those territories, let's briefly discuss what shamanism is. There are many excellent books on shamanism on the market so this chapter will only give a skeleton outline and refer to other sources for further reading.

Shamanism is a set of spiritual practices that puts a connection to spirit at the very heart of human existence. Shamans work from an altered state of consciousness to seek healing and guidance from the spirits on behalf of individuals and communities. Shamanism places a strong emphasis on ceremony, honouring the ancestors and working closely with the Spirits of Place. In shamanism we aim to live a life that is in sacred balance, meaning that it honours the Earth and all sentient beings. Shamanism, like animism, acknowledges that everything has in-dwelling spirit. Not just what we consider animate things, but even inanimate things such as mountains, rocks, the wind, the stars and so forth.

There are many different definitions of a shaman. Here are just a few:

- A shaman walks between worlds
- A shaman restores harmony on the energetic level
- A shaman can look deep into people's bodies, minds and situations by using the so-called *x-ray eyes of the shaman*
- Shamans work outside time, they can travel to both the past and the future
- Shamans are technicians of the sacred
- Shamans were the first priests, doctors and psychotherapists

all rolled into one

- Shaman are soul doctors and they prescribe soul medicine
- Shamans mediate between this world and other worlds on behalf of their community
- Shamans are people who see with their eyes closed

Shaman or Shamanic Practitioner?

The word shaman is a Siberian in origin and derived from the Tungus language. In indigenous societies, certain individuals are called by the spirits to walk this path and they undergo rigorous training and initiations. Eventually they serve their communities as shamans. In Western culture we honour those people and their path by calling ourselves shamanic practitioners instead, to mark the fact that we often trained with Western teachers, in a different cultural context. In essence, we perform the same tasks – communication with spirit, ceremonies, healing work and divination – for and with our communities.

Other Words for Shaman From Different Cultures

- Seer (Medieval Europe or the Celtic tradition)
- Curandero (male) or curandera (female): Spanish word that literally means healer
- Seidkona (female, Norse shamanism), practitioner of Seidr
- Sibyll
- Angakok (Inuit)
- Tang-ki (Chinese)
- P'ago (Andean word)

Global, Masculine and Feminine Shamanism

Shamanism has never been a unified practice globally, though anthropologists studying indigenous cultures found certain core practices. Michael Harner[1] then bundled these together and started teaching them to the West as *core shamanism*.

Barbara Tedlock, in her book *The Woman in the Shaman's*

Body,[2] makes the important point that in indigenous societies there have always been feminine traditions as well as a masculine path.

As a teacher of shamanism, it is my observation that in Western culture many people start off doing some workshops in core shamanism. However, if they commit to this path the spirits often call them to seek out the traditions of their place of origin. This may not even be their personal own place of birth. Many people go on spiritual quests to see where the bones of their ancestors are buried.

When people embark on a spiritual quest they also discover their spiritual lineage and connect with their spiritual ancestors and soul family. My own journey started off within core shamanism, but ultimately took me north, into Norse shamanism in Scandinavia and even to Greenland and the West Coast of Canada.

Suggested Reading about Shamanism

Imagery in Healing: Shamanism and Modern Medicine by Jeanne Achterberg, Shambala Publications Inc, New edition, 2002

Singing the Soul Back Home: Shamanic Wisdom for Every Day by Caitlin Matthews, Connections Book Publishing Ltd, New edition, 2002

When the Drummers were Women by Layne Redmond, Crown Publications, 1st edition, 1998

Gods and Diseases: Making Sense of Physical and Mental Wellbeing by David Tacey, Routledge, Reprint edition, 2012

Shakti Woman, Feeling Our Fire, Healing Our World: The New Female Shamanism by Vicki Noble, Harper SanFrancisco, 1st edition, 1991

Walking in Light: The Everyday Empowerment of a Shamanic Life by Sandra Ingerman, Sounds True Inc, 2015

Soul Retrieval, Mending the Fragmented Self by Sandra Ingerman, HarperOne, Revised Updated edition, 2010

Medicine for the Earth: How to Transform Personal and Environmental Toxins by Sandra Ingerman, Random House USA Inc, 2001

Shamanism: Archaic Techniques of Ecstasy by Mircea Eliade, Princeton University Press, 2004

Notes

1. *The Way of the Shaman,* Michael Harner, Harper SanFrancisco, 3rd edition, 1992
2. *The Woman in the Shaman's Body: Reclaiming the Feminine in Religion and Medicine* by Barbara Tedlock, 2005

Chapter 3

Shamanic Work With Children: The Most Common Fears and Prejudices

A man or a woman who is a medium or a necromancer shall surely be put to death. They shall be stoned with stones; their blood shall be upon them.
Leviticus, chapter 20 verse 27

Beloved, do not believe every spirit, but test the spirits to see whether they are from God, for many false prophets have gone out into the world.
John, chapter 4 verse 1

Let's do Shamanic Work with Children...

So you have done some training in shamanism. Whole worlds have literally opened up. It is obvious that young children naturally operate in this zone. It feels like a great idea and an obvious move to start doing shamanic work with children...

I get emails weekly, often referrals through colleagues: people think the Time Travellers programme is such a great idea. They too would like to run shamanic workshops for children. Could I please give them some pointers or lessons plans? I always reply to those emails. At length. But I am honest. I make a point of telling people about the challenges they are likely to face. To be forewarned is to be forearmed. Let me add here that I have had such emails from all over the world, even people who live in the Bible Belt in the USA.

When I started the Time Travellers programme in June 2012, I thought I was starting small and that the group would grow over time. I expected us to need a larger venue soon and started looking around locally. In reality the TT group started small and stayed relatively small. By this I mean that about eight to 10 children attend the sessions. It has been difficult to get families to commit to this work. For every two children who join, another two generally leave at the same time. In many ways that is fine. Those children have absorbed what they needed at the time and new children arrive to take their place and interact with more experienced children in the group. So the group has not actually grown much in size. But the group still exists four years later and just that is an achievement!

The Time Travellers have their own page on my shamanic website. It is the page that has received the most likes, since I updated the website and put social media buttons on there, including a like button. I just checked: today it has acquired 498 likes since the beginning of this year (I am writing this chapter on 1 June 2015), which is something like a 100 likes a month – but those likes do not amount to a large number of people sending their children to Time Travellers sessions.

Fears and Issues

So what are those fears and issues? Let's list some of the issues people voice and then address them one by one.

- The Bible says: 'Do not talk to spirits!'
- The shadows of the witch hunts and Inquisition still linger today
- It's better not to encourage children's weirdness; instead encourage them to fit in and not draw unwanted attention to themselves

The Bible and Church

Many church buildings are being converted into fancy apartment blocks. Only few of us are practising Christians today. However, in our society there remains a deeply ingrained fear, imprint or inhibition around talking to Spirit. I find that people have associations of Ouija boards and witchcraft when I explain what I do. These issues unfailingly get a mention whenever I am invited as a public speaker by a group of people or professionals in another field. The fear is that I may endanger vulnerable young children by encouraging them to talk to Spirit…or if not endanger them physically, that I may put their mortal souls in grave moral danger. What if they end up not going to Heaven when they die?

There is other vague unease. Is it worth to take the risk?

My reply to this is: 'Does Heaven exist?' Thorny question! I could write a whole book about 48 years of adventures in the spirit world and the fact that I been to many beautiful places, but never to Christian Heaven. My best guess is that Heaven exists somewhere as an energetic realm created by a belief system fed by many people over the centuries. The spirit world is very shape-shifty and elastic. So my take on this as a shamanic practitioner is that Heaven exists as a temporary energetic zone where people go after death, because they expect to find themselves there after death and the world of Spirit will accommodate this. However, eventually human souls move on from there because the soul is on a great cosmic journey home to The Divine and no soul can stay in Heaven (a construct of the limited human mind) forever.

The Time Travellers once asked me: 'Does Heaven exist?'

I bounced the question back to them: 'During two years of exploring the Spirit world, did you even come across Heaven?'

They said: 'No...'

I said: 'You can all make this the intention for a shamanic journey and ask your own helping spirits to show you Heaven!'

The Time Travellers had lost interest at this point. They were busy creating a vortex to go and whirl around Earth with the Storm Spirits… They had more important things to do…

Christianity is a relatively young religion. The message of unconditional love that Jesus Christ embodied has, to my mind, been subject to many grave distortions through the centuries and interpretations by male Church fathers trying to claim and preserve worldly power. I am pretty sure that the spirit of Jesus Christ, which is outside time, in the eternal realm, is horrified at the notion of Holy Wars being fought in his name.

All existing societies and cultures were preceded by shamanic cultures, where people lived in close relationship with the Earth, the ancestors and the Spirits of Place. Connecting with Spirit is our own birthright and the birthright of our children. As I hope this book will demonstrate, it can give young people an exceptional spiritual toolkit for life in the 21st century.

The Shadow of Witch Hunts and The Inquisition

The shadow of the witch trials lingers in Europe. I do a lot of ancestral healing work (with adults, as well as on behalf of children) and frequently I still find the impact of this in the larger family field. People still carry strong fears and deeply ingrained inhibitions around magical abilities and holistic or alternative healing methods. In my practice, I have seen many people who were reluctant to answer the calling to be a healer, because fear and unease remain, but they do not realise where it comes from, whose fears they are holding and living.

The shadow of the witch hunts remains in our culture in other ways too. Calling someone a witch is rarely a compliment today. However, in times past witches often were the healers, herbalists, midwives and medicine women for communities.

In popular culture today we have horror movies and vampire stories that scare the living daylights out of people. I acknowledge the need for such material. Human beings need to experience and express the dark side of things. Our imagination and emotional range seem to require this. And it is better done through movies than through murders! (Chapter 13 in this book explores the impact of violence in the media, films and games on the minds of young people. Chapter 14 describes the conclusions of a youth seminar exploring violence.)

We all need to learn discernment. We need to comprehend that life on Earth is polarised to create a large force field that allows us to learn, make choices and have a wide range of experiences. We also need to comprehend that every physical object on Earth casts a shadow and that even invisible things have shadows too. Everything that exists has both a shadow aspect and highest expression. I can use my own hands to caress someone or to hit someone. I can use my mind to think toxic thoughts or life-enhancing positive thoughts. I can choose to gossip and criticise or to project strength onto other people. That means choosing to see their talents, holding visions of all the amazing things they are capable of.

Even horror movies or crime novels can be a higher expression of something, because it satisfies a human need. I could play Devil's Advocate here and claim that horror movies therefore have a magical or healing aspect. Like a ritual, they allow something to happen under safe and controlled circumstances so it is done and does not need to occur in everyday reality.

It is not fair to project onto shamanism – an ancient and not homogenous global practice far more ancient than Christianity – the shadow of witchcraft and sorcery. Using magical practices for nefarious motives and to fix specific outcomes has occurred and still occurs. Shamanism has a shadow, like all every other thing that exists on Earth. But shamanism is also a path of great beauty with ancient healing modalities that many people walk with immense integrity and dignity. Magical power, once acquired, can be used for good or for bad, but this is why any high quality spiritual training is rigorous and requires profound self-reflection. Personally, I make a distinction between a shaman and a sorcerer, when I teach courses in shamanism and students ask many questions about this.

With the Time Travellers I constantly ask the children to reflect on the effect their actions have on others, to reflect on the true nature of power itself. You could therefore say that I have the privilege of running a group for urban rebels and revolutionaries, teaching me great things in return. One thing all young people in the group have in common is an extreme capacity for individual thought and independence, as well as having an exceptional moral compass at a very young age.

The Weird Web of Wyrd

As a teacher of Norse Shamanism I want to briefly mention the Web of Wyrd

The Web of Wyrd is woven by the Norns (sometimes therefore called The Wyrd Systers). You could visualise this as a massive cosmic spider web where personal threads of life, threads representing destiny, interconnect. So all have our own personal intersection, if you like, of that web where our lives and paths cross those of others.

Our modern word 'weird' comes from this word. There is also an etymological connection with e.g. the word 'worden' in Dutch. Worden means becoming or coming into being. It refers to a being in progress, or even a shape-shifting, and arriving at a different state of being.

Australian Aboriginal peoples speak of the Dreamtime (or Dreaming) where Creation is happening in every moment. This is a totally different concept from a world created by a male God where humans then have dominion over all animal species. The words 'wyrd' or 'worden' express that eternal becoming, where nothing stands still and nothing ever stays the same. Everything is always becoming and evolving.

The word 'wyrd' is related to the name of one of the Norns: Urd and the old Norse word Ur means origin. It is also related to the English word 'word' ('woord' in Dutch, my mother-tongue). It makes us aware that by speaking we create realities. We call thoughtforms into being and send them out in the world by giving voice to something.

In Old Norse the names of all three Norns (often compared to the Greek Fates) are: Urd, Verdandi (literally 'that which has come to pass') and Skuld (literally meaning debt, from the Germanic root skuld, to owe).

The larger web woven by the Norns is sometimes called orlǫg ('or' means out, from, beyond, and 'log' is law). So the Norns are beyond the law. In Norse mythology even the gods are subject to their fate meted out by the Norns. They can appeal, but ultimately the Norns are more powerful than the gods.

Weird!

Me: 'I know that shamanism is my choice and not necessarily yours…'

Son: 'No Mum, I don't feel the need to practice shamanism exactly your way, but I will have you know that I am a deeply spiritual being!'

Conversation with my 15½-year-old son in May 2015

Not Belonging! Not Fitting In! Being an Outcast!

All parents live in absolute fear of this happening to their children. And bullying is an extension of this, where weirdness and vulnerability meet abuse of power. Some parents do not want their children to attend my classes for fear of stigma. They have admiration for what I do, but they don't want their children to be at risk of being perceived as *weird*. Often one parent is open to the child attending but the other partner puts their foot down, saying it is better not to risk it. The most heart-breaking scenario is children really wanting to attend, but their parents not giving permission. As long as children are under age I (or you) cannot teach them anything without their parents' consent. This can be a heart-breaking reality.

In my Time Travellers group, ages have varied over the years and the core group has morphed into teenagers since the programme started. The youngest participant we have had was five and the oldest ones are 15. I find that around the age of 15½ young people need to break free of adults. By then they need to have absorbed whatever they needed, on a spiritual level, and the journey continues in their inner world.

The author Brene Brown[1] has spent many years researching the anatomy of connection. She discovered that shame resilience is the core quality at the heart of living from a place of worthiness and wholeheartedness. This means embracing the fact that we human beings are vulnerable, rather than running from vulnerability, and cultivating authenticity, self-compassion, gratitude, intuition, joy, playfulness. It means letting go of perfectionism, numbing, powerlessness and anxiety as a lifestyle.

Read her book *Daring Greatly* for more, but I will just say here that her list of qualities corresponds extremely well to the issues we unravel in shamanic teaching and shamanic healing work. The work is always about enabling people to live from their True Self or Authentic Self and stripping what obscures this.

Outcast, Weirdness, Being the Oddball

Traditionally speaking shamans have often carried the projection of the outcast. They have often lived on the fringes of the community (but perhaps this was because they needed to have time alone and live close to the spirits of the forest or the desert). In such communities, children who had the energy signature of the shaman would be spotted at a very young age and be offered training and mentoring. Being 'odd' often meant being called to perform a sacred task on behalf of the whole community.

A programme like the Time Travellers caters for children with this signature in our society, but not only for them. The sessions are very exciting and enjoyable. All and every child is welcome. However, I do observe that a certain type of child gravitates to this work.

I am writing this book because I live in London, UK, where only local children can realistically attend my programme. It has been suggested that I need to take this work online and I may get there soon. However, if more people offered shamanic programmes for children in other locations, and some already do, young people with this special interest or special signature (and indeed all and any young people) would have a safe place to go, and experience community, belonging and safe sacred space.

The greatest blessing of this work is that ultimately the children are our greatest teachers. Your own spiritual journey will accelerate once you work with children. Doing this work, you will see the future of our world and the future of shamanism taking shape.

Notes

1. *Daring Greatly, How the Courage to be Vulnerable Transforms the Way We Live, Love, Parent and Lead,* Brene Brown, Avery, Reprint edition, 2015

Chapter 4

The Age of Reason: Parental Consent for all Forms of Shamanic work

A Word of Caution

Doing shamanic work with pre-school children is easy, an absolute joy. The biggest stumbling block is often permission from the parents. We need to operate boundaries around this. When a shamanic practitioner is officially asked to see a child for a session, this issue is taken care of. But a practitioner of shamanism (and here I am speaking in a wider sense, this could include a person who has clocked up a lot of shamanic training or someone who attends a shamanic journeying circle or drum group) can easily find themselves with a group of curious children and get into trouble. Say another family visits your house and their children are fascinated by the rattles and drums you have. I have seen this happen: a shamanic family invites some children from school over on a play-date. The visiting children say: 'What is the drum for? Can you play it for me?' At that point things can get tricky. To pick up a drum and say: 'This is my drum! I use it for my spiritual work. It sounds like this when I play it,' is fine if you then put the drum down again.

However, the temptation is to go one step further and say: 'Let me take you on a quick shamanic journey! I am going to be drumming and you are going to drop down a rabbit hole and meet a very special animal, your power animal!' This is tempting when we are so enthusiastic and the children are *so eager and up for it*. But in that moment we are definitely crossing a line. There are many people out there who will happily let their children play at 'the house of a practitioner of shamanism', but only on a social level. If you wanted to take things further, you would need to ask the parents for permission first.

In Western Europe children are minors until they are 18 years old. The fact that a four-year-old is keen to go on a drum journey does not mean that their parents will support that idea. It is always best to check. You don't want to be carried away and come under a lot of criticism later, or have local families avoid your house, because there is talk about you making their children 'talk to Spirit' without permission.

When our own three children were younger we hired child-minders to look after them for a few afternoons a week, so I could have some studio time and continue to work on painting commissions. At that point I was not yet a shamanic practitioner, but I had long pulled away from my Roman Catholic upbringing. I had decided to try very hard not to introduce certain concepts to my children at all, because I myself had experienced them as limiting or even harmful. Some of these concepts included the Devil, hellfire, original sin and martyrs (the idea of always putting others first and a lifestyle of self-sacrifice). I wanted my children to have a healthy sense of self and clarity about their own visions, needs and boundaries.

One day two young women we hired as childminders took the children out for the afternoon and our boys returned full of stories about the Devil, burning in Hell, purgatory and so forth. Much as I valued their services (they provided competent and loving care for our children) I was horrified to discover that these ladies had just filled our children's minds with the very material I had so carefully edited out in my own parenting. Even today our children still sometimes mention their dramatic introduction to hellfire and the Devil, but they laugh loudly when they talk about this. It didn't stick, thankfully! And the reason for mentioning this here is to make the point that some parents from a more conventional Judeo-Christian school of belief are going to feel about you doing impromptu shamanism with their children *exactly the way I felt about my three children have this unsolicited introduction!*

While on this subject, let's make a quick excursion to the other end of the spectrum: when can young people themselves give consent?

Parental Consent

Consent is a tricky issue. I have just researched how the medical profession handles issues around teenagers and decisions about treatment. In the UK, where I live and work, children are minors until age 18. Meaning that after the age of 18 young people can make all their own decisions about pursuits and medical care, assuming they are of sound mind. I have had 19-year-olds attending workshops or booking themselves in for healing appointments. I have also worked with a lot of 14 and 15-year-olds. The appointment is always made by the parent and I ask the parent to accompany the child to the healing appointment.

With children under the age of about 12, I ask the parents to stay in the room for the whole healing session. I do always say that the child can talk to me alone for a moment if they wish, and then I ask the mum or dad to step out for a short while. But while working with a child I ensure that the parent is in the room so that later on there is never any confusion or debate about what I did or what was said. Often I even record the session, so there is a record of what was said and done, for both parents and myself.

However, young people aged about 14-plus are entitled to privacy, so I will normally offer that the parent can step out and be in a different room for at least some of our work together, like sharing time. Or I give the option that a parent drops off the young person, but waits in the cafe around the corner until the session is done. Teenagers all make very different decisions at that point and I always honour the decision a teenager makes, not what their parents were expecting. Some parents feel excluded when a teenager requests privacy. Well tough! Your child is growing up. Get with it! Most young people that age feel safer and more relaxed when a parent stays. I always make a point of making all sessions age appropriate and as fun and adventurous as possible. I want any child I work with to go home happy and empowered.

In my experience the trickiest age group are the 16 to 18-year-olds. In my work with the Time Travellers I observe that young people go their own way by the age of 16. Often 15½ seems to mark that point of independence and striking out on their own. Young people need to be with peers, they are often dating by then. They actively need to have areas of life where the parents don't intrude. It has not yet happened that someone in that age group requested a healing session without parental consent, or wanted to attend a shamanic group without the parents' consent. I think that all healthy teenagers in that age group are pretty busy with more urgent concerns!

If a 16 to 18-year-old wanted to attend a group or class, I would talk to them and ask how their parents felt about it, but I would let them in. I figure that young people old enough to get pregnant or drive cars can make an informed decision about exploring shamanism, even if their parents do not approve. I would certainly make them aware of any friction and turbulence that might ensue from this. My own 16-year-old son attends Bible studies. Not because he is religious, but because some of his friends attend and he loves debates on the Big Questions in Life. (Apparently the priest finds him a handful and borderline unmanageable because he takes nothing on authority!)

In reality, in my experience, you will meet that age group in shamanic work only if serious problems occur: teenage pregnancy and a family needing spiritual support whatever the outcome or decision, eating disorders like anorexia and bulimia, issues around self-harming and suicidal ideation. At the lighter end of the spectrum you may have people wanting a reading from Spirit when it comes to choosing the right exam subjects for university courses. Sometimes a parent attends a family constellations session and then decides to do more in-depth healing work on specific ancestral issues to set a young person free from various burdens. And often the teenager says to that: 'Fine, you go do this with my blessing, but I am not coming!'

Young people often 'reappear' at some point in their early 20s, often exploring spiritual avenues very different from their parents' choices. They have now *left home*. In every possible sense.

Chapter 5

The Before Life and Spirit Children

If a Siberian woman wanted to fall pregnant, she had to go hunting for the Spirit Soul of her baby and fetch it home from the Spirit Masters. She was expected to go off and live in solitude while she did this. Spirit Souls one level down from the Upper World take the appearance of little birds fluttering from branch to branch. The great Siberian goddess Umai lives by the Tree of Life and sends these birds (the souls of children) into the world.

Caption for one of my own paintings, not reproduced in this book

The Before Life

We speak of an After Life, but what of The Before Life?

Do we exist before we are born on Earth? Or do we miraculously get sparked into existence when our parents conceive a baby?

Everyone is entitled to their own take on this, but as so much of my work happens in this very magical realm, The Before Life, I feel compelled to give my perspective on this.

First let's hear what children themselves say on the matter.

Yellow Land

When our middle son Elliott was just starting to speak (around his first birthday), he talked a lot about *Lalau* and, a bit later, about a mysterious place called Lalau Land. At first we didn't understand what he was trying to tell us. As his speech improved we discovered that yellow was his favourite colour, by far, and that he was trying to tell us about the place where he lived before he was born. By the age of two his speech was very good and we realised that he was talking about a place he called Yellow Land.

Yellow Land is a place in the Other World where everything is made of golden light. There is no pain. Everything is bright and beautiful and bathed in Divine love and light. Elliott used to live in Yellow Land while he was waiting for a placement with a family here on Earth. He had a small yellow house where he lived with his special guardian animals. Elliott says that he would go on outings to play with other child spirits, but he would always return to his Yellow House. Even today Elliott loves solitude and having his own space. He has a den in our garden where he retreats from the world and from his boisterous (more sociable) brothers.

Elliott also remembers how the decision was made for him to be born into our family.

For every place on Earth there are very many souls waiting to go. There was a day when I had to go and tell the Great Spirits that I wanted to be born into a family on Earth. I rode in on my cheetah and there was a very long queue of souls, all wanting to go to Earth. Many souls had their guardian angels and Power Animals with them. Many child spirits were riding their Power Animals like I did. Then there was a meeting and I had to tell them why I wanted to go to Earth and what I was going to do there. I was shocked how many people wanted just one place on Earth! Any place on Earth! Then I rode back to my Yellow House to wait for the decision. I remember when they came to tell me that I had 'won the lottery' (or that is what it felt like!) and that a family had been found for me. I was allowed to have quick look. I saw that they already had one baby (my brother Quinn) who was not yet walking and I also saw a nice big garden. I was over the moon when I heard the news because I knew how rare a chance it was to actually get a life on Earth. Then my mum got pregnant and I was growing in her tummy.

What I remember is that when Elliott was even older (about three years old) he said to me one day: 'Just so you know, you only get one shot at parenting me. I already know that in my next life I am going to a different family and I was with other families before I came here. So…you better make sure you get it right because I will not be your child again!'

Elliott missed Yellow Land very badly for the first years of his life, before he started reception class, the first year of primary school. At night he would often go there in his dreams. In the mornings I would ask him about this. Was his little house OK? What about the giraffe that lives in his garden? How was the duck that lives on the golden pond just outside his window?

Elliott told me that one day, when he dies, he will return to Yellow Land. While he is here, in human body, he can visit the place in his dreams and look after it so his home in the spirit world will be waiting for him when he dies. He says that he is luckier than most people because he knows exactly where he will be going the day he dies. I once asked Elliott to paint his Yellow House in Yellow Land and he did. Today Elliott is 14 and in Year 9 in secondary school, just choosing his exam subjects. He doesn't often talk about Yellow Land any more, but he remembers.

Working with Unborn Children (Babies In Utero)

Occasionally people ask me: 'What ages are your clients? What is the youngest or oldest person you have ever worked with?' The oldest person question is easiest to answer. In shamanism we have ways of helping people prepare for a good death. We are often asked to work with people in the final stage of life. Whatever age they are at that moment: in their 70s, 80s, 90s – and, sadly, sometimes younger of course.

The youngest person is a little trickier to answer, but we can work with a soul from the very moment of conception, or even just before really. I have sometimes worked with people and seen the soul of a child waiting in the wings. Then I know that this person or couple will soon get pregnant.

I have also worked with babies in the womb. Not to do healing work, but because parents wanted to seek guidance on the right name or other requests from the soul of the baby, such as a naming ceremony, preferred godparent and so forth. This is truly beautiful work because the information received is then used to welcome the baby into the world in a way that already respects the soul choices of the baby. In my observation it creates a good foundation for a loving and respectful relationship between parent and child.

This same method can be used to talk to the soul of a baby who chooses to come in with a disability or genetic condition. So if screening during pregnancy throws up such a diagnosis, parents would do well to consult a shamanic practitioner. I observe that these days so much ante-natal screening is done that many children with Down's syndrome, for example, or other genetic conditions do not make it. A termination is performed and the parents try again, sometimes with medical assistance (forms of IVF where embryos are screened genetically before they are implanted). As a shamanic practitioner I have extremely mixed feelings about this. Every prospective parent wishes for their child to be born healthy.

During my own three pregnancies this was our overriding concern too, that our baby would be healthy. And we were lucky because they were. However, on a professional level I am aware of the effect that *lost children* (miscarriages and terminations) have on the family field and psyche of individual people, often for many decades or even generations.

There can be very many reasons why a soul chooses a life with physical or mental limitations. Very often there is an ancestral component to this, perhaps something needs embodying and healing in the larger family field, or a learning component. This soul might be choosing to learn about limitation and their family would learn along with them. There can be a karmic component to this too, not that I wish to foist a belief in reincarnation on anyone. At other times it is none of these things, the soul comes in to teach about giving and receiving unconditional love. This is often said about children with Down's syndrome for example. Their capacity for expressing and embodying unconditional love is literally *not of this world.*

We live in a consumer society with a belief that if something is faulty, get another one. The concept of mail order looms large as well. I have come across books that describe the Universe as a cosmic mail order system: visualise and get ready to receive! There is certainly truth in the power of visualisation, but I profoundly disagree with the concept of the Universe as a massive mail order catalogue because we exist in a larger Web of Life where many different forces interact and shape lives. We all exist at the heart of our own unique spider web of connections and threads.

Please note that I am not making any blanket statement here that abortion is always 'wrong'. As a parent I am extremely aware that parenting is one of the hugest tasks a human being can ever undertake. Even when you actively and positively choose to be a parent, there will be many moments of agony and anxiety. Proceeding with a pregnancy when you know you really and truly don't want a child or that you really and truly are not up to the task of parenting, is not advisable.

The flipside of this is miscarriage: many people badly want a baby, but the pregnancy ends. Often this happens so early on that there is no medical explanation for what occurred. There is no scan picture to prove this embryo ever existed. In situations like this a shamanic practitioner can be of great help. They can facilitate a dialogue between the parent and the soul of the child. They can also assist with performing a ceremony to honour the life that passed through. (You will such ceremonies in Part III of this book.) They can check that the soul of the baby truly did return to the spirit world and that it does not linger in the energetic field of the mother or father. On a spiritual level some souls want to briefly taste life or briefly connect with another soul in the physical realm. They choose a pregnancy that is going to end because it is not the right time for them to stay. On *a soul level* this is understood by everyone involved. However, on *the human level* any lost child, however early in pregnancy, needs to be treated with respect and that child's place in the family needs to be honoured. For instance, if your mother had a miscarriage and then you, spiritually speaking, you are the second child in the family, not the first. And that has big psychological and emotional consequences. You will find some book recommendations at the end of this chapter.

I do a lot of individual shamanic healing work with people where the source of serious personal suffering is a sibling who has gone unmentioned or not received respect.

The last thing I want to say on this subject is that when people cannot have children due to infertility or fear of passing on a serious congenital disease for instance, shamanic work can help see what other unique and important soul task they are bringing to Earth at this time. This does not negate the grieving process at all, but I have observed how this can help people move forward in constructive, and often liberating, ways.

Spirit Children

Many years ago I was called by the spirits to pioneer an unusual, but powerful, form of healing art: painting images of Spirit Children and passing healing messages between them and their parents. I was doing this long before I formally trained as a shamanic practitioner. As always seems to be the way: the Spirit Children themselves came knocking on my door, making their enchanting demands. Spirit Children are essentially spirits of dead children, children who died very young or at any time during pregnancy. On a spiritual level there can be many reasons why a child spirit returns. For the parents this is always devastating event.

When an older child dies, parents have memories of their child: they know what the child looked like, what their preferences were. What made them laugh or cry, what their favourite food or animal was, and so forth. However, if a pregnancy doesn't go full term and the parents have a miscarriage, people are left with very little to show for their loss. Our society has no way of honouring babies lost in early pregnancy.

If a baby is lost after the 12-week scan the parents will have picture of the baby. If a pregnancy ends before that point, nothing tangible remains. This makes it difficult to say goodbye properly and to honour the child in the years to come.

In the year 2011 my colleague Jacqueline Teoh invited me to do a talk about my work with Spirit Children in Geneva, Switzerland. We were not entirely sure how this would go down, if we would even have an audience for this. However, that day we had a full house. All chairs were taken and many people came up to me after the presentation to have a private conversation. It became apparent to me that most people in that room had a personal connection to a dead child. People told me about stillborn babies, miscarriages, abortions, lost siblings and so forth. They all said that they had no idea that it was possible to do shamanic work with the souls of dead children. That it was even possible to visit the spirits of those children in other realms and ask them how they wish to be painted or remembered, if there are any messages to be passed to their parents to bring greater closure to the situation.

At that point I thought that one day I would write a very small book about Spirit Children. Over time I realised that this would become a chapter in a larger book about children and shamanism. This book! For most people these paintings remain very private, for obvious reasons. But some people have given me permission for me to feature their paintings on my website so others can find them and maybe derive comfort from them. You will find my website address and contact details at the back of this book. In September 2014 I also made a small film about Spirit Children. It can be found on YouTube.[1, 2]

I will finish this chapter with a poem I once wrote for a friend who lost a baby.

The Sacred Twins and the Sand Dollar
A child lives outside time
A mother grieves
A child spirit plays guardian angel
leaves evidence
of a sacred twin

A mother to be
Walks on the beach
Speaks to her
Unborn child
Catches a glimpse of a Spirit Child
riding the waves
She finds a sand dollar
A precious moment
of extreme beauty
frozen in time
As a child spirit watches
and smiles outside time
For C 15 August 2009

Notes

1. Spirit Children, a small film by Imelda Almqvist featuring paintings of Spirit Children: www.youtube.com/watch?v=GpSLQLHN2B4
2. Spirit Children, the webpage: http://www.shaman-healer-painter.co.uk/info2.cfm?info_id=126660

Chapter 6

Natural Born Shamans

Mum, do you remember when I lived in your tummy and Tiger was living in my own tummy, waiting to be born?
Our youngest son Brendan at age 7

People think that Narcissus fell in love with his own reflection and drowned. What most people do not know is that he shape-shifted into a merman and started a new life under water…
Our middle son Elliott at age 11

Pre-School Children

Pre-school children *are* Natural Born Shamans! They are naturally 'in the zone'. They talk to so-called imaginary friends. They know that their cuddly toys represent friendly animals that lead exciting lives in Other Worlds. Children still see the colours around objects (you can see this in their drawings sometimes) and they master the art of hearing *what others are not saying.* Children still carry memories from The Before Life. If we are a willing to listen, they may just tell us a magical story. Assuming children have open-minded parents, pre-school children are allowed to play and imagine in our society. They walk between worlds at will. They often have a strong connection to trees and animals as well.

But then they start school...

Starting School

Starting school affects all children differently. Some are bored by life at home and ready for wider horizons. Others are not yet ready for feeling so crowded (standard class size in the UK is 30 children) and following an educational curriculum. Some parents go to great lengths in choosing a Steiner, Waldorf or Montessori school for their children and others decide to home-school. However, for many children starting school is a point where a certain door closes. Starting school and learning to read and write in a classroom with peers also means trying to fit in and learning to perceive things the consensual way. By this, I mean the way that the dominant group in our society perceives and interprets reality. And in Western culture at the moment this is the rational, linear, polarised, scientific, evidence-based paradigm.

While I was at art school in Amsterdam, in the Netherlands, from the age of 18 to 22, I did a special project on children's drawings. I was collecting children's drawings and reading all the books available on the subject. Various authors track different stages in a child's development by the art they make.

When I had my own children one of my greatest joys was observing all three of them as they started making art, and moved through what Piaget called developmental windows. Something that is very noticeable when children start primary school (UK) or elementary school (USA), is that their work loses freshness and innocence. The smiling sunflowers disappear. After drawing horses with eight legs and a rainbow tail they suddenly announce that 'they can't draw animals'. It is heart-breaking to observe! What has kicked in is the unspoken expectation that art must imitate reality. The norm suddenly is photographic realism. And in making that shift, for many children a door shuts on their imagination. Their imagination is the doorway to the spirit world. When the dominant perception kicks in, many limiting beliefs also arrive on the scene. Being told that something 'exists only in your imagination' often means that it does *not exist*. The word 'imagination' takes on more sinister associations. And imaginary friends are not welcome in primary school either. This process can be brutal for many children. I often teach sacred art courses attended by adults who remember moving through this process and it takes a lot of work and commitment to release those limiting beliefs and regain direct access to the imagination and Other Worlds.

How Can Shamanism Benefit Children of Primary School Age (4½-11 Years)?

Primary school corresponds with elementary school in the USA. Children of this age can benefit tremendously from individual shamanic healing sessions where a particular issue or concern is addressed. Examples of such concerns include overeating, insomnia, lack of concentration in school. When I started the Time Travellers group in London, our youngest participant was five years old and the oldest ones were about 12.

For that age the group gave them the following things:

- Community, being with kindred spirits in a safe setting and sacred space
- Permission to express their true, authentic selves and to cast off their school persona, designed to keep them safe and help them fit in, for a few hours
- Exploring their innate spirituality, whatever form this takes. I always make a point of encouraging all forms and exploring all orientations in this process. Some children naturally have Buddhist leanings while others are keen to incorporate the teachings of Jesus Christ into a wider frame of reference
- Regaining the tribal and ancestral experience of meeting around a fire and telling stories, drumming, heating marshmallows in the fire etc. This seems to activate old ancestral memories of belonging from an era before screens and internet
- An opportunity to share issues that come up in daily life and have them addressed as a group. In my group examples of such issues have been nightmares and bad

dreams, bullying, public speaking as in standing up in class and presenting something, doing spirit-led creative writing to help with writing tasks in school
- A growing spiritual toolkit as they move through transitions and initiations

How Can Shamanism Benefit Teens and Tweens?

All the things listed above still apply, but the focus shifts around the age of 11 to 12. Suddenly personal appearance becomes much more important. In May 2015 we did a session on this (see Session Plan 12 Body Imagine, Self Esteem and The Sacred Clown). We explored shamanic ways of raising confidence and creating positive body image. The element of sexual attraction kicks in at this age and that can make sessions more lively. There are opportunities for mentoring and interestingly they work both ways, I discovered that:

- Older children (oxymoron!) with more experience can welcome newcomers to the group and bring them up to speed in terms of what we covered earlier
- Older children can also reach out to the younger ones at the time of transition to secondary school and give useful pointers on what to expect and what to avoid *but...*
- Younger children are often less inhibited. They can show the older ones (i.e. the teenagers) about dropping all inhibitions and having a lot of fun doing shamanic work
- In some ways younger children are more fearless and that can be a great gift to teenagers

I will give an example: we once did a session on shadow work (Session Plan 5) meaning that we engage with all the parts of ourselves that are not socially acceptable and we have pushed far away, into some dark forgotten corner. But a lot of our lifeforce and energy are actually contained by parts of ourselves we reject.

So I took all children through the process of acknowledging in ourselves what we cannot stand in others. The teenagers, obsessed with cool factor, did very poorly in that session. But the younger children just went for it with heart-breaking honesty and great courage. One boy, eight years old, at the time, said:

> *Yes, I have all these things within myself and I know it. Greed, terrible thoughts, wanting to hit people, being capable of bullying others… Really you could say I am a 'Master of Darkness' because I know that all unpleasant things I see others do, also exist within me. But knowing that I get to choose how I behave!*

Children with the Energy Signature of a Shaman

Pre-school children are Natural Born Shamans and that capacity remains alive somewhere within all of us in the adults we become. I spend so many hours a week unlocking that magical shaman child in the adults. I can't help but feel that the spirits were right in the great task they set me: create groups where young people can experience spiritual community and acquire a solid spiritual toolkit as it saves on incredibly long hours of soul searching, psychotherapy and healing interventions in later life. Once people do shut down, opening up again can be an extremely slow and painful process that involves a stripping of many layers of cultural conditioning and family-system conditioning. If people do not shut down, they are mentally far healthier and better equipped to deal with the challenges that life throws them. Such adults are more creative, they have more resilience and they can think outside the box. Most of them will not become shamanic practitioners, but they will display a gift for creative problem-solving in their lives.

However, certain children are born with what I will call the Energy Signature of a Shaman. It is their destiny to be a powerful healer or shaman for their community once they grow up and that talent is clearly visible in their aura or personal energy field.

Here we need to remember that Time is an organising dimension that belongs to Planet Earth, but it does not exist in the spirit world. In those other worlds *outside space and time* the energy signature of a healer of shaman will attract attention. The Western world has lost the ancient art of psychopomp work. The word 'psychopomp' means soul conductor and refers to the art of guiding the souls of dead people to the right destination in the Afterlife. In our culture we choose to believe that everyone who dies goes to Heaven (a Christianised version of the older shamanic concept of an Upper World). However, the fact that we also believe in ghosts and haunted houses indicates that we retain the awareness that the death process can be compromised and that some souls remain Earthbound.

Shaman children can unwittingly attract the attention of Earthbound spirits (maybe looking for healing, trying to follow the Light, trying to transition to a better place). And such children may become brilliant psychopomps (or soul conductors) as adults, but at the age they are now, such attention is neither welcome nor manageable. Earlier in this book I talked about my work in other realms as a very young child. I was lucky to have very competent helping spirits and miraculously the work never frightened me, but I repeat: this is not the norm and I do *not* recommend that very young children do this work.

When I see such children in my shamanic practice I explain to the parents what might be going on. I ask the child to explain what is causing nightmares or an inability to fall asleep on their own. Often we then hear about the child sensing unwanted energies and presences in the room. This frightens the parents and in turn this does not help the situation. The solution for this is that the shamanic practitioner programmes a crystal that acts as a waiting room for souls wishing to heal and move on, so the child can sleep peacefully. The crystal obviously needs to return to the practitioner at regular intervals for emptying and cleaning. Another good idea is to retrieve the child a very special spirit ally that helps with these issues. Dream stones can help too. The spirits will tell you what a child needs. Once a child is free of nightmares and sleeping soundly again, they will obviously function much better in the daytime.

Nightmares and Bad Dreams, Other Causes

And while we are on the subject of nightmares, let's briefly talk about other spiritual causes for this. I have worked with children where ancestral issues were very present. A sensitive child can be flooded with ancestral material at night, meaning that they might be dreaming of things that happened in their family line a long time ago. In that case the solution is to listen very closely to such dreams and then do ancestral healing work to heal and close whatever issue is coming to attention.

An example could be that there is a family story that a great grandfather committed suicide, but actually his death was accidental and he wants to clear his name and for those alive to be aware of the true course of events. A child may then have recurrent terrifying dreams about drowning or being locked in an attic, depending on the specifics of the situation, until a healing ceremony is performed.

In shamanic healing work with children, or indeed adults, it is not always clear what might be ancestral material or what might be material from a previous lifetimes (if one believes in such things). Practitioners need to tread with extreme care here. For whatever it is worth, my own observation is that people choose incarnations where unresolved issues from previous lifetimes (incarnations if you like) are mirrored by the issues playing out in the family they choose to be born into. I see this as seeking a close match on the level of the soul from a desire to heal specific issues. So the long and short of it is that it does not matter if an issue is ancestral or originates in a previous lifetime because the issue will manifest in the same way and will need a similar healing intervention.

Yet another possibility I have encountered is that bad dreams are blessings in disguise. The spirits are trying to bring something to the child's attention, but this is misinterpreted by the child. We saw one example of this in the Time Travellers group: a girl having recurrent nightmares about a tiger chasing her. We acted the dream out and discovered that the tiger was actually her Power Animal trying to communicate with her! In Part II you will find a session plan for Dream Theatre work. There is another example there about a boy being eaten by a dragon, but this dream offering a portal for him to walk through and claim his healing abilities and healing tools.

Autism and ADHD

It is beyond the scope of this book to discuss every possible issue children present with in shamanic healing sessions. What I will say as a very general comment is that things are rarely what they seem. When you look at spiritual cause or deeper picture, no two stories are alike. What looks like one phenomenon in everyday reality will look very different when you are running a psychic investigation for individual people. In shamanic healing work the spirits will always lead us to the right course of action. There is not one pre-determined intervention or solution for any given problem. Something to be aware of is that in shamanism we see the medical diagnosis as a label. We do what is called diagnostic work, meaning that we ask the spirits for a reading on the spiritual cause of any problem. The way we work is therefore very different from a medical doctor.

For example: what medical doctors call Post Traumatic Stress Disorder, a psychologist may call dissociation and shamanic practitioners will call this severe soul loss. I may see two children with ADHD in one week and the spirits will give me a totally different picture and prescription for both. For that reason I cannot make generalised statements about these issues. I often do see children with ADHD in my practice. They cannot sit still, they cannot concentrate in class, other families are weary of inviting such children over because they feel unable to keep them safe and manage them. This can add to a sense of isolation and being different.

My general observation with children with ADHD, or related behavioural issues, is that often they do not feel safe being in a human body on Earth at this time. The child may mirror difficulties the parents are experiencing in communication or in their marriage. Or the child may have a vibration that is not (yet) matched by the surroundings and school the child attends. The child may well suffer from soul loss and not be all here, with a large part of them safe, but lost in Other Worlds.

It may also be the case that the Children of the Future are being born right now and that Western culture has not yet caught up. I strongly sense that this is the case. We have children arriving to be part of a new paradigm that is not here yet. Another intuition I have about this is that planet Earth is not in perfect health just now. We live with overpopulation, global warning, processed and genetically modified foods, polluted oceans and many other issues. It is an illusion to think that we can exist in a safe bubble while the problems are elsewhere. In shamanism we work with mirrors on all levels. We are being grossly insensitive to Mother Earth. We abuse her natural resources. We pollute our oceans. We genetically mess with our crops and food products. So what if a generation of very bright and sensitive children is being born to hold up a mirror for us, to show that extreme state of disconnection from Mother Earth and Father Sky? The microcosmos of this then is: children who have difficulties connecting to their parents and to others. We call this autism. Can we *own our autism*, our lack of connection to others, to plants and animals? Can we see ourselves in the refugees from Syria seeking safety and asylum all over Europe?

Modern life is speeding up. We are rarely unplugged, always switched on. What if children with ADHD hold up a sacred mirror for us saying: is this how we want to live? Can we raise healthy balanced children in a world that bombards us with information and demands? Isn't this creating a form of attention deficit disorder in all of us, on some level? If we see many of the environmental and social problems on our planet as cancers or auto-immune diseases, we have to ask ourselves the question: are sick people bravely making a sacrifice, in terms of their health, to raise the level of awareness on our planet? Do they possibly carry the shadow of illness so the rest of us are free to lead healthy lives? Are sick people heroes rather than the weaker ones? I highly recommend a book by Kat Duff called *The Alchemy of Illness*[1] on this subject. Another author I wish to mention in this context is William Stillman, who writes books about people on the autistic spectrum and, what he calls, The God Connection.[2] Basically he explores heightened spiritual giftedness and the special soul mission of people who are on the spectrum (as the shorthand goes).

Stillman makes a number of very helpful suggestions:

- Always presume intellect! Never talk down to autistic people assuming that their intelligence is impaired or indeed never talk about autistic people to others in their presence. Look them in the eyes and speak to them directly. Give them the same respect you yourself wish to receive yourself from others.
- Doing sincere Forgiveness Work, meaning offering sincere apologies to an autistic person once you realise that you allowed your assumptions to colour the space between you. This can bring about miracles in the connection and communication between you. (This approach generally works miracles with non-autistic people as well, in my own experience!)

Once you are willing to make amends and connect with an open heart, you will find very loving and wise souls in bodies that may seem impaired, showing behaviours that appear odd to neurotypical people, (neurotypical means being wired the dominant way not the autistic way).

Essentially Stillman is a great ambassador for entering soul-to-soul communication with autistic people and for awareness of their unique gifts and teachings. In shamanism we approach things in a very similar way. Stillman is a Christian, but he uses the word shaman in his books. (Chapter 9 in this book is all about using shamanism with children with special educational needs or SEN).

Healing Versus Cure

I will just mention one further issue I have personally encountered in working with autistic children: parents sometimes contact me, not for healing, but for a cure. This means that they are hoping one shamanic healing session will make an autistic child neurotypical (non-autistic). We often see miracles in our work, but that is one miracle I have not yet observed in my practice. However, I have seen autistic children in far better shape after a healing session, doing better in school and the whole family enjoying a more harmonious family life. There is huge scope for healing and transformation. But there is an equally large need for accepting people for who they are, not projecting onto them *what we would like them to be*, and that is yet another sacred mirror of an issue that looms large in our society.

Stimming

Autistic children often engage in stimming (self-stimulating behaviours such as spinning, flapping, humming or head banging). If I take a moment to connect with my Inner Autist (and there is doubt she exists!) I experience the world as a very frantic, noisy and overwhelming place. So what do I do? I create a safe bubble around myself of movements and sounds of my own making. Having said that, I also observe two of my own children (who have not been diagnosed with autism) spinning and flapping and hopping. I have talked to them about this and discovered that it is actually a form of shamanic journeying or talking to spirit. While doing this they retreat to an Other World where they have encounters with spirit allies and super heroes in parallel worlds. This is something I have *not* read in the literature on autism so it might be worth mentioning here.

Notes

1. *The Alchemy of Illness* by Kat Duff, Bell Tower, 1993
2. *Autism and the God Connection* by William Stillman, Sourcebooks, 2006

Chapter 7

Those Who Were Children Before Us: Our Ancestors

Ancestral Imprints and Missing Children in the Family Tree

In the years I have been doing shamanic healing work, a lot of my own learning has been about the influence of the ancestors on our lives. What follows is a summary of some universal spiritual laws or rules that I, and colleagues, have observed time after time:

- Whatever issues or trauma the ancestors did not heal or resolve in their own lifetime are passed on to future generations. In common speech we will speak of issues *running in families*. Bert Hellinger, who pioneered family constellations work, speaks of The Knowing Field. Information can be accessed and healing can be brought through interactions with this Knowing Field.[1]
- Often a very sensitive child with psychic abilities ends up carrying more than their fair share of any ancestral burden because they have made a soul choice to bring healing to the family. However, in everyday reality they may struggle greatly with feeling different and leading a less mainstream and straightforward life than their siblings.
- If such ancestral imprints and patterns are not healed, our lives can be shaped profoundly by events and emotions that do not originate with us. And even if the issue doesn't belong to us, it is still our responsibility to heal it!
- Ancestral imprints can re-create life-and-death scenarios, such as accidents or serious illness. Not healing the underlying issue then means that this is passed on to yet another generation in the family. I often say that we owe it to our

children and grandchildren to heal our ancestral lines. This leaves them free to focus on the challenges their own lives will bring them, without being weighed down by ancient events and trauma.

- Missing children in the Family Tree (meaning miscarriages, abortions, children dying young, children disowned because they were born out of wedlock, children adopted by other families and so forth) feature prominently in ancestral healing work. They must be given their place and their right to belong must be honoured , or else a distortion remains in the family field that inevitably affects the living.

About Children and Grandparents

In his book *Of Water and the Spirit,* Malidoma Some[2] writes beautifully about the special relationship between children and their grandparents. He says young children have just arrived from the realm to which their grandparents will soon return. Therefore grandparents are keen to receive news from the Other World. Therefore they question young children very closely. Malidoma's own grandfather hypnotised him to get the information he wanted!

There are many wonderful books on the market that explain in great detail how ancestral healing work is done and why it needs to be done. (See Further Reading at the end of this chapter). All I want to say for the purposes of this book is that having happy ancestors means the living stand a far greater chance of being happy. For this reason I urge everyone to practise some simple form of honouring their ancestors.

The most basic version of this is to light a candle once a week for maybe 15 minutes and talk to the ancestors; tell them what is happening in the family ('Josie has had her baby', 'Tom is struggling at the moment, please watch over him' etc).

In her book *Medicine for the Earth* Sandra Ingerman[3] emphasises the importance of focussing on the gifts we received from our ancestors. It is all too easy to focus on the negatives and the trauma. But the fact is, we here are on Earth today, in a human body, because of our ancestors and they passed many of their gifts and talents on to us. Take a moment to focus on this and thank your ancestors, rather than choosing a default setting of blaming or pretending they never existed. This practice may well expand over time to collecting and framing old family photographs and giving them a place in your house. In our own house I have created an Ancestor Gallery with old photographs where I light a candle, make offerings, honour the birthdays of ancestors, stand most mornings and speak to them about family affairs and so forth.

As far as children and young people are concerned, take time to show them photographs and tell them stories about their ancestors. One day even you yourself will not be there any longer. You may want to get very creative and make a special photo album with pictures and all the information, or a shoebox with stories and memorabilia. Our children's paternal Swedish grandmother has made ancestral boxes and documents for our children. She has also given them heirlooms for Christmas with the stories that accompany them in writing.

Obviously you will need to operate discernment. You may not want to tell very young children absolutely everything the ancestors got up to. Some ancestors may have been violent or abusive. My approach with my own children has been to start by telling them the edited version of events, but as they grow older I start telling them the less pleasant facts as well. Not because I wish to black-mouth anyone or perpetuate trauma, but because I want my children to have the relevant information to help them understand the cradle for their own lives. If ever they need to seek help in the future, they will have the information.

Recording Information for Future Generations

At the time of writing this chapter (July 2015) my own elderly mother is about to come to stay with us. I have a camera, voice recorder and list of questions ready. I intend to interview her about our family history, my grandparents, her own grand-parents etc. When I asked my mother for her cooperation with this, she said: 'But not everything you hear is going to be pleasant!' And my reply was: 'Mum! I am 48 years old. I daresay I am old and strong enough to handle even the difficult information now!' I am going to put those voice files on my computer, backed up, so if anyone else in the family ever wants to know more, at least the information is stored somewhere.

Further Reading

Connecting to our Ancestral Past, Healing through Family Constellations, Ceremony and Ritual, A Native American Perspective by Francesca Mason Boring, North Atlantis Books, U.S., 2012

Between the Lines: Healing the Individual & Ancestral Soul with Family Constellation by Nikki Mackay, John Hunt Publishing, 2012

Notes

1. *Acknowledging What Is: Conversations with Bert Hellinger* by Bert Hellinger and Gabriele Ten Heovel, Zeig Tucker & Theisen, 1999
2. *Of Water and the Spirit: Ritual, Magic, and Initiation in the Life of an African Shaman by* Malidoma Some, Penguin, New Ed edition, 1995
3. *Medicine for the Earth: How to Transform Personal and Environmental Toxins* by Sandra Ingerman, Random House, USA, 2001

Chapter 8

Shamanic Healing Work with Children

The Psychodrama of the Aspiring Healer

Word of warning! This chapter is NOT about learning how to do shamanic healing work. For that you need to seek specialist training from an experienced shamanic teacher! Before doing any healing work on others (and even more so with vulnerable children) ask yourself if you have the right training and skills and if your own personal healing journey has processed to the point where you can be a trustworthy healer of great integrity for others. Remember that any issues you have not faced or addressed within yourself will inevitably be acted out by your clients or students. This is, what I call in my courses, *the psychodrama of the aspiring healer*. You do NOT want to do a healing session with any child where your own unresolved issues become the focal point and stand in the way of what really needs to unfold.

The Difference Between Working with Adults and Children

This chapter has been written for people who are experienced in doing shamanic healing work with adults, but may wonder how the usual ways of working could translate into a slightly different way working with very young children. Children generally have no difficulties accessing the world of magic and it takes very little encouragement to move into this zone. (With adults you'd need to spend more time cutting through layers of conditioning and limiting beliefs.) I always ask the parents to send me some information about the child's medical history and personal interests in advance. This means that I can cut short the 'boring talking part' at the beginning of a session and it also allows me to use words and concepts familiar to the child. Not infrequently such conversations revolve around a much admired superhero or a favourite animal.

I ask all my clients to undertake a small pilgrimage before their session with me and I ask parents to do a special journey together with their child. This may just be a trip to the local woods or beach to find some special objects and look for signs from the universe. It means that parent and child have already moved into the magical zone together before they arrive, so the practitioner can move faster and use fewer words to explain things. Often these sacred journeys flush out important themes and information for the work. Pay close attention to what people report.

Children have shorter attention spans than adults so you generally need to move *much* faster. I observe this every time I invite a guest teacher for the Time Travellers group. People are used to working with adults and they move way too slow, losing the lively young audience in the process. The most important thing from the child's point of view is that the session is fun, exciting and empowering – and fast-paced!

I treat any shamanic healing session with a child as an opportunity to embark on a great adventure together where magical animals come forward to help us and nothing is impossible. If you practice shamanism you will know that even mythical or extinct animals can appear as Power Animals. So you may have a dinosaur or unicorn appearing in your session to work with a child. If a child really cannot stay still for literally one second and is likely to climb the walls, not just figuratively but because it is so overstimulated by being in unfamiliar surroundings; it is often better to do remote work. Agree a time with the parent and ask the parent to observe what happens. Are there any changes in the moment or in the hours and days immediately following your work? Another thing I often do is I invite the parent to come and we work together, bringing the child in energetically, but physically absent. This is as powerful as working with the child present in the room.

Helpful Hints

With young children I do not use any technical terms, such as extraction or soul retrieval, as I would with adults. I talk about pulling out what hurts or blowing back in special energy that has gone missing for some reason. I did soul retrieval with a little boy recently and I explained that I was going to blow something in that had run to a safe place, while he had some traumatic experiences in school. I tried to get him to understand that he needed to focus on absorbing that I was blowing into his heart and he said: 'Oh OK, you are going to blow me up like a balloon and I will just go OOMPH with all the power that comes back!' (miming expansion). Perfect! Trust the child to find the perfect words for what is going on.

With very young children, or older children with attention deficit issues, you may not have a calm patient sitting or lying still for any amount of time. So you may be working while on the move, following the child around. When I have concerns about a child's ability to focus I always ask the parents to bring something that calms the child down, such as a favourite toy or favourite music or even a snack. This is one rare occasion where I allow iPads in my healing room.

I have found that almost anything can be turned into an adventure. If you need to do spirit release work with a child, say, you can either do it quietly while asking the parent to distract the child for a few minutes or you can involve the child and turn the exercise into a dragon hunt. 'Together we are going to look for a dragon that is hiding and when we find him we send him to his dragon friends who live in a place made of bright light.' This works surprisingly well. Go with the child's own perception of events at all times. If they see an angel dressed as Spider-Man in the room, then that is what is in the room.

I often ask the parents in advance about a permissible treat I can give the child at the end of our session for being brave and co-operative. A small bag of crisps is greatly appreciated by the small adventurer. Obviously after care is extremely important too: check in with the parents how the child is doing, check if there is anything that needs addressing or tweaking.

A Healing Re-Birth Ceremony

Sometimes both mother and child have a very difficult start together in life. A traumatic birth can lead to trauma on both sides. When a mother suffers soul loss due a traumatic birth (maybe forceps were used, maybe an emergency Caesarean was performed, or maybe the mother was rushed to hospital after lovingly planning a home birth), it can be difficult for the mother to be fully present, on the physical, emotional and spiritual level, to welcome the new baby.

When a baby suffers soul loss at birth – and I have seen many examples of this in my practice – the child may feel the urge to run back to safety (meaning: part of the child's soul is not all here, it stays behind in the spirit world) or a child may live with a deep-rooted sense of abandonment and not being welcomed and embraced properly.

I have occasionally seen this in e.g. children diagnosed with ADHD and/or autism, but I have also observed this in people who are very high-functioning, by the narrow standards of our culture, in all other respects. Such issues do not only shape our birth, they can leave their mark on human lives. The guidance I have received from Spirit is then sometimes to stage a Re-Birth Ceremony.

The guidance for me is to engage both mother and child in planning a ceremony of the birth as both had wished it to be, assuming the child is old enough. If not, or if the child is non-verbal, consult the soul of the child. Ingredients might be: low lights, beautiful music, the new-born baby lying on the mother's chest before anyone else holds him or her. The mother may have had sacred dreams about this moment: what feelings did she want to have in the room, what kind of welcome did she want to give her child, is there anything else that is particularly important to her? The father and siblings can be present too. The ancestors can be invited to attend in spirit, and so on. We take all these wishes into account and we enact the birth all over again. In other words, we set a new energetic/template for this experience and then we ask Spirit to transmute the previous experience. It will not be forgotten, medically speaking the first birth obviously happened, but mother and child are given the chance to start again with a loving soul connection and being fully present in this crucial moment of meeting each other face to face for the first time.

With the best intentions (we write birth plans, we meet the team of midwives, we pay a visit to the hospital, or we hire a birthing pool and plan a home birth) we do not always have the birth we dream of. There may even be reasons for this on the level of soul, but the point I want to make here is that in shamanism we work outside time. We can heal even situations in the past or pre-harmonise situations that are still in the future. I have seen relationships between mother and child improve dramatically after such simple ceremonies. A lot of pain and difficult memories are transmuted or dissipated so both parties can then be more secure and joyful in their relationship.

Chapter 9

Using Shamanism to Access the Unique Gifts of Children with Special Educational Needs (SEN)

Please note that this work comes with terminology that has been subject to public debate, strong emotions and opinions. There have been changes over time as not all terms used in the past are now deemed respectful or politically correct. I have therefore chosen to use the term currently used by the UK Government and schools in the UK.

Some Guiding Principles

Over years of shamanic work with children (and often the most challenged children are incredibly gifted and evolved souls in other realms) I have observed certain spiritual principles, or cosmic laws, time after time. It may be helpful to provide a summary of those guiding principles:

- There are no random births and no 'accidents' either. Births are governed by soul choices and higher powers guiding those soul choices.
- Whatever things may look like in the everyday world, children are *not* born randomly to a set of parents.
- This also holds true for disabled children or for children born to parents with few resources to parent effectively (think of mental health issues, addictions, personality disorder etc).
- Disabled children are indeed *differently able* children, as disability advocates emphasise. What makes the situation different from less challenged children is that it can take way more effort and work to unwrap and facilitate those

talents and gifts.

Challenged Children and Challenging Children

There is no question that challenged children pose immense challenges for their parents, families and other carers. It needs to be acknowledged that parenting a special needs child is a task even more immense than parenting an average child. We would do well to reflect on that and extend help to the parents of special needs children.

The modern construct that children are the sole responsibility of their parents is not helpful here as we end up with run-down parents carrying too heavy a load, often feeling lonely and misunderstood on their quest. Who is able to parent well in a permanent state of exhaustion? If the parents feel lonely and misunderstood, how do we think their children feel?

Parents and carers of children with disabilities often have no access to either uninterrupted sleep or babysitters ready for the additional responsibilities. Yet children with disabilities (mild or serious) are the responsibility of, and a gift to, whole communities. They hold up a mirror for all of us. They present an invitation for us to release long-held prejudices and to leave our comfort zone; to truly learn things about the human condition and the world of spirit.

The Diagnosis

Your child remains the same child he or she always was – the child you yearned for and welcomed into the world – even when a devastating diagnosis is made. Your child has not changed, but your expectations are severely challenged in that moment. We all have expectations for our children, even if we don't reflect on those, even if many of those remain unconscious and unspoken. We generally hope and expect them to be healthy and of at least normal intelligence. We assume that they will become independent and leave home one day. Often we even hope, without admitting it, that they will live out some of our dreams and avoid mistakes we made. No child is a blank sheet and no adult is either. We are all shaped by a larger field of influences.

The word diagnosis is derived from classical Greek and literally means *to know thoroughly* or *to learn through taking apart.* We cannot know anything thoroughly by a brief examination followed by pigeon holing a person (meaning we are not learning anything, we are just fitting what we see into what we already know and believe).

Do *not* blindly accept a diagnosis. Seek second opinions. Consult holistic practitioners for the spiritual perspective you will definitely not get from the medical profession. Do your own research. Form a support group of parents affected by similar issues, facing a similar medical journey. Always ask the question: 'Is the diagnosis (label) going to help or hinder my child?' Once a diagnosis is in their medical file, it will follow them through life.

For some parents the diagnosis can be a relief: it puts a name to something, a collection of phenomena, that then becomes easier to explain to others. For example, many autistic children look 'normal' so strangers do not understand why the child is behaving so 'badly' in public. Often a diagnosis also entitles families to special support, help and funding. For some families this is a positive life-changing move as a child then, for example, receives the individual help needed to stay in a mainstream school.

For other parents the diagnosis can feel like the beginning of the end. It can lead to further referrals and more medical opinions that are utterly soul-destroying in the way they focus on everything your child *cannot do* and never on the unique individual with special gifts they are.

Diagnosis or not, always remember and remind people that *your child is not a label.* Behind that label there is an individual who has a unique contribution to make to the whole community.

Even behind individuals presenting with massive disabilities and impairments, we find an eternal soul that is not impaired. Seek help in contacting the soul of your child and exploring the nature of the soul contract between you. A shamanic practitioner can be of great help here. Start unwrapping the gifts in the situation – however dire it may appear.

I urge all parents of seriously challenged children to learn shamanic journeying and the art of soul-to-soul communication. Choose an experienced shamanic teacher, ideally someone who has experience of working with children. This can be the key that opens the door to many new levels of understanding between parents and child.

Please remember too that there is never any need to make critical medical choices, or even life-and-death decisions, on behalf of a child, or indeed anyone of any age. The soul (or Higher Self) of any person, however ill, disabled or even comatose in everyday reality, can be consulted outside space and time. Even if you are competent in shamanic journeying, it is not advisable to do this work for your own loved ones, as emotions and fears will cloud the space. Ask a specialist with a lot of experience to this work *as a compassionate outsider*. Asking a friend is not the best idea either – will your friendship survive if the information passed is tough and not what you hope? Don't kill the messenger and remember that brain surgeons do not operate on their own family members and friends either.

Medication

All of this holds for other medical interventions as well: consult the soul of the person concerned about any treatment choices and about medication. With regard to medication always ask the questions: 'Is this medication truly positive for my child? Or does this medication somehow subdue or control my child? Is this medication 'good for others' perhaps and not at all for my child?'

The same thing goes for educational and medical choices. The dilemma always presents: 'Is it beneficial for my child to keep them on the mainstream track, with all pressures and expectations involved in that, for as long as possible? Or is it kinder to my child to make different choices, place them in a more small-scale caring environment with animals and specialist teachers perhaps?'

For whatever it is worth, my advice is always to try the mainstream route as long as that is reasonable and feasible, because the moment you close that door many future opportunities shut down in a child's life, but look long and hard at alternative opportunities. Just this week I met a woman in Gran Canaria who is sailing around the world with her young daughter with Down's syndrome.

The most important thing of all, perhaps, is to defy the medical profession by never taking any diagnosis or prognosis as inevitable or 'binding'. Remain open to your child surpassing all expectations and doing *far* better than any medical professional is willing to believe right now. If you are not going to hold that vision for your child, who will?

Remember too that our society and culture are changing rapidly. Your child may just have a gift that will help the our planet immensely and perfectly in 20 years' time. We don't always know what is taking shape or what the larger meaning behind events is.

The Ultimate Sacrifice

The last thing I will say here, linking back to Chapter 7 on ancestors, is that not infrequently sick children have made a soul choice or sacrifice on behalf of the larger family, including the ancestors, family members long dead. My own father had a sister called Mientje who died of leukaemia at the age of 14. When I connected with her soul-to-soul (I was born long after she died) she told me that my father's family was seriously burdened by trauma and mental illness. A lot of pain and abuse had accumulated. She made the soul choice to take some of that burden away from the family web by taking it upon herself. She also said it made her sad that her sacrifice was not honoured, because no one in recent times or then understood what she had done. Ever since I was willing to listen and see, I have felt her presence encouraging me, because she says she and I share interests, like writing. Her sacrifice needed to be witnessed. The immense love she feels for our family needed to acknowledged. I make a point of honouring Mientje especially in my ancestral gallery or ancestral healing ceremonies I perform with students. Soldiers are not the only people who make the ultimate sacrifice, not infrequently children do too, but they receive far less acknowledgment than the soldiers.

I appreciate that it will take time for our society to accept the validity of the points I make in this chapter, but this is the course we need to set if we are to fully integrate disabled people into our communities.

Ambassadors

Challenged children present us with great challenges and great rewards. Can you become an ambassador for those unique individuals, changing the dominant view in society?

Some parents become astounding ambassadors and inspirational figures once they answer this challenge and embrace the challenge of parenting a differently able child.

Here I will mention Rupert Isaacson, author of *The Horse Boy,*[1] who embarked on ambitious healing journeys on many continents with his son Rowan. His books are well worth a read. I have had some results with autism families by suggesting that they introduce their child to horse riding, or give the child a pet such as a carefully chosen dog. Truly mind-blowing healing can result from the interactions between children and animals.

Some Questions to Consider

- Is your child served well by you staying in your current location and the environment that predated his or her birth? Are there other places and communities that would allow and encourage a greater unfolding of potential?

  Parents of autistic children may choose to move from a city to a more rural location (less stimulation, wide open spaces) and live with animals who become a valued part of the healing team. For some parents their professional lives may not permit this, but do remain open to spirit guidance. Once I turned my life over to Spirit many things happened that I would earlier have considered beyond belief.
- How do you make choices about what truly supports your child's needs and journey? Are there medical professionals who offer a more spiritual or holistic perspective perhaps? Professionals never failing to say things that drain you of energy and optimism may not be the right experts long-term for you and your child. Listen to your intuition. Don't allow yourself to be bulldozered by specialists who 'know it all'. *You know you own child in a way they never will!*
- Can you find innovative ways of communicating with your child? I have already mentioned shamanic journeying and soul-to-soul communication, as well as animals.
- Are you willing to release the life you had mapped out for yourself (and the expectations you had) and lead a spirit-led life that will bring you untold rewards along with the initiations and challenges? What is the spirit-led life that seeks expression through your family, as opposed to: 'What does my ego want for myself and my family?'

As with any shamanic path, or other committed spiritual

undertaking, there will be huge demands in terms of dismantling existing structures and the human ego. The stripping of egoic attachments can be an excruciating process. However, ultimately you will receive gifts beyond your comprehension today, if you drop into the arms of your helping spirits. Are you willing to take the leap of faith?

There will always be a temptation to trust the medical profession to the point of following all advice to the letter. Medication and a tight schedule can allow life to continue, in some ways, as it was before. But often that is not the highest good. That is not what is being asked of us on the level of soul.

There is no space within the scope of this book to consider individual cases or specific conditions. Every person is unique. I can only paint with a large brushstroke here and identify larger patterns and developments. Maybe I will write another, more specialist, book one day.

Notes

1. *The Horse Boy: A Father's Miraculous Journey to Heal His Son* by Rupert Isaacson, Penguin, 2010 and *The Long Ride Home: The Extraordinary Journey of Healing that Changed a Child's Life* by Rupert Isaacson, Penguin, 2014

Chapter 10

Spiritual Warriors with Water Pistols: Healing Narratives and the Mythology of Fear and Conflict

To be nobody but yourself in a world which is doing its best, night and day, to make you everybody else means to fight the hardest battle which any human being can fight; and never stop fighting.
E. E. Cummings

We must learn to walk through hell with our hearts right open. If we do not, we deaden ourselves while abandoning the victims past and present to hopeless suffering.
Edward Tick in *War and Soul*

Sibling Rivalry

Let's start close to home…

Children fight. I know this from first-hand experience because I have three sons – and I also have two brothers! Adults fight too. Yet anthropologists tell us that peaceful cultures used to exist, and still do, in which people showed no innate desire to fight. However, it seems those cultures are few and far between and they lived in remote locations that did not invite much conflict or attack by outsiders.

Some peace-loving parents ban all toy guns and weapons from their house. For some optimistic early years I was such a parent, just as I was a sugar-free and TV-free parent for the same period. What happens then is that children fashion their own weapons from sticks and found objects. Poof! POOF!! BANG!!!

Of course we can also choose to use our own hands as weapons and children do this. We are all familiar with the popular 'gun' hand position.

So why do children fight? Close observation of my own children tells me that they get into conflicts over toys and resources, that they fight when something feels unfair to them and that they fight to establish rank and pecking order (not unlike a pack of wolves). It goes without saying that the youngest and most vulnerable child usually loses. This can mean that the parents become protective of the family baby. And that can lead to more conflict and fighting because this intervention is seen as unfair by the older children. I myself stand accused of all these parenting crimes!

As my own active parenting years went on (they are still going on!) my views changed from naïve optimist to hard-core realist. I went out and bought them water pistols so they could have water fights – if they now have to fight they might as well have fun doing it. From protecting my babies I moved to a position of thinking that they needed to learn how to stand their ground and negotiate. So I learned to tolerate a certain level of conflict and arguing. Instead of jumping in there with them I started saying: 'I know you can sort this out. Good luck!'

As I grew older I also learned that so-called shadow material (our own aggressive, unpleasant, unpopular side we hide from view, often even from ourselves) needs expression one way or another. So a fun fight with water pistols is preferable to children really hurting each other. Athletics and maths competitions are preferable to playground fights.

In the secondary school my own three sons attend there is a tradition known as The Birthday Punch. On your birthday anyone can come up and give you a birthday punch – and some leave bruises! It is like a rite of passage, my children say. But they also say that many young people take the preventive measure of not telling anyone when their birthday rolls around.

Things get even more intriguing. In spiritual circles there is the concept of the Spiritual Warrior or Warrior of the Light.

The Spiritual Warrior

Do shamans fight?

Do we expect spiritual people to fight?

These days many people call themselves Warriors of the Light!

Anthropology books tell us how in certain cultures shamans are seen as warriors. They fight evil spirits on behalf of their community. This is a belief system people collectively buy into. To be successful in shamanic work, the shaman needs to be seen engaged in battle with 'evil spirits'. For me this raises the following question: are wars and fighting then 'myths' we all collectively buy into? Do they serve a larger soul-purpose? Many spiritual people are fond of calling themselves light workers. Upon closer questioning such people will say that they actively anchor the forces of light and that they are Warriors of The Light. But...does 'The Light' need 'Warriors'? Or is the division between light and darkness something that exists mostly in our own consciousness, reflecting the fact that we live in a polarised world?

And, if that division exists within us, is there any point fighting it only outside ourselves, in externalised form, without going to the heart of the issue and healing the division within us? Then there is the delicious darkness of a mother's womb, of winter evenings, of fertile soil ready for seeds. Like the word 'darkness', or the word 'myth', the word warrior can have almost opposing meanings. You could call me a 'darkness worker'. I love working in darkness or spending time alone in a dark forest at night. I love being up when the world sleeps and doing spiritual work. I often work with clients in complete darkness too, by the light of just one candle.

Warrior[1]

1. a person engaged or experienced in warfare; soldier.
2. a person who has shown great vigor, courage, or aggressiveness, as in politics.

Most people will agree that the words 'soldier' and 'warrior' have different connotations and associations and that a warrior may be a higher expression of a soldier. A soldier follows orders. A warrior makes sacrifices on behalf of his/her community or a cause greater than him/herself. The Time Travellers group once did some constellations work on the theme War and Peace and their conclusion was that the need to fight needs to be transmuted into a higher or healthier expression of martial arts and the Olympic Games, i.e. healthy forms of competition. Great courage, self-discipline, honour and mental focus all have a place in those pursuits and no one gets hurt or dies. This also teaches young people about what I shall call the Art of Losing with Dignity. We can't all win all the time. Learning to respect and find joy in the achievements of others is an advanced human skill not everyone seems to master.

So, my tentative conclusion was that healthy human beings and cultures do not need to go to war and fight, but they need healthy forms of competition so people can test their strength against others, develop skills and learn a lot, but not lose their lives in the process.

Next I read two books that really developed my own thinking: *Iron John* by Robert Bly 2 and *War and the Soul* by Edward Tick.[3]

Robert Bly spent ten years working in the role of mentor with men to discover the 'truth about masculinity' and to get beyond the stereotypes of our popular culture. His conclusion is that without initiation rituals men fail to pass through key stages or windows in their human development and their process of emotional and spiritual maturation. This means that they get stuck in less mature modes of functioning: stereotypes like the tough guy, the mother's boy, the eternal teenager (puer aeternus in Jungian terms, but Bly prefers to call them Flying Boys instead) to mention but a few.

Peter Pan is the archetypal Flying Boy. Living in Neverlands, I frequently meet Peter Pan both socially and professionally speaking. As a blueprint he is very active in our culture.

In a time before this one, as in healthy tribal cultures today, older men held space for and initiated the younger men. Grief, also called The Time of Ashes by Bly, is a doorway to feeling. If men are given sacred space and support to walk this Road of Ashes they can develop their Inner Warrior, whose task is not hostility and aggression, but a healthy and steady resolve to know and protect what one loves.

We tell our children to 'stand up for themselves'. To do so convincingly we ourselves need to be adults who know ourselves and what we stand for. We also need to willingly take the role of the Big Ones allowing our children to be the Little Ones. If this process fails, children end up carrying responsibilities way beyond their age that crush their soul and perpetuate dysfunctional family dynamics for many generations to come. This is my observation as a shamanic practitioner.

Tick's book *War and Soul*[3] describes how post-traumatic stress disorder increasingly afflicts veterans of modern warfare and impacts all areas of life. Tick embarked on a quest to understand the myths of war and the impact of war on the human soul. His conclusion was that the archetype of the warrior is wired into human existence. This cosmic blueprint is visible in the way we order society, in rites of passage for adulthood, in the way social groups operate and compete. Tick says that across epochs, war has caused untold numbers of people to enact vengeance upon one another, I quote:

> *On the surface, worship, belief and the search for meaning seem contradictory to war making. In fact they are not. War and religion have been linked since the beginning of time. Each is a primary expression of our relations with each other, the cosmos and The Divine. Each constitutes a primary expression of mythology and its workings. And each has been used to further the cause and justify the practice of the other. War has fostered religion, and religion war.*

> *We cannot control the existential truths of life or the influence of the archetypes, but we can change our interpretations of them and the way their mythic stories unfold in our lives.*

I could not put this better myself. His words confirm everything I observe in shamanic and ancestral healing work.

Brothers in Arms

Before I move on, I just want to make a few comments about doing shamanic work (individual healing or group ceremony) with war veterans. Speaking from my own experience to offer a shamanic perspective on this, when you work with (ex) soldiers who have done active duty in warzones, their Brothers in Arms (those who did not make it as well as those who did) will be present energetically and spiritually. Make a point of inviting and welcoming and honouring them. Your work is not for the soldier alone, it is for a larger group of people, generally men, who have bonded through experiences so extreme few of us can even imagine. Another party will enter the room too, the so-called 'Enemy'. The other side too will need attention and respect during the work. A third party you will encounter is 'Those Who Gave the Orders'. Not just the field marshal, general or commander, but the politicians and decision-makers in society who declared a war or decided to send the army into conflict zones elsewhere. An army veteran will not find peace until a healing dialogue and energetic exchange occurs with all of these parties.

Then there are families affected by traumatised soldiers arriving home and that trauma splashing all over loved ones: partners, parents, (ex) wives, children and so forth, will all need to brought into the work. Soul connections need to be explored and honoured. Often a healing narrative can be found by looking at soul connections bringing any group together at a specific time. Forgiveness work needs to be done. Ultimately, much of the healing work can only occur in ceremony. Soldiers need to be touched by The Divine. When I do this type of work, I call in great warrior gods and goddesses in their compassionate aspect. My observation is that there need to be shamanic groups for veterans and their families, offering sacred space and powerful ceremony. The same thing goes for children of army officers. It will take hard work by many people to get such groups off the ground. This is a vision I hold and will support in any way I can.

Internal Narratives

I already said earlier, my children fight over resources, attention and for causes they feel passionate about. Children generally can't tolerate any form of perceived injustice. Tribes and nations go to war to fight for the things they hold sacred or most holy. This is where the concept of the Holy War comes from. We have talked about individual children fighting. We internalise the dynamics of our family of birth. We even carry within us the stories, pain and unresolved dreams of our ancestors.

Tick points out that the giving and taking of life are sacred acts. When we have children, we become part of the great cycle of life-giving events. It is an illusion to think that we can give life without dealing with death or that we can teach our children about love but not about war. It is an illusion to expect our children to grow up and reach their full human potential if we do not offer Rites of Passage and the community support needed for young people to survive those key transitions.

We tell ourselves stories. Those stories are based on narratives that played out in our families of origin, either spoken or unspoken and in our culture. We internalise the voices of significant people from childhood. You could call these stories internal narratives. No man is an island unto himself. We all exist in a larger field influenced by the ancestors and by larger themes that play out in our culture today. Courtesy of the modern media, we are also extremely aware of what plays out on the larger world stage.

Healing human consciousness means healing these stories, unravelling old scripts and writing new scripts. In sacred art workshops I teach we open forbidden doors and we unravel personal myths. Guided by our spirit allies we transform those stories. We allow them to shape shift. The word sacrifice literally means 'making sacred', by offering to the gods.

The Mythology of War

In October 2015 I did an Inspiring Youth presentation at Steiner House in London. I had been asked to formulate a response to the question: what makes young people join fundamentalist or even terrorist organisations like Islamic State (IS or ISIS). Is this related to our society's failure to offer appropriate rites of passage to our young people?

In brief, what follows is my take and what I said that evening.

If we do not honour our ancestors and commit to clearing our ancestral lines, our children's lives will be shaped by burdens, events and narratives that do not belong to them.

If we do not offer Rites of Passage, children will either fail to complete crucial developmental stages or they will place themselves in risky situations trying to create communities and initiations for themselves, such as through street gangs, joy-riding, drugs, crime or alcohol.

Tempting as it is to call oneself a pacifist desiring to abolish war, the cosmic warrior archetype is wired too deeply into the blueprint of our human existence. Instead we need to engage with the figure of the Spiritual Warrior and acknowledge the human need for heroism, testing oneself against others, protecting loved ones and working for causes one holds sacred. This larger process gives a human life meaning. A life without meaning is a life of despair and disconnection.

We cannot escape wounds and grief in human existence. But we can support young people (and people of any age) in developing the internal resources to deal with pain and grief, to become stronger for it, to develop compassion for others because of it, to learn resilience and the courage to show vulnerability. We can learn the art of being in our power without reducing others, stealing power from others or putting others down.

We can choose to become conscious of this Inner Warrior and formulate our response to personal provocation, violence, war or terrorism in the larger world, with care. The moment we wage war on war, we are responding on the same level of consciousness. We would do well to remember that any action always produces a counter-reaction. This is one of the most basic laws in physics. So our sacred task is choose our response with immense care so it matches the vibration of the world we wish to create for our children, not the world as we know it today.

Aris, Eris, Eros...

Tick says that we crave war in its mythic dimension. With the Time Travellers group I try to do this work in a light-hearted way by turning things on their head, finding the gift in adversity, working with the figures of the Sacred Clown and the Trickster, breaking taboos, turning laughter into tears and tears into laughter. I also teach the children ways of doing shadow work and how doing this heals all our human relationships.

This way we learn that every story is ultimately one perspective, one point of view. At any given time we are free to choose another point of view. Choosing a different point of view will create a different story. Every story or myth can shape-shift, can be shifted from a wounded or distorted perception to a healthier perception.

Myths from all over the world form a wonderful collective resource of ancient healing stories. They also contain many warnings about what can happen if core human needs are not addressed and the blueprint of human consciousness is not understood.

In Greek mythology three figures (gods, or if you prefer personifications) are relevant here:

Eris: The Goddess of Strife
Eros: The God of Love
Ares: The God of the Underworld

The ancient Greek word Heraclitus used for both war and strife is 'eris'. Eris as strife is an elemental force of the cosmos. Eris as war is the same force playing itself out in the human arena, says Tick.

Ares was the Greek god of war. His name literally means battle. He represents the physical and violent (slaughter) aspect of war whereas his sister Athena stood for intelligence, including military strategy.

Eros was the Greek god of love as in physical love. His name literally means Desire. (Classical Greek had other words for other forms of love, with agape or unconditional love being the highest expression of love, also Divine love or Charity).

I decided to put some of these themes to the test and invited my friend Judith Bogner to present a session for my Time Travellers group exploring violence and the impact of violence in the media and video games on the minds of young people today. Please note that Chapter 14 provides a write-up of this youth seminar. Judith is an actress and shamanic practitioner, as well as many other things, and she starred in the 2015 film Mission Impossible V, Rogue Nation with Tom Cruise. I couldn't resist the word-play and I gave our session the title No Mission is Impossible!

Separation and Division Consciousness

Becoming radicalised goes back to division on all levels: the class system in the UK, the division between private schools and state schools ('a better class of education for a better class of children') but even within those schools: children from immigrant families aren't always accepted. Maybe they are up to a point, if they make a really big effort, but not on the level of 'who they know themselves to be deep within'. So that is where those recruitment programmes 'hook people'. They think they are returning to their roots and then they find they 'return to terrorism and beheadings' instead. So I think the answer lies in healing all divisions, even the divisions within ourselves between our 'true selves' and the selves we show to the world. Anything less than that…is not going to be good enough…' Because for young people to fly to Syria does not solve the problem, but for them to simply stay here doesn't solve the problem either!

My own son Quinn at the age of 15½ when I asked him why young people his age become radicalised

Babies pass through a stage called separation anxiety. In truth I think this issue is cosmic in origin and all humans experience it at regular intervals. I know I feel separation anxiety when I am about to leave a person I love, or a group of people I have really enjoyed being with. I even feel separation anxiety when my students graduate!

Some brilliant authors say that many human problems start with the core issues of shame and/or anger. Others say that those issues create addictions and co-dependency (all of those behaviours are about fleeing and numbing, the very opposite of mindfulness, as in being present to what arises in our awareness in every moment). I resonate with their work and I have learned powerful lessons from their books and teachings. However, as a shamanic practitioner, I have come to believe that there is another issue lurking under the shame and anger etc. and that issue is separation or what my teenage son refers to as *division consciousness*.

In my shamanic healing work I constantly observe many

people move through a profound process of transformation on the level of soul. My take is this: we are all Divine in origin and one day we return to, and reunite with, our Divine origin, no matter how we conceptualise this and what names we give to The Divine. For growth in consciousness to occur we needed to split off and become separate beings. Not unlike the way a new-born baby slowly develops a sense of self, of no longer being an extension of its mother. In that act of splitting and separation, vulnerability and free will enter the great cosmic equation. Where there is free will, there is the option of making misguided or even bad (harmful) choices. Human beings are vulnerable creatures. Such choices can have an immense impact on others. Once we become separate beings, we acquire a human ego (one of my students called this *the air traffic control manager* last week) to keep us safe and focussed. Ultimately, all spiritual work is about dissolving those egoic states of consciousness so we can escape polarised thinking and see the Ultimate Oneness of All That Is.

Many creation stories from all over the world show a point when separation from Divine Unity occurs. An egg cracks open, a dragon or giant is chopped into pieces to make the physical world. Separation allows us to function as souls (i.e. separate beings with a sense of self and identity). However, separation also creeps into our own psyche and functioning:

- Soul and Shadow
- 'Us and them'
- 'Good people and evil people'
- 'There is no space here for those refugees, they will take our jobs and drain our financial resources'

This split allows us to de-personalise, even de-humanise, other human beings. That, I observe, is one of the root causes of many evils perpetrated in our world.

Having acknowledged this, the great gift of free will means that we can start making healing choices and amends at any time, in absolutely any moment. In shamanism we can even work outside time and bring healing, resolution and amends to events that occurred in the past. Likewise we can work on pre-harmonising events that are taking shape in the future. (Please see Session Plan 10 on Public Speaking with Judith.) Collectively we can choose which stories we identify with and which stories we need to rewrite and allow to shift their shape. Individually we can take a step back from our own monkey mind and observe where such splits occur, where our own world is divided and unhealthy.

It has been said that human beings as a collective move through phases of development, just like individual human beings do. I had this discussion with my students recently and asked: 'What stage have we reached today?' I think we are teenagers: we have fiery emotions and make impulse decisions. If that is so, would powers greater than ourselves come forward to initiate us as a collective? I admit that this is a way-out thought…

The Positive Brigade

It would be relatively easy to write a book about doing spiritual and energy healing work with well cared for Western children from good homes. However, as someone who has worked with slum children in Peru and spent time as a volunteer in a field hospital in Bangladesh, I feel we need to set our sights higher. You may call me a naïve optimist. There seems to be a school of thought that suggests being spiritual is about always being relentlessly positive. I am a great believer in positive thinking. I am a mindful user of Facebook and social networks – my personal philosophy is that social networks are what we make of them. I choose uplifting messages and images to put on my Facebook wall, as well as on the walls of our house. Having said that, I am also great believer in being present to what is. Because I believe that denial can be a harmful and even dangerous mindset.

I already spoke about separation and division consciousness in the previous segment. Division consciousness can even *divide us from ourselves* (I see too many clients who have lost track of their true or authentic self and their unique soul task on Earth). The moment that internal crack (or Grand Canyon) opens up, external forces can widen it (peer pressure, conditioning, the dominant culture, making foolish decisions out of a desire to belong and fit in).

I am writing this chapter during the last week of June 2015. Just a few days ago a radicalised young man shot 39 tourists on a beach in Sousse, Tunisia, and the death toll is still rising. One of my own children was attacked in Sousse two years ago. I will finish this chapter by sharing his story.

When Teenage Violence Meets Shamanism...

Our family had a frightening experience in Sousse in 2013, but it had a happy ending and pales into insignificance compared to the shooting on the beach. We rented a car in another town and did a day trip to the Medina, the walled old city of Sousse, one Sunday morning. As we were strolling around, a teenager on a motorbike, with a much younger child as a passenger sitting in front of him, made a beeline for us. We all jumped out of way, but our youngest son, then nine years old, wasn't fast enough. The motorbike knocked him over so he fell backwards, slamming his head on the cobbles, and then drove across his small torso. We were horrified and so were the local people. Some set off in pursuit of the motorbike, but it was long gone. The teenager laughed loudly and hysterically as he sped off. I have never been more angry in my whole life. This was not an accident. It was a deliberate act of one 'child' terrorizing another. I only need to think back to this moment to acknowledge the capacity for violence and murder within myself.

Our son is a Natural Born Shaman – he wrote a small book about shamanism in the months that followed this incident.[4] He told us later that during the moment he knew the motorbike was going to hit him and that there was no escape, he called in all his Power Animals and they protected him. They filled him with their presence and power. He got off with a big bruise on his chest, and a big shock, but no permanent damage. What he said was: *'I have always known that the tiger powers are powerful, but only now do I exactly know HOW POWERFUL they are! Strangely I feel safer than ever after this!'*

Notes

1. From The Free Dictionary on-line
2. *Iron John, A Book About Men* by Robert Bly, Rider, New Ed edition, 2001
3. *War and the Soul, Healing Our Nation's Veterans from Post-Traumatic Stress Disorder* by Edward Tick, Quest Books, U.S., 2005
4. *The Love Hall, Brendan's Travel Guide to his Favourite Places in the Spirit World* by Brendan Almqvist, Polar Bear & Cubs Creations, 2014

Chapter 11

Mudlarks of the Human Soul

Mudlark: *Someone who scavenges in river mud for items of value. A term used especially to describe those who scavenged this way in London during the late 18th and 19th centuries. Mudlarks would search the muddy shores of the River Thames at low tide for anything that could be sold. Mudlarks were usually either youngsters aged between eight and fifteen or the robust elderly. And though most mudlarks were male, girls and women were also scavengers.*[1]

Mudlarks

Here in London people have found untold treasure in the mud of the river Thames. The Time Travellers love going mudlarking, as real Londoners call the art.

In this day and age, events from all over the world are delivered directly to our living rooms. Heartbreaking images of starving children and abused animals flood our screens and social media. I too want to run a mile when I see another picture of someone shooting a lion, abusing a baby elephant or a hungry child with fleas crawling over their face. For me personally the Big Question is: is there anything we can do to make a difference, yet operate spiritual hygiene around the thoughts we think?

The never-ending bad-news-feed can make us feel powerless to the point of depression. After years of shamanic training, soul searching and reading thousands of books, my answer is that within ourselves we can choose to make a shift. From feeling utterly powerless and victimised we can make a gear shift in terms of choosing our attitude and responses with immense care.

We can choose to heal our own poverty consciousness. This is a life-long task, as I am finding. Even after years of spiritual training and inner work I keep finding new layers of poverty consciousness in the mud of my inner world. I have to keep on going back to heal this on another level, and yet another level. It is so deeply embedded... The mudlarking never ends!

We can choose to see all individuals affected by disaster as the brave luminous beings they are on the level of soul. We can see their talents, their sacred soul light, their ultimate luminosity – no matter what pictures of them the media serve up. Some of them may just possibly have chosen to be born in these places to hold up a mirror to the rest of the world. We just don't know. We cannot assume anything. Are we willing to look in that sacred mirror and see them as spiritual warriors rather than victims?

I am editing this chapter on Monday 30 November 2015. My husband brought home a newspaper yesterday. The headline that grabbed my attention, and made me feel sick, was: 'Cameron to order the killing of ISIS leaders. Masterminds of Paris Attack targeted.' For me this goes right back to all the material discussed in the previous chapter: if we are to wage war on terrorists we respond on the same level of consciousness or vibration as those terrorists are operating on. Do we truly want to align ourselves with them, be it on the opposite side? This will only feed polarity and perpetuate a chain reaction of violence stretching into the future.

A Facebook friend, I cannot remember who it was, posted a very different message after the Paris Attacks: 'Every time terrorists commit an act of extreme violence, so much love, healing and compassion is sent to that location that the whole vibration there permanently shifts. They are actually attracting immense love, light and healing to all these locations.'

It is not the whole story, I fully acknowledge the horrific human tragedies and suffering caused, but I think this person is choosing a more evolved response than David Cameron. Obviously a Prime Minister must be seen to be doing something. But let's remember the actions and teachings of Nelson Mandela, Mahatma Ghandi and Auntie Suu in Burma for moment here.

For anyone in the public eye, there is always the option of aligning yourself with a more evolved perspective and using media attention to heal mass consciousness, rather than to wage war. This is *especially true* for people in the public eye. You could call it a *sacred responsibility*!

If we are to heal division consciousness, we must release us-and-them thinking. As in 'those terrorists are evil and we are good'. Terrorists may be fighting for a cause that seems plausible, something that actually is sacred to them. But one person's Holy War is another person's Unholy Undoing.

The real question here is: can we own our inner terrorist and do shadow (inner) work with him or her. Can we heal our own murderous impulses, our own toxic thoughts, the resentments we have allowed to fester, all the ways we have ever thought of others as inferior or unworthy in some way? This will lead us straight to our own hidden reservoirs of self-doubt and self-contempt.

Can we take a moment to even see the luminous soul light of terrorists and war criminals. Who knows, it may just soften or awaken something within them if large numbers of people do this…sometimes we need others to hold a higher image of us, so we can recall ourselves to ourselves...

Sandra Ingerman teaches Transfiguration[1] as a daily practice as well as a healing method. This means merging with our own divinity and making an active choice to see others in their divinity too; choosing to see their soul light, their divine nature, seeing them as 'divine siblings' as it were, children of the same Creator or Divine Parents, however perceived, named or invoked.

100% Responsibility

Another method for polishing the mirror of our soul that deserves a mention here is Hawaiian Ho'oponopono.[3] (See Session Plan 30.) H'oponopono has been used as a form of energy healing for centuries. We perform a form of spiritual cleansing for our entire existence, going back to the very beginning of time, to the moment of Creation itself. It has three vital elements: repentance, forgiveness and transmutation. Essentially we learn to take 100% responsibility for what is in our consciousness. If we are aware of something, we need to find some way of dealing with it!

This is done through a prayer given to us by the late Morrnah Nalamaku Simeona, Kahuna Lapa'au:

> *Divine Creator, father, mother, son as one. If I or my family or my relatives or ancestors have offended you, your family, your relatives or ancestors in any thought, word, deed or action from the beginning of my creation to this present time, we ask your forgiveness. May this cleanse, purify and release any memories, blocks, energies and vibrations and transmute these unwanted energies into pure LIGHT. And it is done. Thank you.*

Please note that when I use this prayer myself I say *child*, not *son*.

This prayer can be used for anything. It can become a mantra we speak under our breath for hours a day. We can also put it on pieces of paper and place it on photographs of people, places, newspaper articles about causes…think of the article about David Cameron.

Contemporary spiritual teacher Dr Ihaleakala Hew Len teaches a shorter, more condensed, version called The Four Phrases:

> *I'm sorry*
> *Please forgive me*
> *Thank you*
> *I love you*

This may look deceptively simple (is that all?!) but those words are like keys that unlock great healing forces beyond our comprehension. The challenge is not in the words, but in accepting that we *must* take responsibility for all that comes to our attention and become willing to apologise where needed and wrap love around what seeks love. No matter how we personally feel about that. No blame and no shame. No focus on who caused this, only ever a focus on: am I willing to heal this by doing spiritual work on this?

Am I willing to engage with these prayers daily, constantly, like a mantra or the rosary beads my Roman Catholic grandmother gave me in childhood? My answer is yes, I am, because these prayers have created tangible results in my own and the lives of my clients and students. So here is one very practical example of something we *can do*, even for situations that seem totally outside our control. May I suggest that you do not overthink it, but try it… Observe and track what happens.

The Sacred Hall of Mirrors

One way to heal separation is making space within ourselves for The Other. To be willing to see that *I am You and You are Me* and ultimately any division or separation is an illusion.

> *A human being has so many skins inside, covering the depths of the heart. We know so many things, but we don't know ourselves! Why, thirty or forty skins or hides, as thick and hard as an ox's or bear's cover the soul. Go into your own ground and learn to know yourself there.*
>
> Meister Eckhart [4]

Are you willing to look at all human beings around you and thank them for the mirrors they hold up? Can you own and hug your Inner Terrorist and your Inner Rock Star along with your Inner Child?

Can you see all the children in our world as your children on some level? (This is hard, I know. Our family has certainly invited children on play dates I have been thrilled to hand back to their parents in the evening!) The children of our world are literally our future. They are our Future Earthkeepers. They are also the nurses, doctors and 'death midwives' who will tend to us the day we die. Therefore our children are everyone's children, they are the children of our global community.

This morning, writing on 14 July 2015, I saw a picture in the news of an 11-year-old Syrian girl mothering three younger siblings because their mother had died in the conflict. We owe it to children, our children, these children, everyone's children to heal war consciousness in our own mind and to anchor the consciousness of peace and Enough For All. We cannot eradicate poverty in our external world without first releasing the poverty consciousness we all hold in our own minds and hearts.

Reality Bites

So today I actually ran the web search: 'What is the Top 10 of most dreadful issues children face globally?'[5] The answer was:

1. Military use of children
2. Trafficking and slavery
3. Internet child pornography
4. Child prostitution
5. Child labour
6. Child neglect
7. Lack of access to education
8. Life as refugees
9. Poverty
10. Violence through indoctrination

Divine Creator, father, mother, son as one. If I or my family or my relatives or ancestors have offended you, your family, your relatives or ancestors in any thought, word, deed or action from the beginning of my creation to this present time, we ask your forgiveness. May this cleanse, purify and release any memories, blocks, energies and vibrations and transmute these unwanted energies into pure LIGHT. And it is done. Thank-you.

I'm sorry.
Please forgive me.
Thank you.
I love you.

Further Reading

How to Heal Toxic Thoughts: Simple Tools for Personal Transformation by Sandra Ingerman, Sterling, revised edition, 2012

Notes

1. Selected and adapted from https://en.wikipedia.org/wiki/Mudlark
2. *Medicine for the Earth: How to Transform Personal and Environmental Toxins* by Sandra Ingerman, Random House, USA Inc, 2001
3. *Zero Limits: The Secret Hawaiian System for Wealth, Health, Peace, and More* by Joe Vitale and Ihalekala Hew Len
4. From http://www.brainyquote.com/quotes/quotes/m/meistereck149160.html
5. Google: Top 10 of terrible issues facing children worldwide

Chapter 12

Not Bad, Not Sad, Not Mad... Shame and Shamanism

Shame itself is an entrance to the self. It is the effect of indignity, of defeat, of transgression, of inferiority and of alienation. No other effect is closer to the experienced self. None is more central to our sense of identity. Shame is felt as a torment, a sickness of the soul in the worlds of Silvan Tomkins.

Shame is a wound made from the inside, dividing us both from ourselves and from one another.

Gershen Kaufman in *Shame, The Power of Caring*[1]

'Shaymanism'

It is a shame that shame is not understood in our culture. We feel it, but we rarely investigate it because we can't bear to dwell on it (or stay with it for any length of time). There is no etymological connection between the word shaman and the word shame, but on a whimsical level I observe many people pronounce shamanism with an ay: shaymanism. (Personally I say shahmanism.) Maybe this tells us that people doing shamanic work need to make it their business to understand shame? I have come to think so over years of being in shamanic practice.

Have a look at Session Plan 12 in this book: Body Image, Self Esteem and The Sacred Clown. Clowns are taboo breakers and so are shamans. Shame is one of the greatest remaining taboos in our culture. It is rarely named or understood for what it is.

The struggle for identity is one of the recurring problems of our age. Each individual inevitably searches for answers to the questions: Who am I? Where do I belong? Inner security depends on feeling whole, worthwhile and valued from within. Identity is rooted both in wholeness of self and in belonging to a larger community.

> *The need to identify is the need for rootedness, connectedness, belonging. It is a need to feel identified with, to belong to particular individuals or groups. From identification spring loyalties, and loyalties create allegiances – to family, friends, religion, nations. The need to belong to something larger than ourselves – to a group, a cause, an idea – is one principal source of identity.*
> Gershen Kaufman in *Shame, The Power of Caring* [1]

What is Shame and What Purpose Does it Serve?

Healthy shame teaches us about boundaries and limits. It warns us about violating social norms. It forces us to pay proper attention to our own behaviour and our relationships with others. However, in recent decades psychologists have coined the concept *toxic shame* for the unhealthy (devastating) side of shame. Toxic shame is internalised. Rather than having committed one shameful act we become ashamed of ourselves, *all* of ourselves.

'Toxic shame says you are unworthy as a human being, you are unworthy of human connection. This leads to violence in an attempt to replace that toxic shame with pride,' says Suleiman Bakhit[2] who is said to fight ISIS with comic books and a diet-healthy heroes and role models for young people in the Middle East.

When shame makes us turn on ourselves, we lose our sense of worthiness. When we lose our sense of worthiness, others cannot see our worthiness either and our interactions with others start confirming what we secretly suspected all along. We start a nosedive and it becomes very hard to change course.

Since about the mid-1990s research has been done into the way shame-prone people behave. They are people for whom life is a never-ending battle. They can never relax. They feel that they always have to defend their place in the world and earn love from others. Do you know someone who fits this description? Sadly I know many people who do...

Some evidence suggests that a high number of people who suffer from depression have unresolved shame as a core issue. Shame hollows us out. We lose our centre, our sense of Self.

> *Shaming begun in early childhood causes a sense of emotional starvation and neediness which demands to be fed. It inappropriately and greedily, gorges on stolen attention.*
> From an on-line article titled Overcoming Toxic Shame by Tova Gabrielle[3]

This quote really got my attention. Don't we all know people who eclipse others around them by talking compulsively or compulsively grabbing attention by acting inappropriately or doing millions of other things that actually makes it hard to remember we love them?

In shamanism we work with symbols, images and stories. Often we need to reframe our experiences. Rather than saying or thinking: 'I am the weird one in my family,' we can say: 'An important part of my healing journey was realising that I chose to be born into this particular family to bring healing and a more spiritual perspective on life.' I use this healing sentence a lot with clients. It doesn't change history or the actual circumstances, but it can instantly change how we feel about ourselves. It can change the story of our life (more correctly, the story of our life as we choose to see and tell it). It releases people from a long-held view that is always saturated with shame.

Research shows that people who survived and recovered from the Holocaust were those most able to derive meaning from their experiences. In this context Viktor Frankl[4] deserves a mention. My students were discussing his work in class last week. He was a neurologist and psychiatrist as well as a Holocaust survivor. He went on to write a best-selling book titled *Man's Search for Meaning*.

Healing Narratives

In her beautiful book *Soul Retrieval*[5] Sandra Ingerman explains what soul loss is and how shamanic practitioners retrieve soul parts or soul essence. She emphasises the importance of healing stories. In reading articles and books about shame I came across the phrase 'soul murder'. If we use shame to discipline young children we can almost literally murder their soul. We can do lasting damage and cause fragmentation of the self. Our word psyche comes from the ancient Greek word 'psykhe', which means both soul and butterfly. Using shame to keep a child in line is, in my personal perception, akin to pulling the wings off a butterfly. You rob that child of their innate ability to take flight and lead a brilliant joyful creative life. Heavy as this subject is, I cannot write a book about shamanism and children without encouraging parents and teachers to *reframe shame.*

Another thing we need to mention here and understand in this context is how toxic shame can be transferred to others. When we were children, others – and not only our parents – may have dumped their own shame onto us.

I have observed my own parents behave with immense discomfort when we children did something that carried shame in their own family of origin. For example, relaxing and spending time 'not working' was a deadly sin in my father's family of origin. He was from a farming background where everyone got up at 5am to milk the cows before school. He could not bear to see me or my brothers idle. He would instantly set us chores or order us to 'to do something useful'. Today I find it difficult to see my own teenagers do *absolutely nothing* for days on end (shouldn't they be doing something productive?! Imagine having *time* on that scale!), but I have now done enough work on myself to think: 'They are great teachers for me in learning to do less.' Not doing anything is rapidly becoming a lost art form. I don't shame my children for it. Not consciously anyway!

Shame researcher Brene Brown[6] explains how imperfect

parenting moments can turn into gifts as our children watch us try to work out where we went wrong and how we can do better next time. Monitoring ourselves and admitting when we go wrong can be a gold mine of alchemical transformation between parents and children. Laughter is excellent soul medicine too.

In shamanic healing work we often need to *give something back to others*: a script they wrote, an expectation they had, a feeling they left us with. In disciplining children we need to constantly ask ourselves: 'Do I have reasonable expectations of my children or is my parenting coloured by my own experiences of being shamed, manipulated and pushed around?' (We will need to polish our soul until the day we die...)

If we have any doubts on such matters, the best thing is always to consult our spirit allies. They will quickly show us the true picture of what is going on in any given situation. If you know how to journey or meditate, build this into your spiritual practice. At regular intervals ask: 'Please show me how to improve my parenting.' Or: 'Please show me what I most need to know about my relationship with my children.' A course in shamanic journeying is a great investment for any parent.

Healing the Dead

One last thing I want to mention here is that sometimes we need to do all of these things with the dead as much as the living. That is what ancestral healing work is: we honour the dead and give them their rightful place in the family. We honour our soul connection to them and the gifts they passed on to us. But we cut and release unhealthy imprints or habits we inherited from them. (Shame will be an active ingredient in many such patterns!) We free ourselves from living out these patterns, blueprints, myths and stories. We become the author of our own stories. You could say that we write a new film script for our own life, often with new actors on stage. We surround ourselves with spiritual family, people who truly support our sacred dreams and the journey of our soul. Not people who push us right back where we came from. We do this type of healing and releasing work for our children and for the children of our children as much as for ourselves. Whatever we resolve and release, our children will no longer need to carry and live and breathe and repeat...

However, one thing I want to emphasise here, going back to Sandra Ingerman's work, is the principle of transmutation.[7] We cannot create or destroy energy, but energy can change form. We can use our intention and imagination to make energy shift shape from something harmful or toxic into blessings, love, something positive.

Further Reading

The Dance of Anger, A Woman's Guide to Changing the Patterns of Intimate Relationships by Harriet Lerner, Ph. D.

Notes

1. *Shame, The Power of Caring* by Gershen Kaufman, Ph.D.
2. Sulaiman Bakhit is a Jordaninan entrepreneur who produces superhero comics in various media for Arab youth. He is trying to change how the West sees Arab youth and how Arab youth see themselves. He does this 'one superhero at a time' through providing positive roles models, heroes and narratives.
3. Online article by Tova Gabrielle http://learninginaction.com /PDF/Overcoming_Toxic_Shame.pdf
4. *Man's Search for Meaning: The Classic Tribute to Hope from the Holocaust* by Viktor E. Frankl, Rider, New Ed edition, 2004
5. *Soul Retrieval, Mending the Fragmented Self* by Sandra Ingerman, HarperOne, revised updated editions, 2010
6. *Daring Greatly, How the Courage to be Vulnerable Transforms the Way We Live, Love, Parent and Lead* by Brene Brown, Penguin Group, 2012, p.15

7. *How to Heal Toxic Thoughts, Simple Tools for Personal Transformation* by Sandra Ingerman, Sterling, revised edition, 2012 and *Medicine for the Earth: How to Transform Personal and Environmental Toxins* by Sandra Ingerman, Random House, USA Inc, 2001

Chapter 13

Learning about Violence or Learning to be Violent?[1]

Can specific media products compel people to violence that they would otherwise not have committed?

... in the lives of too many teenagers, recognition is more meaningful than accomplishment...

Gavin de Becker in his book *The Gift of Fear*[2]

This is the Big Question many parents, teachers and youth leaders are asking themselves today. I would like to thank Gavin de Becker for formulating the question so accurately. In the next chapter we put this question to my Time Travellers group.

The Big Question

What *is* the effect of violence in the media, music and in computer games on young people? My own observation is that young people spend a lot of time in a virtual world that did not exist when I was a child or teenager myself. I certainly spent a lot of time in my own imagination, painting and writing stories, but computers had not yet arrived on the domestic scene. Many people parenting teenagers today did not grow up with personal computers. It can be hard to work out where and how to draw the line. I observe that people in the entertainment industry design ready-made fantasy worlds for young people to step into. To make those worlds exciting, there is incessant fighting. Losing a game makes young people desperate to do another game to *level up*. That way parents, in everyday reality, end up doing daily battle with their teenagers over the issue of screen-time. From that point of view online fighting demonstrably breeds battle in our family homes.

Gavin de Becker is the US leading expert on violent behaviour. He uses PINS (Pre Incident Indicators) to predict violence. Below are just some PINS he has formulated for teen violence, but there are many others:

- Alcohol and drugs
- Addiction to media products (replacing genuine human interaction)
- Fascination with violence and guns
- Getting attention (after a lifetime of being ignored)
- Children learning by modelling and imitation (the 200,000 acts of violence they will witness in the media by the age of 18 therefore pose a serious problem)
- The 'fast track to fame and feeling significant'
- Young people not learning the seven key skills for a human being, as formulated by Daniel Coleman in his book *Emotional Intelligence*:[2] 'The ability to motivate ourselves, to persist against frustration, to delay gratification, to regulate moods, to hope, to empathise and to control impulse.'

In our culture acts of mass violence bring instant recognition and media attention. This poses a problem in its own right we need to re-think. (I will return to this issue at the end of this chapter).

Summary of Findings

I looked at research done on this topic and here is a brief summary of my findings:

- Heavy exposure to screen violence in adolescence is changing the development of young people's brains. Exposure to violent material also activates the brain's limbic system, which is responsible for emotional response and memory.

- Images of violence could be stored in the brain in the same way that post-traumatic stress disorder patients store memories of trauma.
- The two most vulnerable periods in brain development are in early childhood and puberty. The peak age for video game usage is from 11-14 years. (But just looking around me tells me that many young people aged 15-25 do a lot of gaming too!)
- Prolonged exposure to such media portrayals results in increased acceptance of violence as an appropriate means of solving problems and achieving one's goals.[4]

Personally speaking I also observe that even adolescents (aged 18-25) play those games and use the chat button to talk to teenagers much younger than themselves (aged 12-13 and up). I observe how this blurs boundaries that normally exist between these age groups. For example, our own eldest son has thrown some pretty odd ideas at us, picked up from, according to his own description, 'an autistic 20-year-old in Sweden who lives in supervised accommodation for troubled youngsters'. This young man has, apparently, told our son that he should not have a fixed bedtime and that we need to understand that playing World of Warcraft has been classified as a sport now. That is just to mention but a few things! My son has invited us to speak to this young man on Skype, in the hope that his opinions will change many of our house rules. These are scenarios my own parents didn't have to deal with!

And here are a few more conclusions researchers have arrived at:

- Television, movies, and music videos normalise carrying and using weapons and glamorise them as a source of personal power.
- Titillating violence in sexual contexts and comic violence

are particularly dangerous, because they associate positive feelings with hurting others.

- One study of nearly 32,000 teenagers in eight different countries, for example, revealed that heavy television-viewing was associated with bullying.
- Entertainment media inflate the prevalence of violence in the world, cultivating in viewers the *mean world syndrome*, a perception of the world as a dangerous place. Fear of being the victim of violence is a strong motivation for some young people to carry a weapon, to be more aggressive, and to 'get them before they get me'.
- All violent media can teach specific violent behaviours, the circumstances when such behaviours seem appropriate and useful, and attitudes and beliefs about such behaviour. In this way, behavioural scripts are learned and stored in memory.[4]

Last, but not least, here is the most horrifying discovery I made: RapeLay is a 3D eroge video game made by Illustion, released on April 21, 2006, in Japan. This game centres on a male character who stalks and rapes a mother and her two daughters. Three years after its initial release, the game garnered international attention and controversy for its content, and was subsequently banned in several countries.[5]

The Price of Instant Fame

I am aware that our culture values free speech. I am very grateful that we are not living in a police state or dictatorship here in the UK. Having said that, I think our society has gone too far. Sensational stories sell newspapers so any newsworthy story lines pockets in the media world. When acts of terrorism or school shootings occur, these stories make the headlines. On a cynical level I am aware that the would-be teenage shooters or suicide bombers out there must do their research and work out how many deaths are required to make the world news these days. As they unfold such stories are milked by journalists: interviewing neighbours, former partners or classmates etc to keep the story running for as long as possible.

As a society we must take responsibility for the fact that if we allow such events to become a media industry we are actively creating the school shootings and human cause disasters of the future. It is short-sighted in the extreme. If we wish to create a better world for our children and our children's children, we must own the part we ourselves play in this. If we stop feeding the media industry on this scale, giving only a very brief mention of the relevant facts, committing such acts will immediately become less attractive. *We ourselves are feeding the terrorist attacks of the future by not owning the part our own media play in the larger scheme of things!*

This all goes back to the shadow work again: rather than portraying trigger-happy teenagers as complete monsters we must own our collective part in this. How did society (all of us together) fail these young people as they grew up? Are we willing to face the price we all pay for our daily fix of sensational stories on TV and in the newspapers? What diet are we feeding our future terrorists and school shooters? What monsters in our own psyche are we failing to address by acting and reporting like this? If we are to heal the *us and them thinking* these are only some questions we urgently need to ask ourselves. There are many more.

Notes

1. The title of this chapter was inspired by one line in a thought-provoking online article: http://pediatrics.aappublications.org/content/124/5/1495.full
2. *The Gift of Fear: Survival Signals that Protect Us from Violence* by Gavin de Becker, Bloomsbury Publishing PLC, New edition, 2000

3. *Emotional Intelligence: Why It Can Matter More Than IQ* by Daniel Coleman, Bloomsbury Publishing PLC, New edition, 1996
4. From an on-line article http://www.smh.com.au/digital-Life/games/screen-violence-changing-young-brains-researchers-20131004-2uzom.html#ixzz3gG0yXloZ
5. For more information please see https://en.wikipedia.org/wiki/RapeLay

Chapter 14

No Mission is Impossible! A Youth Seminar exploring Violence in Films and Games

Some Personal Background

At age 15 or so I arrived at my secondary school one day and was told: we are going to watch a film! An afternoon off from maths and physics, YAAH! So as a film virgin (barely having watched even Walt Disney films at other people's houses) I found myself watching Psycho in darkened room without any warning about what was to unfold. And yes I will admit that even today (fully 33 years later!) I feel traumatised by that event and I have religiously avoided seeing any horror films since! Do violent films have an impact on young minds? My own experience tells me *yes*. So I decided to organise a seminar with an exciting co-teacher and put this question to the young people in my Time Travellers group.

Violence in the Media Session

Doing my research for this book the question of the influence of violence in the media, films and on-line games on the minds of young people became a pressing concern for me. I decided to invite Judith Bogner once again as a guest teacher for the Time Travellers. Judith is an actress (she plays the role of the Chancellor's Wife in Mission Impossible V, Rogue Nation), with direct experience of action films, as well as a shamanic practitioner.

Here I will provide notes and key observations from this session. *This information does not come from researchers or scientists, it comes from the mouths of young people!*

Judith started by asking the young people what an action film is.

What is an action movie? What do you think?

TTs: 'They are unrealistic stories that push the boundaries, with much fighting and stuff, generally set in the modern era or future, overly dramatic with many entrances and exits.'

Judith herself then summed it up by saying that action films usually are:

- About extreme situations involving danger, injustice and crime
- Something or someone needs to be rescued or protected
- Mission Impossible has this title because the tasks given to the hero seem impossible to accomplish
- Involve pushing boundaries, breaking laws and doing the unexpected

She went on to say that it is important for the action looks real and dangerous but the actors are always protected and safe, that specialists create special effects like explosions or gun shots. That martial arts experts train actors in fights. That the actors themselves need to work out in the gym to be physically in good shape so it is safe for them to run, jump and fight. And last but not least that everything that looks easy on camera actually takes months of preparation, hard training and a lot of discipline! No director wants an actor to die on set!

Q: What is an action hero? Who is your favourite action hero?

The young people immediately talked about *anti-heroes* too and said that action heroes are often almost supernatural in their abilities and in-your-face-amazing.

They agreed that action heroes are generally not a recluse because recluses don't make good stories. If they are not recluses they often are in secret societies and lead a secret life on the side.

Judith pointed out that:

- The hero is indeed either a trained expert or someone 'normal' who rises to the occasion (the definition of an anti-hero)
- The hero can be a man, woman, child, animal etc
- There is a wide range of different types of heroes: muscled, dumb, geeky, smart, ruthless, compassionate, funny, handsome, with superpowers etc
- Generally the hero has their heart in the right place

Many action heroes work as a team so their different gifts and talents are combined to achieve a better result than each can do on their own. Judith explained that human beings do best as team players so impossible tasks can actually be achieved. Next she invited all young people to pay less attention to the main hero and more attention to other actors next time. What else is going on? Focus on the nuances. Looking at one person (even if this person is Tom Cruise) gets boring after a while!

In fact films can be very much like shamanic journeys in the sense that there are no limits and no rules!

Journey to your allies or power animal and ask to be taken to an action hero who is willing to work with you or give you a gift

Our young people all got very different answers to this. The gifts were anything from 'being prepared for anything' to messages about racism and bullying or receiving one key word that is of personal importance. One 15-year-old boy met James Bond who gave him the gift of being perceived correctly by others (meaning that others would always see his true or authentic self).

Judith picked up on this and talked about the importance of *being seen*. She also talked about meeting my own three children when they were about five years younger than they are today and them teaching her how to throw Love Bombs around for anyone in need of love, affection or kisses.

What is a movie from a shamanic perspective?

The TTs said:

- Someone else's story
- It teaches or illustrates lessons and films can carry intentions or messages that affect you or change your perception about something
- Films can help you understand craziness

Judith herself gave the following answers:

- A shamanic journey expressed in images, words and sounds for everyone to see
  Many people watch a movie and think 'it is just a movie, it is not real' but it becomes real when our thoughts, emotions and physical responses are affected
- A movie stays in our awareness long after we watch it
- Every movie has its own spirit, energy and intention, which can be harmful or beneficial
- Films can have the effect of bringing healing or inspiration, causing fears, unlocking memories etc.
- As Time Travellers you are all aware of the invisible world of spirits and power animals so you need to be conscious and aware of the power of movies and how they affect you
- You need to all choose with great care what you allow into your sacred space and your reality
- If your friends or mates push you to watch something you don't like it is OK to say no
- Films can be a parallel reality and make Other Worlds accessible

The group discussed how films are interactive and how everyone will have different responses depending on their own personality, memories and fears. Therefore films can be a double-edged sword: they can nourish us and make us laugh but they can also traumatise us (think of me and Psycho!)

Journey to your Action Hero or Power Animal and ask: 'How do I know if a movie is good for me?' (Is there a sign or signal I could watch for?)

TTs: Anything paranormal… I can sleep on a murder scene if I go with friends and don't force it on myself… being with friends dilutes the impact!

One boy: 'I have an internal alarm system that feels like a pounding in the head.'

One girl in response: 'Yes! I know what you mean. It is like a clock ticking and it announces a nightmare!'

Boy again: 'Yes, I deal with bad dreams by casting a spell.'

Girl: 'It is like a physical feeling creeping up. I sometimes it takes a while for me to notice it and then I wake up. It alerts me to a nightmare.'

Boy: 'This is how I have learned to pull myself out of nightmares.'

Girl: 'It keeps me awake and it annoys me!'

Another boy said that he has (what he calls) an Inner Eye: 'If there is anything suspicious, I always check it out!'

What about a movie showing violence?

Judith explained that the verb to violate means causing injury, harm, damage on something or someone by using force, weapons or a sword.

- Humans or animals get hurt or killed, things or buildings get destroyed

- There is a fine line between destroying something with good intent or by accident and outright malice
- I get very uncomfortable when I see or hear violent scenes. I close my eyes, cover my ears or just switch off
- Just because it is a movie doesn't mean it is OK!
- Please remember that a movie can show dangerous and exciting action without causing harm *(at this point Judith explained how the big explosion in Mission Impossible V was planned and orchestrated for months).*

I asked Judith if she had turned down scripts because of violence or because of them having the wrong signature or vibration. Judith said she has, absolutely!

The next question that arose in the group was: films often glorify violence to some extent – how do we deal with that? Any valuable film generally deals with something dark. What about this aspect?

Judith replied that anger can be very creative in a safe space. Anger can power us through a problem, like music or a ritual can do too.

At this point the group got into a discussion about the question (raised by a 15-year-old boy): is there such a thing as *acceptable violence* and *unacceptable violence*? Does this extinction even exist?

We talked about the portrayal of it. Is it sadistic? Is a larger good being achieved for humanity? (Example: a terrorist is taken out, preventing greater violence at a later point in time).

We talked about how families set (and need to set) their own limits around this issue. There are liberal families and conservative families. There are families with religions or belief systems that say certain things are off limit.

Judith admitted freely that although she stars in action films, certain Walt Disney films have made her leave the room (think of

Bambi's mother dying and there are serious death issues in the Lion King). The children discussed how they have had nightmares after seeing unsuitable movies and how certain scenes can never be completely erased from your memory. Once you see something, you cannot ever *un-see* it again... They said how seeing some films was almost equivalent to 'offering yourself for an attack'.

Can watching violent movies make people commit violent acts?

The children disagreed on this. Some said yes they could and others said no, deep inside most people know 'where the line goes'. They went on to say that some people have mental disabilities though, or a mental illness. Shamanic journeys are very real so a disturbed person could equally well perceive a film as 'reality'. The line between everyday reality and 'other or non-physical parallel worlds' can blur for some people.

All the children agreed that these people (including young people) are an absolute minority, but one person committing an act of violence has a huge impact on a very large number of other people. School shootings were mentioned and the children talked about the recent terrorist attacks in Paris.

The discussion moved on to generations. Old people have more life experience so they can be involved in handling the effect violence (in films and life) has on young people. All of our lives will be touched by violence at some point. This is part of the human condition, unfortunately.

Then we talked about ancient stories and myths. There is violence in the great classical myths and fairy tales too can be very dark. Think of the Greek god Zeus raping women or Red Riding Hood and the wolf in grandmother's clothing.

Is there such a thing is becoming numb and learning how to tolerate too much violence? Can we learn to give violence a place and respect in some other way in our lives and reality?

Judith decided it was time to hand these issues over to Spirit and she announced another journey.

Journey: How can I protect myself from something that makes me feel uncomfortable?

The answers included:

- Visualise myself embraced by my Power Animal
- Project a pillar or tower of light (or angel) between myself and a person or event
- Transmute an event by using our own imagination to change the outcome
- One boy suggested we use our imagination to see scary creatures shape-shift into teddy bears (this is a bit like imagining a person you don't like or a scary teacher sitting on the toilet!)
- Trusting your inner stillness and breathing through it
- Humour: deliberately seeing the funny or cheeky side of something
- Call in your Power Animal; he or she will not be scared of anything!
- The oldest boy present (15) said: 'I feel an obligation to weather scary things. Encountering something like that is a life lesson. It trains me up to later on cope with something worse.' (Judith summed this philosophy up as *initiating yourself into adventures*!)

We then talked about the need to become hyper-sensitive and having our internal warning systems on alert because technology is making huge strides and impinging on our privacy and confidential information about us held in databases etc. This discussion segued into a discussion about illusions of safety. Judith pointed out that many things that are reality for us first actually appeared in movies like Star Wars. So we would do well to pay attention to those films as they show us aspects of the future.

What about violence in video games?

This is different from films because you yourself are actively involved in creating outcomes. The children talked about progression (as in building a higher skill level) as a form of entertainment.

The 15-year-old boy talked about the kill score mechanism. Basically this means that many kills and wins means you move up to the next level of the game (and you gain prestige with peers along the way, for being good at a game).

The discussion moved onto war for a moment.

Does war have positive aspects?

The group agreed that strategy and planning are positive skills learned by military people.

Judith pulled the discussion back to the issue of self-control. How much time passes while you are playing a game? Do you forget to eat or go to the toilet? Most children agreed that they play until a parent pulls them off their screens. Using a timer was discussed. The importance of having a balanced life was discussed too.

Judith announced the final journey for the day. The younger children were looking extremely tired at this point!

Ask your spirit allies: what do I need to remember from tonight's session?

- To be more aware of my surroundings and use my

intuition to stay safe
- Being able to tell the difference between virtual reality and ordinary or everyday reality
- The importance of leading a balanced life and not being sucked into virtual worlds for too long periods
- Not taking films overly seriously
- Actively creating a calm Eye of the Storm within us

No Mission Is Impossible!

Chapter 15

Things That Have a Positive Impact on Young People

Having listed so many negatives I would now like to list and discuss some things that have a positive effect on young people.

Mentors

Research has demonstrated that having a compassionate mentor can make a huge difference in a child's life. One person (a grand-parent, kind teacher, neighbour, older cousin etc) showing interest, providing encouragement, a listening ear and so forth, can turn a young person's life around. Gavin de Becker (please see the previous chapter) talks about the moment a child sees his own worth reflected in the eyes of an encouraging adult. We can choose to be that adult, even (especially!) for other people's children. I have already said earlier, we need to dissolve the idea of children belonging exclusively to their parents and family of birth. Children need to be seen as belonging to the whole community.

Peer Mediation

In December 2015 Judith Bogner and I did a presentation at Steiner House in London, as one in our series of Inspiring Youth Talks, titled Mediation and Compassion. We were exploring how mediation can be used to arrive at compassion and how peer mediation has been successfully introduced in schools since the 1980s. A mediator will typically assist two parties in resolving a dispute or disagreement. The idea is to find a compromise or common ground, an outcome that both parties can live with.

I remain convinced that most human conflicts can be solved

through genuine dialogue conducted with a spirit of openness and reconciliation
Dalai Lama, Speech before the European Parliament, 14 October 2001

Mediation is the attempt to help parties in a disagreement to hear one another, to minimise the harm that can come from disagreement (e.g. hostility or demonising the other parties), to maximise any area of agreement and to find a way of preventing the areas of disagreement from interfering with the process of seeking a compromise or mutually agreed outcome.

Elders and Rites of Passage

Our culture fears old age (i.e. is in denial about death) and has done away with the traditional roles for old people. If we allow them to once again become the highly respected Elders of our communities, they can reach out to young people and spend time with them in ways parents aren't always able to do. In doing so they may literally save our future and turn around the lives of vulnerable teenagers. Ideally they would also provide Rites of Passage and facilitate the ceremonial transfer of spiritual wisdom and knowledge.

Spirit Allies and Spiritual Toolkit

As I have already said elsewhere in this book, other than good parents and teachers, what children most need is a strong relationship with their own spirit allies. Power Animals and other spirit teachers are with us day and night. They can be asked for guidance and support at any time, in any place.

Spirit World as an Anchor for the Virtual World

We live in a 24/7 world where we are bombarded with feeds of information. Young people need help in learning that this is an important part of contemporary life, but the virtual world can never replace the world of everyday reality: meeting people in person, unplugged time around the family dinner table, switching off all iPhones to have a good night's sleep, and so forth.

I have always had the sense that the true purpose of the internet is *not* to abolish libraries because the answers are only a click away or to do my shopping online. My feeling is that the internet prepares us for a paradigm shift where human beings come to terms with the fact that we are multi-dimensional beings. That there is more to all of us personally than we can see in this reality. There is more to reality than we can perceive with our earthly senses. Just like websites are places you can visit in a virtual world, we can visit places in energetic parallel worlds.

My observation is that computer games provide ready-made worlds that stimulate aggression and fighting spirit, but do not engage young people's own imagination, or stimulate their innate ability to enter parallel worlds at will, or to create worlds in their own imagination (those things can amount to the same thing). Therefore my advice is to marry online games with grounding in a sound spiritual framework.

A Sound Spiritual Framework and Belief System

I just wish to expand on this for a moment: for me a sound spiritual framework means committing to a belief system and sticking with it. In my shamanic practice I see many people who dabble in shamanism, then do a course in Buddhism, they have also explored Wicca… All of that is fine. We all need to explore several things to find out where we truly belong, spiritually speaking. But the day inevitably comes when the need arises to make a commitment and take the hardships along with the magic and inspiration. Every committed spiritual path serves up challenges along with the soul food. For Jewish people this means having newborn baby sons circumcised. For tribal shamans this means surviving ordeals and initiations. Buddhism requires approaching what you fear most and extending compassion to the people you most want to avoid. Roman Catholics used to confess all their sins and transgressions to a priest on a weekly basis. The list goes on.

To shamanic parenting we can bring an awareness of initiations that occur naturally in the lives of our children and the importance of those transitions. Rather than protecting our children from challenges we can support them through their challenges and send them the message: 'You can do this!'

Noah's Ark and Spirit Canoe

Many people tell me that they loathed the religious upbringing they received and decided not to pass this on to their children. I myself chose not to bring my children up in the Roman Catholic faith of their Dutch ancestors. But to choose away one thing without making a positive choice for another thing is akin to not building your child the equivalent of Noah's Ark.

If your child has no spiritual compass, how will they sail into the unknown and weather the storms of life? My philosophy is, build them a spirit canoe! They can reject your offering and decide to build themselves a different spirit boat. But at least they will realise that they need some kind of boat to navigate the waters of life.

'Power Full'

The previous chapter has demonstrated that online games give children the concept of weapons as a source of power. True personal power has nothing to do with weapons. It has everything to do with feeling worthy and loved, having focus, healthy personal boundaries and a viable spiritual toolkit.

It is more about being 'power full' than about being 'powerful' as that often implies exerting power over others. That is not the kind of power shamanism works with and teaches.

Part II

Thirty-Two Session Plans

Brief Introduction to Part II

Part I of this book has introduced spiritual and shamanic work with children. I have discussed many issues that occur frequently. I have named obstacles and prejudices that make can make this work challenging. I have also talked about how to work with what I have called lost children: spirit children and children lost to families due to various causes.

Part II of this book describes my work with the Time Travellers group in London. You will find 32 session plans and suggestions for anyone interested in using shamanism creatively with children. Parents and grandparents will find ideas here to use with their own children and grandchildren. I hope that the voices and wisdom of the young people I work with shines through these plans, as many sessions were prepared in response to themes requested by the children themselves.

I am aware that shamanic work with children is extremely time/location/age and person specific. What works a treat with one group of children will not work at all with children of the same age in a different location, or children speaking a different language, or young people in a different climate, and so forth. The session plans you will find in this book are just a starting point, to get you thinking, adapting and ultimately flying free. I repeat: *there are no limits to what is possible!* The most important thing by far is creating a safe container where children themselves are able to receive guidance and support from spirit. Equally important is you receiving the right guidance from your spirit allies in every moment, allowing you to wear the robe of teacher/facilitator, *always remembering that the spirits are the true teachers in this process.*

Work with children is always 'in the moment' (even more so than with adults), so you are going to be flying by the seat of your pants. Often you will come away feeling they taught you more than you could ever hope to teach them. Sometimes you will plan a session and something urgent happens that means you need to change course. Sometimes something happens in the everyday world that the children are concerned about, that needs naming and addressing in a session. So you can't ever make rigid plans... But you can arrive well-prepared.

From this point of view it could be argued that it is pointless to publish session plans. However, from the volume of emails I personally receive I know that the most common request is for session ideas and inspiration, where to start? What to do and what to expect? What to avoid?

Last, but not least, many people want a mentor who can provide support and answer some questions along the way. People also crave a community of kindred spirits. Right now a colleague and I are working hard to put such a network in place.

Inspiring Youth – Feeding Spirit, Finding Self

At the time of writing (September 2015) I am working on a project called Inspiring Youth, Feeding Spirit – Finding Self with Marion Briggs, who is the co-ordinator of the Alliance for Childhood in the UK. The aim is to connect people all over the world who are passionate about working with young people in fresh and innovative ways. Many of these people are parents and grandparents who care profoundly about the next generation. Others work with young people as paid professionals in manifold capacities (teachers, nurses, therapists, youth leaders etc). Our intention is to map and summarise what people are doing and where they are based. In doing so we are creating a larger forum where people can share experiences and get in touch with each other. The most important thing is obviously young people themselves creating the spiritual structures of the future, their voices being heard and their visions coming true. We have created a Facebook page by the same title (feel free to find and join us) and we are also working on a listing that will appear on the Alliance for Childhood website.

We are organising monthly Inspiring Youth Events at Rudolph Steiner House, in London, to bring people together physically and create a forum and platform for issues affecting young people all over the world. We hope that this will lead to focus groups and events in other locations. Long-term plans include a conference in London followed by a larger international conference in Sao Paolo, Brazil. We are also hoping to publish a small book presenting the visions and dreams of young people today and resources for those who live or work with young people.

Help! Where to Start?

In an ideal world your own spirit allies will provide all the ideas and information you ever need. However, in the world of everyday reality I get frequent emails from people asking for ideas and session plans and inspiration. I invite you to use my ideas in this book for inspiration, without any need to follow them to the letter.

The absolutely most important thing is allowing the children themselves to voice what they need and what they need from you in the role of facilitator. Run frequent checks on this. Remind them you are always looking for cool session ideas. If you have planned a session on plant spirits but, heaven forbid, a school shooting occurs and the children need a spiritual perspective on this or wish to do some shamanic work on this, the plant spirits will agree to wait another week.

Authorship, Copyright and So Forth

I am very happy for other people to use these ideas, but I do ask that you give credit where credit is due. If you use any Time Travellers Group material I thank you in advance for referencing my name and that of the group in London. As you will see from the credits and links organised at the bottom of most chapters, I myself am indebted to incredibly many other people whose work I have used loosely as inspiration for fun, but transformative, sessions with children. If you use this material, please reference their work or name too as and when appropriate. Thank you!

Where to Start if You Feel Called to do Something Like This

Just the logistics can be overwhelming. You will need:

- A group of eager children with consent from their parents
- A venue that has both indoor and outdoor space
- Ideally a fire pit or fire bowl, firewood and kindling
- A designated Fire Keeper is a good idea. Ideally this person will also assist with all other things *(you can ask adults to volunteer for this, it may be different people for different sessions)*
- If you are working outside in a place with no direct access, you may need a door or gatekeeper person as well
- A remo drum (meaning a rain-proof and weather-proof drum)
- Any other props for a particular session
- To sort out money matters

You will need to work out a reasonable fee for your sessions, unless you can afford to work for free. In shamanism we honour the principle of energy exchange. If you are going to be paying for a venue, your students will need to pay a session fee for you just to break even. If you have never done anything like this before, do your homework and some research. What do parents pay locally for other classes their children attend, such as art classes, woodwork, karate, music or swimming lessons? I decided to price my sessions as comparable with local woodwork or art classes. However, I soon realised that this would barely cover the train fare or petrol cost of any guest teachers I invited. But I also learned that many people are willing to come and generously share skills with young people if you pay their travel expenses. If you make the sessions too expensive it may well stop families from attending. You could consider operating a sliding scale.

I made one big mistake, which I then had to correct later: I did not announce the sessions as a block and charge for them as a block. So children were constantly missing sessions and not paying for the sessions they missed, but I still had to show up, prepare and teach etc. Therefore my suggestion is announce a block of sessions for one school term (perhaps five to 10 sessions, depending on how often they run) and ask people to pay in advance for the whole block. If children don't show, you still get paid for your time/preparation and you are not out of pocket with either venue or a guest teacher needing their train fare refunded.

It is generally a good idea to allow new children to attend one session for free as a taster, but after that, make it clear that they need to commit to a block of sessions and the tuition fee. You can make exceptions in dire circumstances and offer discounts for siblings.

Some General Pointers

Weather

A true shamanic practitioner may be tempted to work outside in all weathers, but I work with city children and once it starts raining seriously, which is not uncommon here in London, UK, the children want to be able to run for cover or they get extremely miserable indeed. I have tried to take a tougher approach ('Let's dance with the rain spirits today') and parents have then contacted me about their children having asthma or health issues etc. City children aren't very weatherproof it seems! For that reason it does not work to run all sessions in local parks, woodland or other outdoor venues. I usually manage to use parks, cemeteries, ecology parks and the bank of the River Thames as locations for summer sessions, but in winter it is too cold, too wet and too dark. So I end up doing indoor sessions. They are less fun than the outdoor sessions because the kids can't go feral in quite the same way or go wild on the trampoline before and after the sessions, but I keep reminding them that we will be outside again as soon as the weather allows.

Managing Age Difference in the Group

If you are lucky enough to attract a very large group, you could decide to teach them separately in age groups (say five to 11 years and 12 to 16 years). Having said that, there are considerable obstacles in attracting children to this type of work, so more likely you will find yourself with a smaller group of children/youngster varying wildly in age. I have had sessions where I have had both a five-year-old and a 15-year-old present.

What then kicks in is teenagers not being overly keen on being taught alongside younger children. The way we have managed this in our group is to try to allocate some special roles. Meaning that the older ones get to mentor or assist the younger ones. The energy of discontent is then transformed *into feeling grown up and being useful, taking on a mentoring role.* I see this as part of creating a sense of community. In tribal communities different age groups still have and always had their roles and made different contributions to society.

I also spend a fair amount of my time reminding all children that everyone is allowed to engage on their own level. Some will move fast, others are more cautious. A seven-year-old will share in a different way from a 14-year-old. In our group we celebrate diversity, on both a personal and cultural level.

The Parents

In the early days of the Time Travellers I allowed and even encouraged parents to stay. Some of them were driving a long distance and home again. Others wanted to know what I was teaching their children so they could continue practising the material at home and continue doing shamanic work together with their children. I still think that for a time this worked surprisingly well in creating a bonding experience for parent and child, but there are things children will not share while there are parents around. The day came when I asked parents to leave and return at the end of the session. As I run courses for adults as well, parents can be directed to those courses for their own learning process. I have also invited some parents to be guest teachers for a session and share a skill. This is a very positive way for them to stay involved.

Teaching Your Own Children

I think it is very common for a shamanic parent to have a vision of doing shamanic work with a larger group of children. For me personally one of the challenges has been having my own three children in the group. We have had many amazing sessions and they have made fantastic contributions, but they have also mucked around big time. If your own children are in the group, they are going to be testing you to the very limit. It is good to be aware of this. Having an assistant or co-teacher (who is *not* the other parent of those same children) can ease this dynamic.

Personal Limitations and a Reflection on Gender Issues

I am a woman and mother of three children in the Time Travellers. Teenage boys need to be encouraged to break free and make their own way in the world. They need independence and privacy. I cannot Initiate my own children, who all happen to be boys, and I cannot host Initiation for teenage boys, full stop. Here I call on male colleagues and ask them to organise things like a night of sitting out, vision quests, wilderness camps off the grid etc. (You will find more information about this in Part III of this book).

If you are a man you cannot host a Rite of Passage for teenage girls who have just had their first menstruation. I myself cannot offer experiences of Initiation to teenage boys. I can be in the background or at base camp, but the actual role needs to be performed by men for boys. In indigenous/tribal societies this is done by the Elders of the community. Old men take teenage boys away from the village and from their mothers and Initiate them, so they then return to the community as young adults.

The women in turn provide Rites of Passage for the girls, celebrating menstruation, witnessing death and assisting with childbirth. This is how girls learn from an early age about the close links between midwives and shamans. And often the midwives are also *death midwives*. They assist at times of birth *and* death.

Building Community, Sharing Skills and Resources

If you want to do more than offering a programme of exciting classes, you will need to reflect on your own gender, resources and limitations and then actively look for partnerships with people who can offer those vital things that you cannot bring to the group. For me this has been an important part of working with the Time Travellers. I have learned a lot about my own strengths and limitations. I have slowly built a group of wonderful people who support the work I do with children and are willing to make guest appearances and share skills with the group. It is my sincere belief that raising and teaching children takes a community, not just one or two individuals.

Examples of this have been:

- A TV presenter teaching the children about public speaking using shamanic tools
- An animal communication specialist teaching the children how to do animal healing work
- An artist friend teaching them about pyrography and working with wood
- A shamanic practitioner friend demonstrating the use of different kinds of drums and explaining how shamanic frame drums are made

The possibilities are endless. Many people *love* being asked to share their skills with children! I hope that this book reflects how my own community has made the work with the Time Travellers possible. I could *not possibly* have done it alone.

Session Plan 1: The Great Cosmic Egg

Introduction

As this was our first ever session I wanted to achieve the following things:

- For the children to have fun, so they would want to come again
- For them to learn a safe basic healing modality, so they could go home and practise on willing family members
- For them to have some free time at the end to run wild and connect with others in their own way.

The first session our London group did was based on the concept of the primordial or cosmic egg.

I wrote to all the families who had brought me individual children for shamanic healing session and invited them to bring their children to this class. My colleague Nick Taylor, who committed to being my co-teacher for the early months of the Time Travellers, came up with a great exercise where we prepared threads in all colours of the rainbow. Those threads became soul connections made visible and vibrant, as we stood around the fire. We talked about eggs and new beginnings and how this group represented a new beginning.

I showed the children how eggs are commonly used by healers in Central America. The Spanish word for healer is curandero (man) or curandera (woman). The official name for this method is La Limpia de Huevos[1] (meaning egg cleansing). You run a raw (unfertilised) egg over the body of the client with the intention that the egg absorbs any intrusions, unhealthy energy, stress or even illness held in the body.

All the children, and the parents who stayed, teamed up and took turns doing this. It was very interesting to observe how some of the children really got the hang of this. They really took their time, their hands would sense that the egg needed to stay longer in certain places.

All children present observed that the eggs felt much heavier after use and that their clients felt lighter and brighter. Our large garden, where we were doing this work, backs up to a railway bank that is part of a small local nature reserve. Many city foxes have their dens there. They exercise their cubs in our garden. A day rarely passes without a sighting of foxes in our garden! There is a particular area of our garden where I told the children to leave all eggs that had been used as *an offering for Mr Fox*. There was some concern about Mr Fox falling ill, but I explained that any energy unwelcome to humans is not going to affect Mr Fox. He'd just be happy for the free meal! The children were so intrigued by this that even now, four years later, they still talk about *Feeding Mr Fox,* meaning that sometimes the Earth or certain animals can receive and transmute something that humans need to release.

I also explained that the eggs can be used for something called divination work in shamanism. So we cracked some of them open in a bowl and tried to understand what the egg yolk was telling us about the person we had worked with.

Teaching Notes

The Fire Keeper arrives early and starts building a fire assisted by arriving children.

Gather around this fire, holding hands. Take a moment to arrive and be fully present (meaning that our monkey minds are not running off to other locations and concerns).

Ask everyone to introduce themselves (our name and age) and say whatever they wish to share with the group.

Reinforce the message about safe sacred space where young people are free to share anything they wish in the community of young people here, as long as they do so respectfully. However, *whatever we share there, stays there!* Make a point of explaining what confidentiality is.

Get out the rainbow threads and allow those threads to connect everyone up, so the energetic connections in the circle become visible.

Introduce the concept of the Great Cosmic Egg and how it appears in creation stories from all over the world.

Introduce the egg healing method and demonstrate on a volunteer.

Do two rounds: everyone gets to be practitioner and receive healing.

Mention the word 'extraction', a key term in shamanic healing.

Say that you can even perform an egg healing on yourself.

Extraction

Shamanic extraction means taking energy out of the body or personal field and returning it to the Earth or the elements. Extraction deals with energy that is in the wrong place. Energy in itself is neutral, but we can send energy and with the intention it acquires a direction. Talk about the difference between sending and expressing energy.

In our country eggs are not fertilised – in other locations they might be. The spiritual rule is that *energy always happily follows a life form*. The egg is a universal symbol for life.

Share observations: how did it feel to be client and practitioner?

Do we ourselves feel different afterwards? Did the eggs feel different after use? Any other comments or questions?

Leave the eggs out overnight as an offering for Mr Fox or other wildlife in your area.

Gather around the fire again to close the group for the day.

Thank the Fire Keeper, thank Grandfather Fire, thank the parents for driving a long distance, thank all the Spirits of Place.

Remind everyone when the next session is and what the theme will be, close the group, then call 'feral time!' (slightly wilder than free play time, meaning permission to run wild).

Notes

1. I was introduced to this method by shamanic teacher Ruth Aber in Santa Fe, NM, USA

Session Plan 2: Meeting My PA! Session about Power Animals

In shamanism we love playing around with the abbreviation for Power Animal: PA. Let me check with my PA...my personal assistant! Most people love knowing what their Power Animal is, but children especially love connecting with their Power Animals. Many children instinctively know what their Power Animal is. Often, but not always, it is their favourite animal. Their special animal since they were tiny.

Power Animals play a central role in shamanism and in shamanic work with children. As not everyone reading this book may have done courses in shamanism, I will start by briefly introducing the concept.

What is a Power Animal?

A Power Animal is an evolved being that makes the commitment of being with you 24/7 and helping in all areas of your life. It is not actually an animal (say a panda that died in China last week), it just takes animal form to allow you to draw on the strengths of a particular animal species. In some ways a Power Animal is not unlike the Christian concept of a guardian angel. It is an evolved being guiding you and watching over you.

The Shaman's Map

At this point the children have committed to attending sessions in shamanism. As children want to be active and not do too much listening, I give an extremely brief introduction to the three worlds of (core) shamanism: Lower World, Upper World and Middle World. And sometimes I show them the shaman's map drawing I use in classes with adults. But I try hard not to talk too long – and keep the session action-based.

Children work extremely fast. Any shamanic journey

generally only lasts about four minutes tops and they will pack in more adventures and guidance than most adults doing a 25-minute journey. This is something I always have to alert guest teachers to. They think that they will stand there drumming for 15 minutes and the session simply explodes if you do that. You have just lost your audience completely! Everything runs much faster than when covering the same material with adults. The moment children return from a journey they get bored and twitchy. They may start tickling the feet of other children for dramatic effect etc. The key words in this work are *fun, speed* and *action.*

Teaching Notes

The Fire Keeper makes a fire assisted by arriving children.

Meet around the fire. Open the group.

Ask: 'How has everyone been?' Go around the circle and share.

Say that today is going to be all about Power Animals.

Ask: 'Who knows what their Power Animal is? And how do you know?'

Say: 'Power Animals are often found in the Lower World so today we are going to learn how to make our first shamanic journey.'

Say the following:

We can visit the Lower World by travelling down into the Earth. This means that we need to find a way of going down, like a rabbit hole, a hollow tree trunk or a tunnel. I will be drumming and that will help the journey along! When you come out the other end, you will be in the Lower World. This is nothing to do with the Under World you hear about in mythology. It is a vast place where you find different landscapes and many animals.

Now I will demonstrate what shamanic drumming sounds like.

Plus (very important) I then demonstrate what the call-back signal sounds like. I need to be sure that everyone is going to return from their adventure.

Next I explain that we are going to set a strong intention by speaking it aloud:

My attention is to travel down to the Lower World and meet My Power Animal!

Then call everyone back and check how they got on.

Generally they are very excited and have many stories to tell.

Ask them if they have any questions.

Ask them if this was a new animal or if they had met this animal before.

If there is time left, make another trip down and get them to try asking their Power Animal a question.

Share what happens.

Close the session and announce the next session, then call feral time.

Session Plan 3: A Shamanic Toolkit for Bullying

Years ago a local mum told me that her daughter's school had called her because bullying had been observed. She automatically assumed that her child was the victim and told me how rattled she was to discover that her daughter had actually done the bullying. This taught me a *huge* lesson about bullying and personal shadow that we would all do well to observe!

Introduction: Why a Session on Bullying?

The Time Travellers Group was born on 5 June 2012, the day of the Venus Transit. An auspicious day! I ran fortnightly sessions throughout the summer and in September all the children went back to school. Some started new schools (secondary school or what in the USA is middle school). This is a turbulent time for most children and some of the parents reported cases of bullying and asked me to run a session on that. Sandra Ingerman gave me one piece of invaluable advice at this point. She said that it was extremely important for *the children themselves to receive guidance and tools from their own spirit allies to handle bullying*. As the teacher and adult there is a temptation of knowing 'what is there in shamanism' and teaching young people what you think they might find useful. This has its place, but the most precious thing you can give a child is a close relationship to their own spirit allies so they can always ask for support and guidance.

A related point I wish to make here is that teaching shamanism, in any form, is always about taking students to a new level of consciousness. One level of consciousness that is very much alive in our culture is, what I will call, *victim consciousness*. What I mean by that is that if you say the highly emotive word '*bullying*', any parent will have a fear reaction and automatically see their own child as the one being picked on, never as the bully. Parents will also have flashbacks to times they themselves were bullied. With the amount of bullying that goes on in schools (writing this as parent of one child in primary school and two teenagers in secondary school) there are obviously *parents of bullies* as well. And the line between victim and bully is not always clearly drawn in the sand. Even the line between friend and bully is not always clear-cut, as we found with our youngest son a year ago.

As a shamanic teacher I feel very strongly that we need to own *the part of us that hurts others* as much as *the part of us that is wounded*, or *wishes to heal wounding*. Think of all the people in 'the helping professions'. That is the only way we are going arrive at wholeness, owning both the benign and shadow expressions of our own humanity (that is all any human being is capable of).

One year ago we discovered that our youngest son was being bullied in school. One of his friends visited one afternoon and spilled the beans. So we contacted the class teacher and a school protocol kicked in. For our son, and for us, the most shocking thing was that the boy doing the bullying (making our son look ridiculous at play time, getting other boys to laugh at him and humiliate him) was someone our son had thought of as a close friend for five years. The class teacher was excellent and spent many lunch breaks mediating and talking with all children involved. In the end the issues were resolved. On a personal level I was angry that the school never called in the parents of the bully, but the school was adamant that there were sound reasons for this. Over a period of weeks peace was restored. Over a period of months our son gradually became friends again with this boy. This boy's parents do not know what happened there, unless the boy himself has told them, but we see no evidence of that.

Bullying brings out all sorts of big issues and emotions in parents; it activates the memories of all the times we ourselves were humiliated or treated badly. There is an instinct to protect your child at all cost and 'make the bully pay' for what he or she is doing. (I admit that I had fantasies of going around to this boy's house and taking his parents to task over this!) The class teacher calmly followed school protocol and lovingly restored peace. The fact that the boy's parents didn't know made the process easier perhaps. There was less awkwardness in the aftermath. It is hard to arrive at a definite opinion on this.

The larger point I am making here is this: our children are not always the victim in a bullying situation. And if our children go through a period of bullying others (not necessarily as the instigator, but as part of a larger group or being present in the role of observer) we are not always going to know about it. I talked about this to a friend and she said: 'I can relate to this. When I was Brendan's age the person bullying me was also my best friend. These things are so complicated!'

The last thing I want to mention here is that in 2014 LA-based film maker Hannah Beadman filmed the Time Travellers Group doing a session in which they received guidance from Spirit on camera about handling and resolving bullying.[1]

Teaching Notes

The Fire Keeper builds the fire assisted by arriving children.

Open the group.

Introduction

Say:

Today we are going to work closely with our own spirit allies to receive spiritual tools that protect us from bullying and help us deal with bullying when it does occur.

Remind everyone that we have opened safe and sacred space. What is shared here, stays here and remains confidential.

What IS Bullying?

Ask: 'Has anyone here today experienced bullying?'

(In my experience no school child exists who has not experienced bullying or at least witnessed other children being bullied.)

What Does Bullying Look Like from the Shamanic Point of View?

This will generally flush out the themes of personal power, power loss and power theft. What our group arrived at was the realisation that losing personal power can make a person attempt to reclaim power by stealing power from someone else.

Talk About the Nature of Power and Talk About Power Animals

Drum a journey for the children to visit their Power Animal and ask for guidance or a method to handle or resolve bullying.

One method our children received was merging with their Power Animal so their power was fully up. Say: 'People around you will not consciously see your animal, but something in your 'field' will make them back off.'

Shamans can call their helping spirits really fast. They can power up in a split second if they have to! However, one obvious concern is children attracting unwanted attention to themselves while doing this. So, we did some practice runs on powering up quickly and discreetly.

Another method received was creating and wearing an Invisibility Cloak. Harry Potter wears such a cloak. We talked about animals using camouflage to protect themselves and we did some work creating invisibility cloaks in the Other World.

Next we all of us went outside and we gave the children the instruction to become invisible. We had some parents present for this session and one shamanic practitioner father decided to become invisible by merging with a tree. The children did not find him. Even today the children still speak fondly of The Tahir Tree!

Close the group.

Follow-Up Sessions

The bullying theme was not just a one-off session. When you teach a group of children over a period of years this theme needs to return at regular intervals. In follow-up sessions we have built on what we did before. Follow-up sessions have also allowed new arrivals to catch up on what we did before.

In such follow-up sessions we have explored the following things:

- Projecting strength and divinity on to someone
- Choosing to see them as a luminous being and Child of The Divine – even if they are not behaving exactly like that in that very moment
- Doing a meditation to call back any power that others have taken from us
- Psychic protection: using things like a blue egg or bubble of light all around us and setting intentions around thought forms from others bouncing off, transformed into love and blessings
- Sending others a strong telepathic message that bullying is not on

Further Reading

One teacher asks her students to write down the names of four children they want to sit with during the upcoming week as well as one student whom they believe is 'an exceptional classroom citizen'. However, she does *not* do this so students can sit next to their best friends. Rather, she analyzes the papers for patterns. She looks for the names that are not being requested, the ones that go from several requests to none, and the ones who leave their sheets blank. She looks for the lonely children, and then rearranges the seats to help them connect with their classmates and, hopefully make some new friends. The teacher began this activity 14 years ago. More specifically, the day after the Columbine High School shooting. Realising that 'all violence begins with disconnect,' she has found a way to break the pattern and, hopefully, saved several lives.[2]

Notes

1. The link for the film is https://vimeo.com/138086974 Google Hannah Beadman and her personal website will come up.
2. As reported by author Glennon Doyle Melton in her blog but abbreviated slightly by me. Google her using the key words 'momastery' and 'share schools'.

Session Plan 4: The Ones Who Came Before Us, Our Ancestors

Introduction

In tribal or indigenous societies honouring the ancestors is a huge part of spiritual community life. Ancestors are venerated, consulted about important matters and kept alive in memory. As a shamanic practitioner I do a lot of ancestral healing work. Most clients I see know surprisingly little about their ancestors.

In our society we hold certain beliefs that are too simple and naive, almost childish:

- *When people die they go to Heaven.*
- *Why would I connect with my ancestors? They are long dead. I never give them any thought.*
- *Death can be a great release. Once people die they take all their unresolved issues to the grave with them and those issues no longer affect anyone else.*

As a shamanic practitioner, walking between the worlds daily, I observe that this dominant view in our culture is not in alignment with my own experiences of Other Worlds or indeed with what most shamanic cultures have always taught us about the after-life and the spirits. I felt that it was important to invite the children to explore their connection to the ancestors. As the children were relatively fresh and inexperienced at this point, I was also curious to see what guidance they would receive from the spirits with me only giving a very sketchy introduction of what ancestors are. The results, as always, were both surprising and life affirming.

Teaching Notes

(This makes a good 'winter indoors session' if you are weather

dependent, like me. We gathered around a candle instead and did this session the week after Halloween.)

Open the group and reconnect.

Ask: 'How has everyone been since we last met?'

Then say:

Who are the ancestors, the Ones Who Came Before Us?

In our culture we often behave as if dead people do not exist any longer. Many indigenous peoples believe the opposite thing, that our ancestors still love us and care about us and watch over us from their new home in the spirit world. Ancestors also come forward to assist shamans during healing work and ceremonies. Another thing to remember is that the Earth is not our permanent home. One day all of us will die and return to our true home, the spirit world, and we ourselves become ancestors.

Today we are going to start by travelling forward in time. After all this group is called The Time Travellers!

Imagine a time in the future when you are not alive any longer, but your children and grandchildren will be. Do not even try to think about your own death. It has not been written at this moment in time. Don't even look for that moment on the time line. Go much further into the future instead!

I will drum for you. Please undertake a shamanic journey into the future at some point on the time line where you will have joined the ancestors.

J1: Journey to a time where the journey participants have become ancestors. Observe what that feels like. All should ask: 'What do I want from the living?'

(In truth I thought I was reaching very high by setting this journey. However, the children completely met the challenge and really enjoyed doing the work.)

Go around Circle and share.

This journey sets the stage for the rest of the session.

Say: 'Next we are going to travel back in time. I will drum again and you will all do the following journey.'

J2: Journey to meet an ancestor (from the recent or long ago past) and ask them to tell something about themselves and the time in which they used to live...

Go around the Circle and share.

J3: Journey out to meet this same ancestor and ask for guidance. All should ask: 'How do my ancestors wish to be honoured by the living members of my family?'

Go around the Circle and share.

Close With a Small Group Ceremony

Give all children a tea light in a holder and take turns lighting them all individually. Then all the children take a turn to speak a prayer to the ancestors. Say this is for: 'The people you have memory of and the ones you never met. It does not need to be long but it needs to be sincere, speak from the heart!'

Then move all the tea lights to the very centre of the Circle.

Tell the ancestors that we hold them in our heart and that we honour their place in our family tree.

Ask:

What did we learn from our ancestors today?
Are there other things we would like to learn or find out?
How can we research those things by talking to family members, or online, or by doing more journeys ourselves?

Thank all the young people present for excellent work done.

Say: 'Thank you too for being here today, ancestors!'

Close the group by talking about ancestors some more and sharing some funny stories about them.

Brief Discussion

Though I had given them very little information, I was blown away by the fact that the children returned with guidance and insights completely in line with what tribal people with strong ancestor traditions report and what spiritual teachers know from their own shamanic work with large groups:

- Most of all, the ancestors wish to be *remembered*. They wish *to live on in our memory*
- They would like to be *honoured* on special days of the year, such as their birthdays, special occasions like Christmas or other festivals
- They would like to be *invited as guests of honour* at weddings, funerals, christenings and other important events in the life of a family or tribe
- They would like *to receive an occasional offering*: a thimble of wine or whiskey (our own children sometimes give them some of their cake or sweets), a very small amount of the family dinner, incense, flowers etc

I was impressed by how utterly fearless the children were. Below are some of their comments.

One girl (11): 'OK so when I go on that journey to see myself as an ancestor, does that mean I will also get to see my own death in this lifetime?'

Me: 'No, your death has not yet been written. You have much living to do and many choices to make before then that will shape the course of your life. So no, give that no thought, go much further in time please and then look back!'

One boy (eight): 'This is so COOL to be an ancestor! It's great to see what they are doing on Earth… I think I am going to have a large family because I see so many descendants! (His face drops.) But to be forgotten is awful… I really would not like that… It makes you feel like you never lived…'

Other children said things like:

I met my own ancestors and I have no idea who they were. But they really liked me visiting them and connecting. I could feel that they care about me.

I just use this vortex and takes me absolutely anywhere I need to go. The past! The future! And once I live in the spirit world myself again I will be able to zip all over the cosmos, astro-travel, it's great!

The children surpassed my expectations by a long stretch! But this session also had one unexpected side effect: they all seemed to feel that death is not such a big deal, it is just a doorway into a place where we can have adventures without being limited by our human body…

Session Plan 5: Meet the Monster! Shadow Work

Compassion is not a relationship between the healer and the wounded. It's a relationship between equals. Only when we know our own darkness well can we be present with the darkness of others. Compassion becomes real when we recognize our shared humanity.

Pema Chodron[1]

Introduction

Please note: this session took place in the aftermath of the Sandy Hook school shooting (on December 14th, 2012) in Connecticut, USA. A 20-year-old young man called Adam Lanza fatally shot first his own mother, followed by 20 children and six members of staff, and then committed suicide by shooting himself. At that time this was the deadliest mass shooting in a school in the USA by one single person and the children in my group were much affected by this incident. For that reason it felt important to weave in ceremony to honour those who lost their lives. This session, announced before Sandy Hook occurred, was all about shadow work.

What is Shadow Work?

Shadow work means actively working with and embracing all parts of ourselves that are not pretty, not acceptable and not liked by others. Over time we have pushed those qualities far way and hidden, often even from *ourselves*. This is a human survival strategy: we all need to belong and to be part of a community. We all need to be loved, liked and accepted by our family and our peers. But the thing is that a huge amount of life force is locked away in those parts of ourselves we deny and divorce, as it were. Vital energy and life force becomes lost to us and we, quite literally, become *shadows of our true selves*. And we don't lock away only the so-called bad things, usually we also hide talents, good things about ourselves we are not ready to own for some reason.

Our session was loosely based on a book written by Debbie Ford, called *The Dark Side of the Light Chasers*.[2] She gives powerful exercises for individuals and groups to engage in shadow work and reclaim both life-force and personal power. We gain a lot of knowledge and self-awareness along the way, doing these exercises.

Teaching Notes

The work included shadow work and a small ceremony for Sandy Hook: flying a sky lantern that carried our prayers for the children who died, the children who survived and all families and other people affected.

Preparation

Have sky lanterns, black markers and matches ready and some chocolate.

Choose a wide open space. Never use sky lanterns in a place where there is drought or in wooded areas as they could cause a forest fire or do great damage. Do not use where there is any risk of them falling on animals, by the sea as they can be mistaken for ship distress flares, or close to an airport.

Session

The Fire Keeper builds a fire assisted by arriving children.

Open the group.

Ask: 'How has everyone been since we last met?'

Say: 'Today we are going to be doing shadow work, as well as a small ceremony for the children of Sandy Hook *(here substitute any other event that seeks loving attention and healing at the time of your session).'*

Explain what shadow work is.

Go around the circle and get all the young people to say what annoys them most about other people. Mention one thing in particular that drives you *completely crazy*...write this down or sketch it.

Ask for one volunteer and get him or her to stand up and darken the room. Use a candle to project this person's shadow onto the floor or wall. Say: 'We now all welcome our shadow into the room!'

Say: 'Hello (name's) shadow! How are you! Nice to meet you!'

All wave and the shadow waves back.

Explain that our shadow contains parts of ourselves we disown (i.e. hide, even from ourselves or pretend we don't have).

Then pass around a small mirror and ask all the young people to have a good look at themselves. Say:

> *Now it is time to meet our own shadow. I will do some soft background drumming and you will all write down one occasion where you did or presented the very thing/quality you cannot stand in the other person. This means being very brave and honest!*
>
> *We are not going to ask you to share this – unless you wish to, and are brave enough to, then it would be very interesting to hear.*

Ask for a show of hands: 'Who admits that they have the despised quality somewhere deep inside themselves. Is anyone brave enough to share what they worked on?'

The title of this session is Meet the Monster. Who IS the Monster?

In the session mentioned, all the children shouted ME! As Sandy Hook had been mentioned many times, the children could conceivably have shouted *the school shooter* – but I was pleased to see no one did.

Explain *projection*: what we don't like about ourselves we project onto others. This is not fair perhaps, but it is better to be aware of this process than to be unaware of it.

Last but not least, link this session to the work on bullying done earlier.

Say: 'Thinking of what we learned today, what do you think is going on when some children bully others?'

This is followed by a discussion.

Mention that projection of unwanted characteristics is an aspect of bullying.

Sky Lantern Ceremony

Next we all spent some time writing prayers for the children and adults killed at Sandy Hook on our sky lanterns. We went outside and launched the sky lanterns. Doing this in our own garden turned out to be a grave error because we have many mature trees and so do our neighbours. One sky lantern was slow taking off and, once it finally did so, it managed to snag itself on the top of one tree in our neighbours' garden. This set the whole tree on fire, which was quite dramatic. The children are still talking about this years later!

Obviously I was mortified, but my first responsibility was to the children. We said more prayers. The children asked: 'What will happen now our sky lantern has burned up and set a tree on fire?' Improvising madly I said that fire is traditionally one of the ways we send prayers and communications to spirit, and that every tree is a son or daughter of the Tree of Life. So the spirits will collect all the prayers that landed in the tree. The children were happy with his. I closed the group.

After the work, tell the children: 'You have all been very brave today. Well done!'

I had some pieces of chocolate ready to sweeten the bitter medicine we had all tasted.

It is a good idea to give all the children a small reward at the end of this session because shadow work takes guts and honesty.

Say: 'Now take what you learned into everyday situations –

but please don't set any trees on fire!'

Discussion

Afterwards I immediately went on a mission to apologise to our neighbours. They were amazingly kind. I explained that we had performed a small ceremony for the children of Sandy Hook and they said: 'You do beautiful work Imelda, please keep going!' And that was *all*. It could have been so much worse. So if you are going to be using my idea of sky lanterns, please learn from my mistakes! For once I was very grateful for the damp British weather.

Notes

1. *The Places That Scare You: A Guide to Fearlessness* by Pema Chodron, Element: New edition, 2004
2. *The Dark Side of the Light Chasers: Reclaiming your Power, Creativity, Brilliance and Dreams* by Debbie Ford, Hodder Paperbacks, 2001

Session Plan 6: Animal Healing: Invite a Specialist!

For my group, animal healing work is in the top five of all sessions we have ever done and we revisit this work at regular intervals, building on what we learned before. Most children love animals and they can learn a lot from doing animal healing work. For that reason I wanted to include this session concept in my book, but I will not provide a session plan.

If your group of children is interested in animal healing work, I strongly suggest that you invite a guest teacher with expertise in this area, unless you are experienced in this work yourself. That is the only way this work will come alive and inspire the children. This work cannot be taught from a session plan or a set of notes. In my experience people doing animal healing work all have unique ways of working. There is not one universal way of approaching this. Personally speaking I am very lucky to have a partner here in my shamanic practice in London. Her name is Jill Hunter and though she mostly works with humans, she does great work with animals as well. She is our guest teacher for this work.

We always work with animals long distance, with permission from their human family. Bringing the animals to class would be too stressful for the animals and working long distance allows us to work with different animals all over the world. So far the children have worked with dogs, cats, horses, donkeys and a parrot. Mostly the healing requests we receive concern cats and dogs.

There is quite a lot of preparation work. I start by announcing a session date and I post a request for animal volunteers on one or two spiritual forums. I then ask those families to send me pictures of their animals for the children to hold and focus on. After the session we send all families some personalised feedback. The children are all teamed up with one animal they focus on for that session.

You may remember how the first session plan in this book is about using an egg for healing purposes. In one session the children learned how to use eggs to heal animals. Next we broke those eggs into bowls and did what we call in shamanism 'diagnostic work' by looking at the egg yolk. What does the egg yolk tell us about what is going on with the animal?

One of the most wonderful aspects of this session is seeing how children soon develop their own unique ways of working with animals. One girl merged with 'her' dog and used her own body to feel where the dog felt pain or discomfort. (A word of caution: she dropped this merged state again as soon as she had the information – we can *not* heal animals or people by carrying their pain for them! We also need to be equally aware that our pets often try to carry our pain for us!)

One boy tuned into a dog and was shown very clearly how this animal was carrying the family stress of an imminent divorce. The dog was healthy in himself, but he was buckling under the stress that the whole family lived with. Another boy shape-shifted into a dog so he could make a soul travel visit to this animal and have a conversation about issues such as tail-biting.

Someone reported a missing cat, so we all tracked him by remote viewing, using our shaman's x-ray eyes to see things long distance as a group, and we saw him walking around Soho in Central London. When we told the cat's mum this, she said that the cat was born in Soho so maybe he was visiting an old stomping ground.

One boy tuned into a dog and said: 'This animal is perfectly healthy and absolutely fine! I really don't know why the mum sent us a healing request!' So be careful, children are not easily fooled into finding problems with healthy and happy animals.

Some Words of Caution

For me it was rather a shock to discover that some well-meaning adults sent us the most gruesome animal causes for the children to work on. This included the trade in cat and dog meat in Vietnam, because there is a belief that the more an animal suffers, the more tender the meat is. My personal take on this, after organising about five animal healing sessions with young children, is that it is fine to put such causes by the candle at the heart of the group as a prayer request, without sharing the gory details. The whole group can generate a lot of light and love and hold all suffering animals in prayer and there is no question at all that those animal need and deserve love and attention. But, personally speaking, I do not think it is appropriate or necessary to share truly horrifying images and information with a group of young children.

This work is about empowering children in a world that often misunderstands their spiritual needs and makes them feel powerless. It is a judgment call. After all, I could not keep out of their consciousness what happened at Sandy Hook (see the previous session), but as a mother and teacher I feel there is a limit to how much children can be expected to absorb. So I put limits around this.

Another issue I want to raise is that some people can have extremely high expectations. You may want to be aware of that and pitch things at the right level. When I was asking for volunteers, some friends of colleagues from all over the world wrote in and said things like: 'I live in a very remote location so I hope that the work done by your children's group can spare us a long drive to the vet.' In this work we see more than our fair share of miracles, but it is not fair to burden a young child with the expectation that he or she will work a miracle that will save a trip to the vet.

Not all children will want to continue working with 'their' animal once the session is over either. Others happily do. Be quite clear about the boundaries and expectations all parties involved bring to this session.

I wish you luck planning a truly great session!

Session Plan 7: Dream Theatre: Working with Dreams and Mining Nightmares for Treasure

It seems that there is no right way of spelling the word 'theatre'. American English mostly (but not always) uses *theater* while UK preference is *theatre*. Among those in the know (in the world of drama) theatre refers to the performance while theater refers to the building the shows takes place in. After much thought I have decided to stick with *theatre,* as a UK resident who puts on a dream show outdoors with children.

Along with animal healing work, dream theatre work always gets a top-five rating in discussions about our favourite sessions. I keep a box in the room where the children can leave feedback, session requests, or share something they'd rather not throw in the whole group. One day I found a note in that box. One boy was having severe nightmares and this made him nervous about going to bed. It also made him tired in class. Could I please run a session on shamanic ways of actively working with dreams and nightmares? The great thing with this box – or often emails from parents behind the scenes – is that I never know what will ask for attention next. It pushes me right out of the comfort zone and I have become a great deal more adventurous when it comes to covering new ground, running sessions on subjects I have never taught before. Having said that, I *do* have my limits and my community of guest teachers will always have their place. Only fools rush where angels fear to tread, as the saying goes.

When this request came in, I consulted Robert Moss,[1] who devotes his whole life to teaching shamanic dream work. I also posted a request on our global forum for shamanic teachers[2] to request helpful suggestions. Robert Moss and my colleague Jacqueline Teoh both pointed me in the direction of dream theatre work.

Some General Pointers on Dreaming

I ask all clients to pay attention to dreams before their shamanic healing appointment with me, because often dreams cast light on important issues. Often ancestors or spirit allies appear in dreams too, to share important information. My sacred art students are always set dream tasks as part of their training and shamanic work with me.

It is extremely important for parents to listen closely to any dreams a child shares. It can provide a great window on the inner landscape (soul-scape) of your child. Dreams can flush out anxieties the child is not ready to share in everyday reality. Scary teachers could appear as monsters and this indicates where a child may be suffering stress that is unacceptable and avoidable. Obviously the 'monster' might also be a Power Animal that has arrived to help or symbolise something else altogether. Only spending the time and being fully present to your child is going to allow you to get to the bottom of things. It is not always easy for parents to accept that even very young children live with a high level of stress. We like to think that we protect them and that they live idyllic and innocent lives. We are often surprised to learn what really goes on in both their lives and dreams.

With very young children it is important to get any scary stuff out straight away. The energy can be moved by taking them outside and literally spitting it out, or making a picture and then burning it (or tearing it up, burying it and so forth). Sandra Ingerman suggests that children call on their Power Animal for protection during the night. It is also possible to make a talisman for a child to sleep with, followed by a ceremony to call in protective spirits. Parents do not need a lot of shamanic training to do this with their child. In my shamanic healing sessions with children I have sometimes made them a dreaming stone that keeps them safe and attracts healing dreams. Native American peoples make dreamcatchers. These days we find them in shops all over the word.

Children and young people can be encouraged to keep a dream journal, just like adults. One great spiritual practice is for a family to share all dreams over the breakfast table. (Our youngest son Brendan once had a dream about a machine that churned out Barbie doll versions of his older brothers. That dream had us all in stitches for months!)

Robert Moss suggests that we give every dream a title and make an action plan. For instance, dreams can be told as stories, painted or acted out. He calls this technique Sacred Theatre, where the dream is used as a portal for dream re-entry, to obtain more information or clarity on what is going on. Other people in the group can then act as dream trackers to get more information for the dreamer.

I decided to put Moss's suggestions to the test with my Time Travellers group.

Teaching Notes

Preparation

Before the session email the group and ask everyone to pay attention to dreams and to bring a dream, or dream fragment, to our session. Nightmares are welcome too.

Session

The Fire Keeper builds a fire assisted by arriving children.

Ask: 'How has everyone been since we last met?'

It is important to always weave the fabric of the group together by linking back to what they have already done and linking forward to what they are going to do in future sessions. This particular session started with me giving the children an update on how all the animals we worked with in our previous session were doing.

Open the class by reminding the group that we all dream the world into being.

Talk about the Australian Aboriginal concept of The Dreamtime or The Dreaming.

Get all children to journey to their own power animal and dream friends to ask for individual guidance on handling frightening dreams. Remind them that their Power Animal is always there and that they already know how to do shamanic journeying, therefore they can access information and help for themselves.

J 1: Journey to our Power Animal to receive personalised guidance on a frightening dream

Next choose one dream for dream theatre work.

Do several rounds with dreams different individuals have brought.

For the children who do not get to see their dream enacted, tell them everyone will revisit this work in future sessions.

One thing that can be an issue here is that some children want to be the superstar in all sessions. Keep it fair, make sure that your choices are guided by Spirit and actively encourage quiet or shy children to contribute in sessions. Give them all their moment of glory and individual attention. Tell shy children that you know that they too can take the lead role.

The idea is that all children in the group become a cast, acting out parts or roles in the dream. This needs to be done in such a way that, if you are dealing with a nightmare, the fear starts dissolving and any anxiety is resolved.

Ask:

Maybe something or someone needs freeing or rescuing?
Maybe the 'monster in hot pursuit' can be asked to state its business or to shape-shift?

Often things are not what they seem in dreams. It always pays to take things a little further (in a safe way) and find out what is really going on.

Sit in Circle and ask everyone to share what they learned in that session.

Close the group followed by feral time and wild running or trampolining to wind down. This session brings on very high levels of excitement!

Discussion

In our sessions over the years we have made some remarkable discoveries.

One girl used to have recurrent nightmares where she was on the run from a tiger. When we did dream work on this, we discovered that the tiger was actually her Power Animal trying to talk to her!

A boy had a dream about a dragon chasing him and trying to swallow him. He spent several dreams running for his life. When we used dream theatre to enact this dream, another child volunteered for the part of the dreamer, meaning that the boy could watch from a safe distance. The dragon was now allowed to swallow this boy and he reported that he had landed in a beautiful cave, where many crystals and gems were waiting for him. We all asked him questions, as this boy was in the dragon's stomach:

What are those crystals and gems for?
They are spiritual tools for me to use, they are beautiful!
Why did the dragon need to swallow you?
Because I was supposed to die in the dream and be born again as a shaman!

The boy who had presented the nightmare got so excited that he asked to play the role of dreamer himself. We allowed him to join the other boy in the dragon's stomach (so we had two dreamers now, double dreaming you could say, reporting all discoveries).

They had such fun that everyone wanted to experience being swallowed by the dragon and going on a treasure hunt in the stomach of the dragon.

In shamanism there is a process called *dismemberment*: the spirits take us apart and give us a complete going over, cleaning out all dark corners, before they put us back together again. This boy had had a spontaneous dismemberment dream. Dismemberments are common when indigenous shamans undergo ordeals and initiations into the profession. To me it was very interesting that a city boy had this dream, but was completely cured of his fear by group dream work. In the Dragon's Cave (stomach) he received the calling to be a shaman one day. So that is what a nightmare can turn out to be!

Notes

1. *Conscious Dreaming: A Spiritual Path for Everyday Life* by Robert Moss, Three Rivers Press (CA), 1996. Robert Moss has many great books on dreaming out but this book makes a good starting point.
2. I would like to thank Sandra Ingerman and my colleagues on her global network of shamanic teachers for all the pointers and suggestions that helped me write the first ever dream theatre session for the Time Travellers.

Session Plan 8: Heartbeat of the Universe: All About Drumming

Preparation

I have a selection of drums and different beaters laid out on a blanket. As a surprise I had ordered remo drums for all the children and painted their Power Animals on those drums. Not for them to take away, they belong to the group, but for them to use when we are in Circle. Some parents are happy to buy their child a drum and help the child paint their own drum.

Session

The Fire Keeper builds fire assisted by arriving children.

Open the group. Ask: 'How has everyone been since we last met?'

Say:

Today is going to be all about drumming! And we will all be drumming, but first I want to talk about the drum as a power tool. Drums are sacred objects for shamans and we never touch another person's drum unless we have permission.

Why do Shamans Drum?

Shamanic drumming is a quick and safe way for slightly changing our state of consciousness and that makes it easier to reach the dream-like state we need for both shamanic journeying and for healing work. Some people call this process sonic driving. Shamanic drumming uses a repetitive rhythm played at a tempo of three to four beats a second.

Drumming is also a very good way of summoning helping spirits. You could say that a shaman uses the drum to build a bridge to the spirit world so we can talk to the spirits and they can talk to us. The key to understanding drumming is realising that everything in the Universe is made of vibration.

In our group, one of the fathers has a Tibetan Chod drum and a friend gave me one too. He and I demonstrated together how Chod drums are used. The children were already a familiar with *dismemberment* so now we talked about Chod (an extreme dismemberment practice from Tibetan shamanism).[1]

Say:

Now we are all going to have a go at shamanic drumming, first individually and then as a group

Pass around the drums and ask everyone to take turns to express how they feel right now by drumming. Make a point about handling drums with care: pounding too hard or aggressively can damage a drum (and it can also damage our ear-drums!) Every drum has an in-dwelling spirit: so please treat any drum as you would treat a living being.

Do people feel:

Happy? Tired and S-L-O-W… Excited? Jumpy? Mellow?[2]
Drum it!!!
Everyone has a go…
Can we understand from the way people are drumming how they are feeling?

Next all hold their drums and practise the classic shamanic journeying beat together

Then do a round to see if everyone can do this correctly on their own. Say: 'Let's have a listen…'

Then do something even more advanced. Say: 'Let's see if we can do a journey while drumming for ourselves.'

J: My intention is to speak to the spirit of this particular drum and hear what it wants to tell me.

Go around the Circle and ask: 'What did our drums say?'

If time allows, do another journey, where everyone asks a question of their own choice.

Share!

Close the group and call feral noisy time to burn off the energy that has been raised.

Notes

1. *Chod Practice In The Bon Tradition* by Alejandra Chaqul, Yongdzin Lopon Tenzi Namdak and Tenzin Wangyal, Snow Lion, 2009
2. Thank you dear friend and shamanic teacher colleague Janet Elisabeth Gale for this suggestion!

Session Plan 9: The Weather is Always Perfect: Dancing with the Storm!

Mum, do you think that the clouds talk to each other, just like we humans do here on Earth?

My son Brendan at age 3

Introduction

Weather shamanism is another theme on our top five and we return to it at regular intervals. This work can really only be done outdoors. Children love being encouraged to run wild, but make sure they absorb some instructions first!

The first journey we do, to see how weather is created, usually produces amazing journeys. The children have spoken of great cauldrons stirred by weather spirits and of weather spirits taking outlandish shapes to talk to the children, just because they can. Young people quickly realise that good weather for one person or group is bad weather for someone else. They appreciate variety and realise that weather spirits have consciousness. If we are always complaining about the weather, how are the weather spirits going to feel about that?

This session is about moving away from any concept of fixing the weather to being properly attuned to the weather and in communication with weather spirits.

Teaching Notes

The Fire Keeper makes fire assisted by arriving children.

Open the Circle. Say:

Today's session is going to be about weather shamanism. What is the first thought that comes to mind when I say that? Exactly! Most people think about fixing the weather, but actually today we will introduce the concept weather dancing. This concept was coined by two shamanic teachers called David and Nan Corbin.[1]

The weather spirits want us to work with them. They want us to take an active and healthy role in the functioning of the planet. They want us to exist in harmony with them. It is from that harmony that true healing of our eco-system occurs.

The Salish people on Vancouver Island have a word for existing in true kinship with nature: when nature and people are in perfect harmony. They call it skalatitude.

The Yurok people of Northern California used a rain stone to manifest rain. This stone was so powerful that they were forced to hide it! Then one day it was found by a road crew. What do you think happened? Yes, it caused a flood.

Some indigenous peoples say that the weather expresses the emotions and moods of Mother Earth.

So now let's see what we can find out ourselves from talking to the Weather Spirits.

J: Journey to witness how weather is created

J2: Journey to the Weather Spirits and see what they tell us

Say:

Next we will do what we do best and go feral! We are going to connect to the Storm Spirits and merge with them, meaning that we ourselves shape-shift into storm. In other words, we become the storm!

Teachers should try to make it dramatic with loud drumming etc.

Try to find out what the gifts and blessings of storms are… Share!

At this point mention how people who practise weather shamanism will merge with a storm or even a hurricane to divert it… Explain how and why this is done…

As we are getting to the end of the session, it is a good idea to calm the children down a little now.

J: Dancing with the Cloud People and learning from them

Say:

Now we do the same exercise with clouds. We will all merge with a cloud and move around the garden like a cloud.
How is this different from merging with a Storm Spirit?

Mention cloud divination at this point. It means you can ask a question and read the shapes of clouds to receive an answer.

Conclusion

There is no such thing as bad weather. There are only many different kinds of good weather. The weather is always perfect! Here in the UK we often complain about the rain but many parts of the world (Africa, New Mexico) suffer from drought and they yearn for rain. Ask:

What would happen if it never rained? Would we like it if every day was a hot day?

Talk about the rain dances of Native American tribes in the South Western states of the USA.

Many Native American tribes in the USA do rain dances even today. They wear special headdresses and clothing. The colours and patterns all have significance. The rain dance is meant to bring rain for an entire year or for a particular occasion. The costumes worn are passed down in the family as heirlooms for many generations.

Every time the weather changes form, power is released in a

process that balances chaos and order.

Say:

From now on, spend at least five minutes a day outside and do not complain about the weather. Instead ask: 'What is the weather telling me? What can I learn from the weather?' As you get to know the weather, the weather gets to know you… Have fun!

Close the group.

Notes

1. *Weather Shamanism: Harmonizing Our Connection with the Elements* by Nan Moss with David Corbin, Inner Traditions International, First Printing edition, 2008.

With gratitude to my shamanic teacher colleague Cynthia Crisp who recommended this book and told me about the concept weather dancing. She suggested I explore this concept in a session with my Time Travellers group.

For more information Google 'Native American rain dances' and a lot of material will appear.

Session 10: Public Speaking = Shamanic Secret Agent and Warrior of the Light, with Guest Teacher Judith Bogner

Introduction

The seed concept for this session was one mother writing to me about her teenage daughter and telling me that the girl nearly fainted from anxiety every time she had to present a project or piece of work in class. She asked, could I organise a Time Travellers session on this theme? I knew just the right person for the job: my friend Judith Bogner is a TV presenter and actress and she agreed to do a guest session.

Judith talked the children through the whole process, but somehow the most important new word and concept they all learned was *pre-harmonising*.

Teaching Notes

What is public speaking?

- Allowing yourself to be seen in all your glory
- Allowing yourself to expand
- Allowing your teamwork with Spirit to create magic

It is also an opportunity to:

- Practise fearlessness
- Practise shape-shifting
- Educate yourself and your audience

Any public speaker has three tools:

- Intention
- Imagination

- Focus/will

And you need to set up your presentation in three stages:

- Preparation
- Pre-Harmonising
- Practising

The First Stage: Preparation

Your preparation begins well before the opportunity to speak in public arrives. As a Time Traveller you can expand into the future and ask Spirit/the Universe to send you opportunities that serve your journey. Request a topic that serves you and lights your passion.

If a subject seems strange or uncomfortable for you, find something about that subject that feels like fun for you. The best presentations are infused with passion and light, this is what inspires people!

Learn everything you feel is important about the topic and allow your intuition to guide you to unexpected sources of information. Put the information together and allow breathing space (i.e. do not overwhelm the audience).

The Second Stage: Pre-Harmonising

This is setting your intention + calling in your spirit allies + sending your energies to the point in time where you deliver your presentation.

For instance: *'My intention is to teach The Time Travellers all that is useful for them to know about speaking in public.'*

- Call in your allies to assist in setting the energies for your event to ensure it flows beautifully and meets your intention.
- Then move into a place of well-being (thinking lots of

joyful and happy thoughts).

- In your own mind, travel to the point in time where you deliver your presentation or speech. In your mind's eye: see the room, see your audience, paint rainbows or hearts or other happy things all over the walls (only in your imagination remember?!).
- See the event go perfectly, see the audience with happy faces, you feeling happy and pleased with the way your talk went.

Do not just do this once. Repeat it many times until you feel at ease, knowing that your intentions are anchored and the scene is set for the best possible outcome. This is called pre-harmonising!

The Third Stage: Practising

You need to invest time and energy to practise your presentation until it rolls off your tongue and you feel comfortable with the way it flows.

Think about what you want to say and write bullet points, perhaps add props.

Memorise it and maybe add images.

Practise by speaking out loud, ideally on an *ally free of human ego* (meaning on a pet or a tree for example).

While practising, keep focus on your introduction and the headlines/key elements (where am I in my presentation? What comes next?).

Practise a preparation routine for the Big Day: breathing exercises, warming up your vocal cords, remember to pre-harmonise one more time, fill the room with light, become the tree...

Select your outfit and choose your appearance. Choose something that matches the energy of the event and/or the location, that makes you look the part. If you are expected to look dressier or more elegant than you normally would, *shape-shift* into it!

On the Day of Your Presentation or Event

No eating or drinking sugary stuff because it makes your saliva flow. Drink water.

Have a printout with your bullet points/images in your hand and any props.

Before going on stage, or in front of the classroom, do your preparation routine to anchor yourself.

When go you on stage, take a deep breath, be the tree, anchor yourself, expand.

Be present and shape-shift into your role as presenter.

Be fearless and allow the energy of the event, and the energies present in the room, to support you!

Notes

These teaching notes have been reproduced with permission from Judith Bogner with gratitude. You can Google her name to find her website.

Session Plan 11: Shamans and Superheroes

Introduction

In London this was an Easter session. My eldest son (aged 15) likes playing World of Warcraft. When he tells me about this online game I am always struck by how many characters are *shamans*. It seems quite obvious to me that the designers of such games have been raiding both world mythology and even shamanism big time for interesting heroes and concepts.

Teaching Notes

Preparation

Put out:

- Some masks and costumes
- Bananas, chocolate and marshmallows plus aluminium foil
- Alien Egg or other items for a Treasure Hunt
- Some chocolate (Easter) eggs
- One small hobby knife for sharpening sticks
- Drum

Session

The Fire Keeper makes fire assisted by arriving children.

Open the Circle around the fire. Ask: 'How has everyone been since we last met?'

Say: 'Today's session is going to be about shamans and superheroes.'

What is the Difference Between a Shaman and a Super Hero?

Talk about power. Ask: 'What is Power?'

Power is the ability to use and direct energy! Ask:

What special powers would you all like to have?

Discussion, then ask:

Do shamans have special powers that other people do not have?
And how do they obtain those powers?
Now see if we can generate some power here in the garden…

Get out the masks and costumes. First get the children to play a game of tag in their everyday clothes. Then get them to dress up in superhero clothes. Ask:

Does this change the outcome? Do you feel more powerful?

Remind the group of the magic wands they made and the talk about empowering objects. Ask:

Could we think of another game to play while wearing superhero outfits and masks?

Say that when they have all worked up a heroic appetite they will have a picnic and make chocolate bananas in the fire!

Then ask them to go to find sticks for toasting the marshmallows…

Talk some more about power, then say:

Some of you have attended these sessions for several years now. Have you developed any new powers or skills? Like, perhaps…

- *Seeing the dark*
- *Working with power animals*
- *Finding solutions for bullying*

- *Learning about healing both animals and humans, and so forth*

Enjoy the snacks!

Play a game to find the Alien Egg or run a treasure hunt.

(At this point I had hidden a plastic egg with a (toy) alien inside in the garden. I invited all the children to find this and then tell a story about the special powers of this egg.) Say:

Act out the story. Have fun!

Close the circle followed by feral time.

Session Plan 12: Body Image, Self Esteem and The Sacred Clown

Heyókȟa are thought of as being backwards-forwards, upside-down, or contrary in nature. It was manifest by doing things backwards or unconventionally — riding a horse backwards, wearing clothes inside-out, or speaking in a backwards language. For example, if food were scarce, a heyókȟa would sit around and complain about how full he was; during a baking hot heat wave a heyókȟa would shiver with cold and put on gloves and cover himself with a thick blanket. Similarly, when it is freezing he will wander around naked complaining that it is too hot. A unique example is the famous heyókȟa sacred clown called 'the Straighten-Outer':

He was always running around with a hammer trying to flatten round and curvy things (soup bowls, eggs, wagon wheels, etc.), thus making them straight.

John Fire Lame Deer[1]

Introduction

The idea for this session came from working with young teenagers in private shamanic practice and observing great struggles in terms of body image and fitting in. At this point the Time Travellers Group had been running for exactly three years and some of our young people, who had been there from the beginning, were transferring to secondary school (equivalent to middle school in the USA) when appearance suddenly becomes a much bigger concern than it is in primary school.

On a larger level I am also aware that in society at large many young people are in crisis. Unheard of numbers of people have eating disorders such as anorexia or bulimia. Here in the UK children as young as five years old are receiving medical treatment for anorexia.[2] Many teenagers are self-harming too (for example, cutting their own arms and legs to release tension).[3]

Our February 2016 Inspiring Youth Event at Steiner House explored this challenging topic as it is important not to avert our eyes from this.

Here in the UK it is believed that one in five teenagers has inflicted self-harm on occasion. As a mother of three teenagers I find this statistic most alarming. Most often this is done by cutting and biting. Young people as young as 12 years old engage in this.

Rather than worrying about the possibility of my own children doing this one day (worrying = visualising negative outcomes and projecting them onto someone – I am not a great fan of worrying and actively ask people to never worry about me!) I felt I had better take this particular bull by the horns and put together a session plan that introduces a different perspective on body images and self-esteem.

Invitation

Anyone who wishes to use these session notes in any way at all has my absolute encouragement to do so. The only pragmatic thing I will say is that obviously one session is not going to shift young people's perception forever. If you run a shamanic group for young people, I believe you'd do well to revisit this theme in different (creative) ways at regular intervals. I also believe that it would be of immense value to create specialist groups for young people affected by the issue I described above. It is extremely important to do ancestral work and to unravel and transmute these issues for once and for all, so our children's children don't end up carrying these ancestral imprints. We need to develop a very specific toolkit and safe sacred space for this specialist type of healing work with young people. They urgently need community too: being with other young people who 'have been there' in safe space where they are not being judged or criticised.

Teaching Notes

Preparation

You need face paints, glow in the dark bubble solution and wands, sparklers for the transmutation exercise, a mirror, a print-out of quote about the role of the Heyoke/Sacred Clown.

Please note that you can make glow-in-the-dark bubbles by mixing glow fluid (from glow sticks for children's parties) with bubble solution. About 50% of each.[4] Wait for darkness or do this session at a dark time of the year and enjoy the great clouds of bubbles glowing the dark, with many children blowing them, and floating into the night sky.

Session

The Fire Keeper makes fire assisted by arriving children.

Open the group. Ask:

How has everyone been since we last met?

Today we are going to arrive at a shamanic perspective on the issues of self-worth, self-esteem and body image. How do we develop our sense of self, do you think, as we grow from baby and then a toddler to teenager?

Can things go wrong when we develop our sense of self?

At what age do we become extremely aware of the way we look?

Who are we really? Can we be ourselves in everyday life, in school?

Is there another Self hiding behind the role we play in public? Behind the image we try to create for ourselves? In shamanism we speak of an authentic self or true self. And sometimes we lose touch with our authentic self because we get so busy pleasing other people and trying to fit in.

Share experiences, then say:

In shamanism we also speak of a Higher Self outside space and time. Something that is larger than our limited awareness in this reality. When a problem occurs, or people have a hard time, it often means that we need to shift to a higher level of awareness and look at the problem from that perspective.

Where does our body come from? Our human mother gives birth to us. But where do the building materials for our body come from? Indeed, Mother Earth! And when we die, our body returns to Mother Earth (if we have a funeral). Or maybe we have a cremation and we are scattered to the winds. Either way the very Lego blocks of our body return to Earth or the elements and become building blocks for something new.

Do we love living on Earth? Do we love the Earth?

If we love the Earth, we must love our bodies too, because they are part of the Earth and creation. Do we love our bodies?!

In shamanism we say that 'the world is as we dream it'. There is a book by John Perkins by this very title.[5] As young children we often get accused of day-dreaming, but as adults we need to remember that we all dream the world into being!

J1: Journey to see the Soul Light of a Person

Do a journey to our Higher Selves outside space and time. This self will see the larger picture and may even remember things like events from before this lifetime (if you believe in such things!)

J2: Journey to see another person's Higher Self, for a person of your choice. Does it look different from their everyday self?

Say:

Now look at the person on your right hand side and ask your Power Animal to show you their Divine Countenance. Essentially you are looking at their soul. And their soul is pure Divine Light and essence.

Pass around a large mirror. Say:

And now look in the mirror…has anything changed? Do you feel changed by someone seeing you at your most beautiful and amazing?'

J3: Transmutation of something I do not like about myself

Say:

Now think of something you don't like about yourself. It does not need to be physical. Could be impatience or a bad temper or a compulsion to play too many computer games.

Who can remember what transmutation is? We have discussed it many times before, but often we have new children in our group who didn't attend all the previous sessions. Can someone explain transmutation to the newcomers please? Thank you!

We are now going to use sparklers to burn the thing we don't like and see them transformed into sparks and blessings.

Everyone uses the sparklers. Then ask:

How does this feel? Is this a fun way of releasing something back to the Universe?

Introduce the concept of The Sacred Clown. Say:

Sometimes we take ourselves a little too seriously. And sometimes women paint their faces to look more attractive. Can we think of another person who paints their face, but not to look more attractive?

Indeed: clowns!

What do clowns do? What is their role in our society?

Yes… They fool around. They ask difficult questions. They make fun of serious things. They say things others are afraid to say! They actively do things other people would feel ashamed to do.

They turn things on their head. They make sad people smile and they make confident people feel uncomfortable. They make everyone think again and arrive at a fresh perspective on things.

Another thing they do is that they break taboos and clear the path for change. They force everyone to ask, like small children do: 'But why? Why? Why?' They force people to look at everything in a brand-new way and to think again…

And that is something any society really needs or things get very stale. Just like individual people need to keep on growing and arriving at a new level of awareness, societies and culture need to do this too.

This is called a Change of Paradigm!

Get out the face paints. Everyone paints someone else's face.

Take some photographs. Have a good laugh!

(At this point we had a girl with a moustache and boys with animal faces. Children just love shape-shifting!)

Close the group.

Notes

1. John Fire Lame Deer was a Lakota holy man, member of the Heyoka society, grandson of the Miniconjou head man Lame Deer, and father of Archie Fire Lame Deer.
2. http://www.dailymail.co.uk/news/article-2020765/Children-aged-FIVE-treated-anorexia-Doctors-blame-ultra-slim-celebrities.html
3. http://www.theguardian.com/society/2014/may/21/shock-figures-self-harm-england-teenagers
4. You can find instructions on-line for making glow-in-the-

dark bubbles, e.g. http://chemistry.about.com/od/glowinthedarkprojects/a/glowingbubbles.htm

5. *The World is as you Dream It: Shamanic Teachings from the Amazon and Andes* by John Perkins, Destiny Books, 1994

Session Plan 13: Coyote Crystals and Mythic Memory

Coyote and the Stars

Coyote is just being coyote when he sees the Creator placing the stars in the sky from a bag in a very orderly manner. Coyote asks if he can help and the Creator lets coyote place stars in the sky reminding him to be sure and put the stars up in an orderly manner. Coyote does it correctly, but, as is his nature, coyote becomes impatient and throws the whole bag of stars into the sky distributing the stars helter skelter. The Creator scolds him for his carelessness and for the mess he made. Coyote leaves with his tail between his legs. Soon, however, Coyote goes back to being a coyote, only after that he howls at night when he sees the mess he made with the stars.

Native American Creation Story[1]

To understand the concept of Mythic Memory you only need to have a brief conversation with a child! Last week I was talking to our youngest son Brendan (aged nine) about the years just before he was born. He asked: 'Where was I when all this happened, mum?'

I said: 'You were not yet growing in my tummy then, this was before you existed.' For a moment there was an incredibly spacey look on his face and then he informed me, very firmly, that 'he has always existed, but maybe not in the human form he has today…' And of course he is right and my choice of word was wrong!

Introduction

In shamanism we acknowledge an invisible but eternal Other World that lies just beyond our perception. This is the place where the ancestors reside, where the gods and goddesses live.

The Land of the Dead is there and many other places too. It's an infinite energetic realm.

I did this session with The Time Travellers in February 2014. We were working with the Spirit of Coyote. The children themselves made journeys to Other Worlds and returned with some very interesting information. My son Quinn (aged 14) visited Great Coyote Spirit in the Other World. There he was told that once upon a time, in Mythical Time (i.e. long before recorded human history or human memory) coyotes and human beings both had great shape-shifting powers and in fact this was true for all animal species. They would shift between human and animal states at will ('like werewolves, but less scary!'). Then something happened: a veil came down between worlds and humans and animals became different species, more permanently fixed in their bodies. My son said that the teaching of Great Coyote Spirit was that outside time and space, (in mythical time, what Australian Aboriginal people call The Dreaming or The Dreamtime), coyotes and other animals are and remain ancestors of human beings, but our species has lost that knowledge and we now view all animal species as separate beings from ourselves. Quinn says that Great Coyote Spirit invited him to re-think and re-vision this and work closely together in dissolving that sense of separation between humans and animals. This is his unique soul task on Earth.

Our middle son Elliott (aged 12) was told that Coyote is a creator god and that he helped create our world as we know it.

I love doing shamanic work with children and young people because they do not yet carry the full load of prejudices and programming that we grown-ups do. In linear time (here I mean in terms of their own human lifespan) they are still closer to the mythical realm, the spirit world. After teaching this session I went to bed and found myself dreaming all night about Power Animals. Through dreaming I came to understand more deeply what Power Animals really are. My understanding of Power

Animals evolves as I evolve and working with children deepens and accelerates this process. I have a deep inner knowing that the children in my group are right in saying that animals and humans are much more closely related than we like to think in our scientific worldview. Here I am not speaking of humans and apes, in the more limited Darwinian sense!

Power Animals are evolved beings, pure spirit, that *choose* to take the form of animals to help us in our lives. Over the years many clients have asked me: 'Why animals, why not angels?' And angels are a subject in their own right. I won't digress, but I work with angelic beings too.

After this session I found myself wondering whether or not Power Animals hold the archetypal memory of the proper relationship between animals and humans. Perhaps they hold that wisdom for us, ready to bring us the sacred teachings of animal species when we are ready to heal the rift? They certainly bring back to us the unique qualities animal species possess that have become lost to us human beings. What a gift!

Teaching Notes

Preparation

Have enough Citrine crystals for all children present, or ask them to bring one themselves.

Have a selection of coyote myths and stories at hand.

Session

The Fire Keeper makes fire assisted by arriving children. (This session also works well as an indoor session).

Open the group. Say: 'How has everyone been since we last met? Today we are going to be working with Coyote Crystals!'

Talk about crystals in general. Ask: 'Who has worked with a crystal before?'

Give everyone a Citrine crystal to hold.

J1: Journey to the Spirit of the Citrine crystal and ask about its properties and gifts to us

The Time Travellers came back with very similar information: sunlight, wards off negativity, lemon yellow, cleanses groups/rooms and situations, power/courage/finding voice. This all seemed to dovetail nicely with what is known about Citrine.

Then introduce the Great Coyote Spirit.

J2: Journey to meet Coyote

As I already described earlier, the children returned with many stories about a mythical time where humans and animals could shape-shift into each other. The coyote qualities they returned with were: transforming, leaders of the pack, represented instinct, cleverness and communication/pack/groups/families.

Say: 'So now let's bring the spirits of Coyote and Citrine together!'

J3: Bringing together Citrine and Coyote to create a Coyote Crystal

Suddenly the room was full of coyotes with Citrine eyes and Citrine crystals bright as the sun with coyotes in them ('like the man in the moon!'). The kids all ended up with powerful Cloaks of Invisibility (or in their own language: immense force fields around them, hiding, shielding or powering them, depending on the situation. Proper Invisibility Cloaks shape-shift all the time, along with their owners, as do coyotes…

J4: Journey to the Spirit of our Coyote Crystal to ask how to use it and look after our crystal

One girl was told to make herself a bracelet, but not to keep it on her body the whole time (it was too powerful). One boy was given a symbol to communicate with his crystal. I asked him to draw it and it turned out to be the Nordic rune Sol (AKA Sunna or Sowilo in the Anglo-Saxon system, a rune representing the

Sun). That was an interesting detail in the context of working with Citrine!

Another intriguing thing is how often the stars and the night sky cropped up in their journeys. They were *all* shown the night sky and the whole cosmos was blown into their crystal (by Coyote). They all agreed there is a big connection between Coyote Crystals and the stars/galaxies/cosmos.

All the young people did great work. One boy took on Coyote Energy big time and acted as the trickster (and clown) in class the whole evening. (He says his Power Animal is wolf, this type of behaviour comes naturally to him… Taming that energy all evening comes a bit less naturally to me as a teacher!) I was forced to greet and name the Coyote Energy and ask it to calm down a little. Had I left it the whole group would soon have been yapping and howling at the Valentine Moon sailing over our heads!

Our session ended in very high spirits.

Close the group. Some feral time is advised after working with Coyote!

Notes

1. There are many different stories online and in books about Coyote and the Stars. Unfortunately, I could not find my way back to the site that had exactly this version up. It is an ancient tale and you will find many different versions of it.

Session Plan 14: The Knowing Field: Exploring Family Constellations Work

The Fire Keeper makes fire assisted by arriving children.

Open the group.

Ask: 'How has everyone been since we last met? Who has heard of family constellations work?' *(In our case: no one!)*

Give a brief introduction to this kind of work.

Explain the concept of the Knowing Field, coined by Bert Hellinger, and how this field holds information. We can access that information by taking up a position in the field and speaking for what we feel, sense and perceive in that place. This technique can be used to gain insights you cannot get in other ways.

In a constellation you can have people take the place of people long dead, or even institutions and world situations. For example, a person could represent the Government, the oceans of our world or world poverty and give voice to that issue.

First we did a trial run where I lined the children up in order of age. I then asked everyone to rotate and speak for the person whose place they had now taken. This exercise helped everyone tune in. The information they received could be tested for accuracy because the person concerned was present.

Next we felt ready to explore larger issues, where it is harder to obtain evidence one way or another. This involved a big drop into trust.

Our group chose to explore the following issues:

1. *The polarity between World Hunger and Consumerism*
2. *The relationship between War and Peace*

We decided who was going to speak for War, for Peace and who was going to be asking some questions.

Then we arranged everyone and we had War and Peace facing

each other.

War and Peace said there needed to be some distance between them so they stepped back to make the field larger.

Next we did another round where we repeated the procedure with World Hunger and Consumerism. These issues had a dialogue, voiced aloud by the children, and we all learned a lot in a short spell of time.

Our Conclusion

Our conclusion was that the concepts War and Fighting need to shape-shift into Healthy Competition and Sports. Martial Arts and Olympics, not War! Our other conclusion was that we all need to be properly rooted in our local communities and live/work in close partnership with the spirits of the land there. By buying things flown in from all over the world, even our food, we are adding to local and global imbalance on every possible level. *That disconnect from local land and local people allows shadowy things to grow in the place where our food and identity should be growing instead.*

Family constellations work can be used to map anything. You can bring in representatives for groups, families, individual people, causes, ancestors. The possibilities are endless.

See Chapter 8 in this book for more information about doing healing work for and involving ancestors. That chapter also lists some useful books on this subject.

Close the group and call feral time.

Session 15: Here Be Dragons! Geomancy and Dragon Lines

> *Our personal healing process is linked to that of our planet. We know this to be true when we develop a relationship with the Living Landscape, when we tap into the experience of the interconnectedness of all life.*
> Karmit Evenzur[1]

The idea for this session came from working with my colleague Karmit Evenzur. We teach rock art courses together in Andalusia, Spain, where geomancy meets sacred art.

The word geomancy literally means *divination of the earth* and originally referred to a form of divination work where a handful of soil or other material was scattered on the ground and the resulting pattern was 'read' for meaning. Geomancy explores the Earth's vital energy flow. Every landscape has an identity and consciousness and this is not a difficult language to learn. All it takes is some effort and stillness, some *deep listening*. Karmit has made it her life's work to help people deepen their connection to the Earth and to enter into a new relationship with Place. Geomancy is the art of being in deep communication with the spirits of place and all the layers of history, memory and emotion held in land.

When I first started working with Karmit, I discovered how similar this work is to shamanic healing work. Where I was used to working with human beings and scanning them with the so-called x-ray eyes of the shaman. I now discovered that I could use those same skills to read land and landscapes and to enter into a dialogue with all the layers of history, memory and emotion held in land.

Geomancy teaches that there are Dragon Lines in the land. In our culture we often call them Ley Lines. The term Dragon Line originated in China. These are lines of magnetic force, also known as dragon currents (*lung mei* in Chinese). They can take two forms: the yin (negative) current is represented by the white tiger and the yang (positive) current is represented by a blue dragon. It has been claimed that animals use these lines as a natural compass on their migration journeys over large territories.

Karmit came to London as a guest teacher on a two-year sacred art training course I teach. We took our group on a field trip into London where all of us had the privilege of seeing London through completely new eyes. We connected with the dragon that lives in the river Thames. We saw a glimpse of an ancient temple devoted to Diana right underneath St Paul's Cathedral and so forth.

This work is so magical and amazing that I wanted the Time Travellers to have some experience of this as well. I took them on a field trip to Greenwich. Here we first connected with the Zero Meridian, which our family practically lives on, and then went to a small city beach by the River Thames. When it is low tide, the Thames has small sandy beaches all over the city, even right by St Paul's Cathedral. It was a beautiful day and this was in the Easter holidays. All the children were thrilled to be off school. On this small city beach we found the bones of some big animal (a cow?) as well as many big white stones that all looked like eggs. Our young people got busy finding other bones and trying to put the skeleton back together like a big puzzle. Once they had enough of that they got busy with the big white stones.

We all stood in a circle and I had them tune in to the river. Things took a very magical turn. Our young people said: 'Easter Bunny is a myth but that there is a very real dragon living in the River Thames.' She is not a myth and she showed the children how she had been laying and hiding eggs all over the city because she wants us human beings to enter into communication with the Spirits of the Land again.

One boy said that this dragon was yearning for a hula hoop to play with. Sometimes, at night, when no one is looking, she plays with The London Eye (a huge Ferris wheel on the South Bank that provides marvellous views over the Thames and the whole city).

We brought the bones and the stones into our work. We talked about death and rebirth and Easter. The children said: 'Forget about chocolate eggs, this year's Easter eggs will all have baby dragons in them!' We agreed that the baby dragons represented changes in human consciousness.

The children wanted to do some drumming for the river dragon, but I had not brought my drum on this occasion. So we all took a big stone each and used the animal bones for beaters. We did some decent shamanic drumming (and it must have been quite a sight, and sound, for other people on the small beach, or higher up on the Thames towpath). I was extremely aware of all of us holding white stones that looked like eggs. One boy said: 'Every time a ship passes it makes those big waves and ultimately one of those waves will crack open all the eggs that the dragon has laid. It is only a matter of time until all these eggs *hatch* and there will be baby dragons all over our city!'

Teaching Notes

Field Trip

If you are in a position to invite a geomancer, this work will be a real eye-opener for young people. Take the children on a field trip to a place where there are powerful currents in the land. If the group is large, take some parents as volunteers too.

Open the group in the location of choice.

Take a moment to do some grounding exercises. Maybe everyone becomes a tree with their roots growing deep into the Earth and their arms like branches reaching for the sky.

Now pay attention to the mood and the feeling quality of this place. Have we asked the Spirit of Place for permission to enter and be here? Do we feel welcome?

Explain what geomancy or energy work with the land is, but don't give the children too much information. Invite them to tune in for themselves. Ask:

What is here? What would like to communicate with us?
Is there anything this land needs or wants from us today?

Then roll with whatever guidance the children receive.

Is there a ceremony to be performed?
Are there any dragons here? How can we find them and communicate with them?
What role do dragons play in the land?

Generally dragons represent the great forces of creation. A friend of mine likes saying that there were dragons long before there were angels!

What other beings are here? What beings can we perceive with our eyes closed?

Allow this session to unfold.

Is there a song that wants singing?
Is there a story that needs telling?
Is there an art installation to be made from objects found in nature?

Close the group.

Ask the children to go home and paint those dragons or other beings they met and write a story about them.

Notes

1. To read more about Karmit Evenzur's work Google her name and 'Earth speaks'.

Session Plan 16: Message in a Bottle

Yesterday (writing this on 23 June 2015) we did a session that followed on from Here Be Dragons.

My plan was to teach the children about connecting to the Spirits of Place at a small ecology park in Greenwich and then visit another Thames beach next to the Thames Path. The ecology park is a small nature reserve with a thriving bird population. It is right on the river, near the Greenwich Yacht Club. There is charming small beach there, where other children have already made an art installation.

Hidden in this art installation our group found a message in a bottle that another group had left behind. This brought on a sudden urge for everyone to write a message in a bottle themselves. I tore up my teaching notes to produce paper. Someone had a pen in their pocket. Sadly there was no shortage of bottles because this beach had a fair amount of litter on it. The children were secretive about what they wrote, but from what I gather, they wrote clues for people on a spiritual quest or treasure hunt.

One of the girls drew a dragon's egg in the sand. A boy then found the perfect egg: an egg-shaped white stone. The stone was ceremonially buried within the dragon's egg outline. I was told that one day it will hatch and there will be another river dragon in London, but not just yet...

Nearby was a heavy chain sunk into the sand, possibly an old anchor from a ship. The children attempted to dig all the way to New Zealand to see what was at the end of the chain. 'Stop digging or you will pull the plug on the river Thames and our whole river will drain!' said one Dad. 'No! No!' Said the children. 'There is dragon tied up deep in the Earth and we are going to free him today!'

I called this session *The Spirits of Place,* but really it became

Message in a Bottle instead as soon as I tore up my teaching notes (very literally)!

The most important thing is always dancing joyfully with what the children themselves receive from Spirit.

Session Plan 17: Omen Walk

Introduction

The session plan for this session is extremely simple: give a group of children a notepad and pen. Then take them on a walk wherever you are and get them to pay close attention to absolutely anything that comes into awareness: signs, symbols, notices, trees, the way people and cars are moving…

Session

Welcome everyone and open the group.

If you have a fire, make sure that you have a Fire Keeper who does not join in the Omen Walk as it is important that the fire is always attended. Say:

How has everyone been?
Today we are going to explore omens. What is an omen?
Omens are signs that tell us what is taking shape in the future. In ancient times people believed the omens were divine messages from their god or gods. Where can we find omens?

Tell the story about a man who was driving along pondering a big question: should he marry a woman, yes or no? In that moment a car overtook him and slotted in front of him. The number plate was, mixed in with some numbers, NO. He realised that he had received his answer!

Go around the circle. Does anyone have experience of a powerful omen?

Explain that the whole universe communicates with us and that answers can be found literally everywhere: clouds, trees, behaviour of people, names of shops and car number plates etc. Say:

Pay attention to absolutely everything!
We will bring paper and pens – so make note of what you see.
Then we will return and share experiences.

This was one of the most hilarious sessions ever. We had such fun! Everyone found signs, messages and symbols that meant something in the context of their lives.

Close the group.

Session Plan 18: Shamanic Divination

Preparation

Ask all the children to bring three small objects of their choice. These could be found objects like a twig or stone/shell or small toys.

Session

Open the group.

Ask: 'How has everyone been since we last met?'

Show a crystal ball and ask: 'What are balls like this one sometimes used for? What does the word divination mean, does anyone know?'

Name other examples of divination methods and show a set of runes. Examples might include Tarot cards, I Ching, angel cards, oracle bones etc.

Ask: 'Does anyone here have experience of using any of these?'

The key themes of divination work are:

- Doing a reading on a question
- Telling the future
- Seeing into the heart of a situation
- Seeking guidance from the spirits

Ask if everyone brought three small objects and say: 'We will now do three short journeys where you will ask the spirits about the meaning of your objects. Also ask how you are to use them.'

Write this down or draw it so you are quite sure before you see a client.

J: Do three short drum journeys to the spirits of the objects the children brought, including how they are to be used.

Then team all children up in pairs.

One has a question and the other one does a reading, using the objects and guidance from Spirit.

Demonstrate. Someone asks a question and then pull a rune.

Say: 'Your turn now! Then reverse roles.'

After they have done that, gather in the Circle again. Ask: 'How did everyone get on?

Are you keen to learn more about divination? Remember the Omen Walk we did last time? Any other questions or suggestions?'

Close the group.

In my group a lot of children chose to give each other readings on managing the imminent transition to secondary school.

Session Plan 19: The Night Sky

Preparation

Choose a dark winter night and location away from big cities for this session.

Bring a torch for pointing at the night sky.

Check in advance what the night sky will look like in your location and research some stories behind the star constellations you will be able to see.

Session

The Fire Keeper makes a fire assisted by arriving children.

Open the group. Ask: 'How has everyone been since we last met?'

Say:

Here we are, sitting around a fire with the night sky overhead. We have talked about this before. This is how our ancestors lived. They did not have TV or the internet, but they had the fire to warm themselves and a great storybook overhead, the stories that the planets and stars and their movements tell us in our night sky.[1]

Who has kept up with the news, including the summer 2015, Pluto flyby? Pluto used to be a planet, but was demoted to dwarf star status in 2006. New Horizons is a NASA spacecraft that spent years making its way to dwarf planet Pluto. It scooted by Jupiter in 2007. After passing Pluto it will head farther into the Kuiper Belt, a massive zone of icy bodies beyond Neptune. On July 14th, 2015 New Horizons completed the closest flyby of Pluto performed so far. It sent fabulous photos of Pluto and its moons back to Earth. Pluto's largest moon is Charon. One of the more surprising discoveries was a frozen heart-shaped region on Pluto. The photographs even show a whale shape on Pluto![2] *So we live in exciting times and this session is going to be all about the night sky.*

What is the largest body we can see in the night sky? Yes, the Moon!

What else can we see in the night sky? Star constellations, yes. Can you recognise some star constellations we can see right now?

People all over the world have felt inspired to attach their own stories to those constellations.

Talk about the Great Bear or Big Dipper and some stories associated with this constellation that never dips below the horizon in the Northern hemisphere.

Below I provide a few stories.

Some Mythology

Ursa Major is a well-known and prominent constellation in many cultures. It is one of the oldest constellations in the sky, with a history dating back to ancient times. This constellation is mentioned by both Homer and in the Bible. A great number of tales and legends across the globe associate Ursa Major with a bear. The Ancient Greeks associated this constellation with the myth of Callisto, the beautiful nymph who had sworn a vow of chastity to the goddess Artemis. Zeus saw the nymph one day and fell in love. They had a son, and named him Arcas. Artemis had already banished Callisto when she had learned about the nymph's pregnancy and the broken vow, but Zeus had a very jealous wife called Hera. Hera decided to take revenge by turning Callisto into a bear. Callisto lived as a bear for the next 15 years. She was roaming the forest and always on the run, hiding from hunters. One day her son Arcas was walking in the forest so mother and son came face to face. At the sight of the bear, Arcas quickly drew his spear because he got scared. Seeing the whole scene from Mount Olympus, Zeus decided to intervene to prevent disaster. He sent a whirlwind that carried both Callisto and Arcas into the heavens. Here he turned Arcas into the constellation Bootes (the Herdsman) and Callisto into Ursa Major

(The Great Bear). In another version of this same myth Arcas becomes the constellation Ursa Minor (or The Little Bear). This only infuriated Hera even more and she persuaded her foster parents Oceanus and Tethys never to let the bear bathe in the northern waters. This is, according to legend, why Ursa Major never sets in the Northern Hemisphere.[3]

We often see robins in our garden. They won the competition for *most popular bird in the UK* recently. Why do they have a red chest?

The Micmac Indians of Nova Scotia and the Iroquois Indians along the St Lawrence seaway share one story about the Great Bear. In this story, the quadrangle of the Big Dipper represents a bear that is pursued by seven hunters. The three closest hunters are the handle of the Big Dipper. As autumn approaches, the four farthest hunters dip below the horizon and abandon the hunt, leaving the closest three hunters to chase the bear. The hunters are all named after birds. The closest hunter to the bear is named Robin, the second closest is Chickadee, and the third is Moose Bird. Chickadee is carrying the pot in which the bear will be cooked. The second star in the handle is actually two stars, and a famous double star system, called Mizar and Alcor, which represent Chickadee and the pot. In autumn, as the bear attempts to stand up on two legs, Robin wounds the bear with an arrow. The wounded bear sprays blood on Robin, who shakes himself and in the process colours the leaves of the forest red; some blood stains Robin and he is henceforth called Robin Redbreast. The bear is eaten, and the skeleton remains travelling through the sky on its back during winter. During the following spring a new bear leaves the den and the eternal hunt resumes once more.[4]

My maiden name means 'son (or child) of a bear' and I have always felt a special connection to bears. You can follow the night sky throughout the year and observe if the Great Bear is walking on all fours, standing up, or lying on its back dead and dismembered, awaiting rebirth. Corona Borealis (a crown-like star formation near the Great Bear) is said to be the den where the bear hibernates.

J1: Do a Journey to the Spirit of the Big She Bear in the sky

Then talk about Orion, the Great Hunter, recognised by the three evenly spaced stars in his belt.

J2 Do a journey to Orion, the Great Hunter in our night sky

Say: 'You Time Travellers know that there are other ways of visiting far off planets than travelling in a space rocket!'

J3: Do a journey to Pluto. What do we see? What is the Spirit of Pluto like?

Afterwards ask: 'While you were there, could you see the heart on Pluto? Or the Whale?'

Close the session and call feral time.

Notes

1. *Planets for Pagans: use the Planets and Stars for Personal and Sacred Discovery* (formerly titled *A Magical Tour of the Night Sky*) by Renna Shesso, Weiser Books, 2014
2. See the Nasa Space Flight website http://www.nasaspaceflight.com/2015/01/new-horizons-pluto-observations-july-flyby/
3. To refresh your memory of Greek Mythology: http://www.greekmyths-greekmythology.com/ursa-major-in-greek-mythology/
4. From http://www.aavso.org/myths-uma

Session Plan 20: Lunacy and Luna-See

Introduction

The Mid-Autumn Festival or Moon Festival always falls on the 15th day of the 8th month according to the Chinese lunar calendar. The fact that it is always celebrated in the middle of the autumn gives it this name. The Moon always appears big and very bright at this time of the year.

Preparation

Choose the dark time of the year for this session and check when Moonrise occurs on the day you are teaching. Will the Moon be up?

Bake or buy Chinese Moon Cakes.

Session

The Fire Keeper makes fire assisted by arriving children.

Open the group. Ask: 'How has everyone been since we last met?'

Say:

Today's session is going to be all about the Moon. Can we see her just now?

All over the world we find stories about the Moon. Early peoples, who did not wear a watch or have our internet, used the Moon for time-keeping. Tribal people might say: 'I will see you seven Moons from today!'

What is most noticeable about the Moon? Does she look the same every night?

And is she always up at night or can we see her at other times of the day?

Fact: the Moon is up in the daytime as much as at night. We do not always see her because the light of the Sun is so bright. Often clouds obscure the Moon too, as they do at night.

How would you keep time if you didn't have a watch or any modern technology? How would you keep track of the days , nights and the seasons?

For early peoples the waxing and waning of the Moon was about death and rebirth, about dying and resurrection, about disappearing and reappearing. In many ways the Moon was a symbol of hope. Her phases inspired a spiritual and cyclical way of thinking where death is always followed by rebirth and new life. Now let's do our own journey to the Moon.

J1: Journey to the Moon Spirit to have a conversation. What would she like to tell us today?

Afterwards ask: 'How did the Moon Spirit appear to you? What did the Moon Spirit tell you?'

Chinese Moon Cakes

Talk about Chinese Moon Cakes.[1]

Years ago I was studying Mandarin Chinese. At my teacher's house I got to eat Moon Cakes for the first time. They had Chinese characters on them, so eating them was very educational!

Once upon a time in China a woman called Chang'e and her husband Houyi were immortals living in the sky with the Jade Emperor. The Jade Emperor had 10 sons who became stars in the sky. They were so bright and hot that they made life on Earth impossible. Chang'e and Houyi shot down nine of those stars. The Jade Emperor was furious and sent them down to Earth to live as peasants. Houyi was determined to stay immortal. The Queen Mother of the West gave him an immortality pill that would make him and his wife eternal if they ate half each. However, Chang'e accidentally ate the whole pill. She got so bloated that she floated up to the Moon, where she found a rabbit to live with. Chang'e became the Moon Goddess. People pray to her for blessings and a good harvest of crops.[2]

We may talk about the Man in the Moon, but Chinese people have always seen the Rabbit in the Moon!

Moon Cakes have evolved over the years to encompass many different flavours, materials, and traditions. But they are generally sweet, moist, and somewhat dense cakes. Many moon cakes have a salted egg yolk in the middle to symbolise the full moon. There is a crust around each cake that is thicker and harder than the inside. Atop each Moon Cake there is generally a Chinese symbol that translates to either 'longevity' or 'harmony'. It is also common to find the name of the bakery it came from somewhere on the cake. There may also be other additional designs such as a moon, a rabbit, flowers, or Chang'e, the Moon Woman.

What is Lunacy?

Lunacy is a state of craziness, insanity or extreme folly! We could also spell it Luna-See. Shamans often have a special relationship with the Moon and they use their x-ray eyes to see what remains hidden from most people.

Say: 'Now look at the Moon with your shaman's x-ray eyes. What do you see? (Use your Luna See!)'

J2: Do a trip to Chang'e or the Moon Woman

Afterwards ask: 'What does she look like? What did she tell you? Is there anything she wants from us today?

'Will you look at the Moon with different eyes after our work today?'

Eat or bake Moon Cakes around the fire.

Also mention that shamanic drums are sometimes said to represent the Moon. I hope that the Moon Woman likes crows because my drum has many crows painted on it!

Close the group.

Notes

1. To find a recipe for making moon cakes: http://www.wikihow.com/Make-Moon-Cakes
2. More information about moon cakes: http://keewah.us/what-are-mooncakes.html

Session Plan 21: Talking to Plant Spirits: Session in the Herb Garden

The Fire Keeper makes fire assisted by arriving children.

Welcome the group. Say: 'How has everyone been? Today we are going to work with plant spirits. Has anyone here worked with plant spirits before?'

Where Does a Lot of our Medicine Come From?

When Western scientists arrived in the rain forests of South America they were amazed by how much the local people knew about plants. They did not have our laboratories and microscopes, yet they knew all about the plants in their surroundings.

How could they have so much plant spirit knowledge?

Tricky Question: What is the Difference Between Herbalism and Plant Spirit Medicine?

Say:

Herbs can be used in a variety of ways: culinary (meaning for cooking, in the kitchen), medicinal and in some cases spiritual. For example, I like burning dried sage in my bee smoker and I use this in purification and healing work. You could say that Plant Spirit Medicine is more like plant shamanism. It recognises that plants have spirit. Those in-dwelling spirits of plants can speak to us directly, if we know how to listen. So the answer to my question is that native peoples in the jungle know about plants because they speak to plant spirits.

One well-known Plant Spirit Medicine Teacher, called Elliott Cowan,[1] *says that 'the active ingredient in plant spirit medicine is friendship'.*

Do you think you could all form a friendship with a plant spirit?'

In our session today we are going to be connecting to some plant spirits right here, in my own herb garden, to see if we can gather information or knowledge directly from the plants themselves.

Team children up with different plants such as lemon verbena/oregano/rosemary/thyme/basil/dill etc. Say:

I am going to be rattling very gently. I want you to close your eyes and just sit with your plant for a while. Maybe the spirit of the plant will appear… Maybe you will feel something. Maybe you will just have a deep knowing in your heart that cannot be explained... You may even hear words, or a story…

How this unfolds does not matter! If you give this your full attention there are no wrong answers. But you need to go very quiet within yourself for long enough to receive the information. You have talked to trees and clouds before, I know that you can do this!

Rattle… Then share information received…

Next do it again with a different plant. Then say:

Having done this twice, how do you feel about Elliott Cowan's active ingredient? Do you feel it is possible to be friends with a plant spirit? I know this is possible because some of my art students have become very close friends indeed with plant spirits!

Now let's ask the Spirit of Lemon Verbena for permission to make tea, so we can make a potion and drink it! Or maybe you choose to ask another plant.

Only if you have permission from the plant spirit, pick some leaves and let's go to the kitchen.

Everyone makes tea. Maybe put some honey in it as well. Say:

How does it feel to drink this after you have met the plant spirit?

And now you know that you can follow this procedure with

plants in your own garden.

Just one important word of warning: not all plants are edible and some are very toxic. Now obviously the plant spirits themselves will tell you this, but you may still want to check with a parent or teacher before you eat a plant or make tea, OK?!

Ask if there are any questions.

Close the group.

Notes

1. The website of Eliot Cowan is http://plantspiritmedicine.org/
   My favourite book about plant spirit communication is:
   52 Flowers that Shook My World: A Radical Return to Earth by Charlotte Du Cann, Two Ravens Press, 2012.

Session Plan 22: Mild Pyromania

Elemental beings can be likened to units of consciousness of the Earth. If we look at nature as a complex system of processes and relationships, we can see that at certain levels of complexity, an intelligence arises, an elemental consciousness; from basic units to more complex intelligences 'overlooking' larger systems.

Their consciousness arises from the element and the process in nature they are connected with, so we can say they are tied to a 'task' and do not have 'free will' like we humans know it. They exist on the etheric level and on the astral level, communicating to us mostly through the emotional realm. Their vibration is very subtle, and responds to ever so delicate changes in frequency and so responds very rapidly to our own emotional state. When connecting to any nature spirit the best way is to be present with an open heart and show our love and respect to these intelligences that are overlooked by most modern people.

Karmit Evenzur, 2015[1]

Introduction

All children LOVE fire! And that is love deliberately spelled with capital letters! We have met around the fire in all seasons and in nearly all weather conditions. We have danced with smoke spirits and done divination work by staring at the fire.

Session

The Fire Keeper makes fire assisted by arriving children.

Open the group. Say:

Today is going to be all around fire. Why is fire so fascinating? What does fire give us? (Reasons include warmth, cooked food, transformation and transmutation. Smoke is also often used in purification.)

Does fire have dangerous aspects as well?

What does the word pyromania mean?
Are there any pyromaniacs present here today?

Let's do a journey to the Spirit of Fire.

J1: Journey to the Spirit of Fire

Say:

How can we honour fire?

Do people in our society respect Fire as a living being? No. Why not?

Fire is one of the elements. What are the other elements, can we name them?

That is right: fire, earth, water and air. Some people say that spirit is like a fifth element. In Norse shamanism ice is considered a fifth element in its own right, separate from the element of water. But of course we all know that ice is one of the forms that water can take. Can you tell me other manifestations of water?

Who has heard of the word elemental? What are elementals?

I asked my colleague Karmit Evenzur to describe this for me. Her reply, as a professional geomancer and specialist, is at the start of this session plan. Translated into my own words she says that elementals are beings that look after the Earth and all her ecosystems. They are spirits of the earth, fire, air and water (even of snow and ice). They are always trying to bring things into balance. However, what they call balancing may look like a drought, flood or storm to us! They are not human beings but they are extremely present wherever we find ourselves. They are always open to communication with us, as long as we approach them with an open mind and open heart.

Ask the children to try this.

J2: Journey to the Elementals

Afterwards ask: 'How did you get on? Did the elementals have a message for us today?'

The elements can be very good teachers for us when it comes to balance. Too much or too little can cause big problems:

- Too little water = drought.
- Too much water = floods or tsunami
- Too little fire = a frozen world.
- Too much fire = a forest fire
- Too little air = living beings can't breathe
- Too much air moving = a great storm, cyclone or hurricane
- Too little earth = lack of grounding if humans do not feel Mother Earth under their feet
- Too much earth = a landslide or earthquake perhaps

This tells us a lot about leading a balanced life, about eating right and being in the right relationship with our own bodies and the body of our Ultimate Mother, that is to say Mother Earth. Ask:

How do we feed fire?

How much wood (or coal) does it take to keep a fire burning all night? More than you'd think! And that tells us something about the amount of fossils fuels we are using up today.

Discuss human management of natural resources and how all eco-systems need to be in balance.

After all the hard work everyone then makes chocolate bananas and roast marshmallows over the fire.

Close the group and call feral time.

Session Plan 23: Masks

Introduction

All children love working with masks and costumes. This session can be timed around Halloween when masks are on children's minds anyway and easily available in the shops.

Preparation

Have spare masks at hand. There is always a parent who doesn't read the instructions you send out.

Below is some background information for the teacher to bear in mind.

Though masks are found all over the world, the word to describe a mask (and the purpose of a mask) does not translate in any straightforward way between languages of nations that have mask-making traditions. In English the word mask emphasises concealment, covering up and hiding something. We also have the word unmasking and we associate this with spies, dirty secrets and corrupt politicians or public figures. A masquerade is literally a costumed dance, but more commonly refers to an outward show, pretence. Wearing a mask strips someone of their personal identity (think of bank robbers wearing balaclavas so they cannot be identified on closed camera footage). Someone wearing a balaclava exudes menace. A friend, or child, all dressed up for a party can startle us by looking quite unlike their everyday selves.

Session

The Fire Keeper makes a fire assisted by arriving children.

Open the circle.

Say: 'How has everyone been since we last met? Has everyone brought a Halloween mask? I have some more right here!

'Let's hold up our masks and go around circle.'

Everyone says a few words about their mask.

Say: 'When I say the word mask, what does that make you think of? Why do people wear masks?'

Then talk a bit about how masks are used in shamanism.

Below is some information about masks from all over the world. Pick out some interesting bits for your group of children.

Masks are a very widespread phenomenon. They appear in cultures all over the world and they were used in civilisations dating from antiquity to the present. In Medieval times, when Europe was plagued by the Black Death, the people who came to collect the bodies of the victims wore masks with a large hooked nose. This striking feature of an exaggerated nose was not developed to hide the face of the person wearing the mask. Instead it was stuffed with sweet-smelling herbs in order to conceal the stench of death and also to prevent infection and spreading disease. This is how in our day and age masks with prominent noses have become part of the fun and spectacle of wearing masks. In many parts of Central Asia the generic terms makishi or nkisi refer to a range of masks and to the performance of which masking is part. These are normally spectacles that take place in the context of male circumcision ceremonies. But makishi are also said to be *the dead in resurrected form*. This is how the term came to be translated as *ancestral spirit*. Something similar happens in Inuit or Native American ceremonies where the wearer of a mask *becomes* the spirit whose identity he assumes.

In the days before photography people often made death masks. This was about preserving someone's appearance in time. The mask would remain after the body was buried. Today we tend use photographs to capture such moments.

The religious calendar provides a cycle of annual events in which masks are sometimes used. This still happens in many predominantly Catholic countries in Europe and Latin America. Think of Carnival!

In the Ancient World masks were used in the tragic and comic theatre. Think of how a sad mask and a smiling mask put together are still in use as a symbol for theatre today.

Last but not least, in medieval Venice masks were common and extremely fashionable. The law allowed people to go about their daily life wearing masks for several months of the year. Fancy that and imagine what everyday life would look like! These masks were a great leveller. They put everyone on an equal footing: rich and poor, law-abiding and criminal. Men wore masks when visiting brothels, princes wore masks to walk around anonymously, nuns (in this context often women forced into convents against their will) wore masks to meet their lovers. This all contributed to an ambience of moral decadence. Things are different today, but the Carnival in Venice, with the masks and costumes involved, has become world famous.

For the Inuit people seeing was the ultimate act for their shamans. Some wore masks and others hid their faces behind seal-skins. The idea was to banish the obstructions of ego, greed and self-importance.

Say:

Now let's do another round where a masked person goes looking for those who have hidden. Then we reverse things and we have an unmasked person looking for those who are hiding but wearing their masks.

The last thing we will do is put on our mask and become a different person for a while. Let's try this! Who is this person you become when you wear your mask?

(For us things took a spooky turn because we were using Halloween Masks! There were references to ghouls and the walking dead, and so forth).

Gather around the fire and discuss.

Was there a difference? What difference did the masks make? Did it make things more fun or scarier or just different?

In this session the children then asked me to wear a mask and chase them. They said that a masked adult chasing them is *deliciously scary.*

Close the group.

Session Plan 24: The Spirits of Courage and Resilience

What does not kill me, makes me stronger.
Friedrich Nietzsche, German philosopher (1844-1900), *Twilight of the Idols (1888)*

Preparation

Have a collection of rubber bands ready to demonstrate the concept of stretching and pulling back to the original shape – or breaking.

Also have chewing gum for demonstrating both stretching and so-called *stick-ability*!

Session

The Fire Keeper makes fire assisted by arriving children.

Open the group. Say:

Today we are going to be working with the Spirit of Courage. What does the word courage mean?

It means 'The ability to do something that you know is difficult or dangerous'[1]

And as I happen to be Dutch, what is Dutch courage? Yes, becoming brave through drinking alcohol. Does that really work, do you think?

Here is a more serious question: does being brave mean feeling no fear? Discuss!

The children will quickly realise that anyone who does not feel fear is not truly being brave.

J1: A shamanic journey to the Spirit of Courage

Ask: 'What does the Spirit of Courage look like? What did he or she say to you?'

J2: Ask the Spirit of Courage where in our lives we need to be braver just now

Ask: 'We are in safe sacred space here. What would be an act of bravery right now? Can anyone think of something?'

Some of the younger children in the group I ran were still afraid of striking matches, so they decided to strike a match and throw it in the fire, encouraged and witnessed by the group. Say:

Does being brave mean always pretending to be strong? Or does it mean sometimes admitting that we are scared or find something difficult?

And what does the word vulnerable mean? Explain that it comes from vulnus, the Latin word for wound. Why is vulnerability a good thing?

There is a quote: 'When we were children, we used to think that when we were grown up we would no longer be vulnerable. But to grow up is to accept vulnerability. To be alive is to be vulnerable'[2]

Why is it so hard to be vulnerable? What could happen? Yes, we could end up in scenarios where we end up feeling great shame. And that is really uncomfortable!

Raise your hand if you have ever felt ashamed? What does it feel like?

What would you do if you could not fail? [3] *Discuss!*

Has anyone here heard of the word resilience? What does it mean? [4]

Resilience:

1. *The power or ability to return to the original form, position, etc., after being bent, compressed, or stretched; elasticity.*
2. *The ability to recover readily from illness, depression, adversity, or the like; buoyancy.*

Hand out rubber bands. Say:

So let's experiment with this: how far can you stretch a rubber band and still have it snap back to its original shape?

Now that is resilience! We all have that ability!

But what happens if you stretch a rubber band too far? Indeed, it may snap.

So that shows us what too much pressure can do to people.

Brene Brown uses a phrase: 'shame resilience' and it is a really helpful quality or ability to have. So let's explore what makes people shame resilient. She found that (some of) the following things were very important:

- *Being whole-hearted and knowing our own worthiness*
- *Being authentic and letting go of what people think*
- *Self compassion and that means letting go of perfectionism*
- *Cultivating a resilient spirit: letting go of numbing and powerlessness*

I am not going to run through her whole list, but it also includes things like gratitude, letting go of certainty, more play and rest and letting go of the need to control. Discuss!

So the important thing is to grow all these qualities within ourselves (sort of like the plants you see in the garden) and stick with things.

J3: Ask the spirits to show us about developing resilience and stick-ability

Get out the chewing gum. Ask: 'Can chewing gum teach us about *sticking to things?'*

Ask the children to take home some chewing gum and reflect on sticking with the things we discovered in the session…like stretching and growing and snapping back to our original shape.

My group loved the chewing gum prop.

Close the group.

A few weeks later some of the Time Travellers spoke about the importance of having a spiritual toolkit during a presentation at Steiner House in London. One boy spoke about courage and resilience – and about chewing gum!

Notes

1. From http://www.merriam-webster.com/dictionary/courage
2. Brene Brown quotes Madeleine L'Engle in her book: *Daring Greatly: How the Courage to be Vulnerable Transforms the Way we Live, Love, Parent and Lead*, Penguin Group, 2012
3. This is a question Brene Brown asks in her book, same as footnote 2
4. Taken from http://dictionary.reference.com/browse/resilie nce

Session Plan 25: Psychopaths and Psychopomps! Field Trip to Local Cemetery

Introduction

In my Wheel of the Year for the Time Travellers, this is the session that closes the academic year. It traditionally takes place in mid July, just before schools break up and the summer holidays start in the UK. Perhaps surprisingly this is a very popular session.

However, this is not so with adults. It is much harder to fill a course exploring shamanic perspectives on Death and Dying for grown-ups! Children have no such inhibitions.

We are fortunate to have Nunhead Cemetery right on our doorstep. It is the twin sister of the more famous Highgate Cemetery in North London. It was built in the Victorian era with ornate, almost Gothic, tombs and mausoleums and it is very overgrown and set in old woodland. This is by far the wildest place I have easy access living so close to Central London. I cannot see myself running this session in some overly tidy modern cemetery. I have brought groups of adult students here as well, dressed in bear suits and drumming. Almost anything goes in this magical otherworldly place.

The first time we did this, I gave this session the boring title A Shamanic Perspective on Death and Dying, but the children themselves quickly christened it Psychopaths and Psychopomps instead. A far better title! This was on our first visit. The children were having a fabulous time. They all climbed a tree and I spent a lot of time standing under that tree hollering at them! We explored the Tree of Life as well as Death. From high up the tree a small voice called down: 'Is a psychopomp the same thing as a psychopath?'

That gave us the meat for our session right there. A psychopomp is a soul conductor, a being (it can be angelic or an animal spirit as well as a human being) that accompanies souls on their final journey to the Land of the Dead and ensures that they are taken to the right place. (And just for the record: A psychopath is a person who appears outwardly normal, but seems to possess no empathy or compassion, or any related concept of ethics, when it comes to fellow human beings). In our session we played around with that. Once a psychopath kills someone, a psychopomp is needed. Children love a bit of gruesome detail.

Some Things My Group Said or Asked

'Where is the place Christians called Heaven located on the Shaman's Map?'

Some of the children had just studied Ancient Egypt in school and they knew that Anubis weighs a human soul after Death on his scales. To make a full transition into the Afterlife, the soul needs to be as light as a feather. What kind of stuff makes your soul too heavy for the spirit world? We talked about soul parts, resentment, unhealthy connections to the living, the desire to still control events on Earth from the grave, as it were.

'We all die and then we are born again. What is that called again: recycling?'

The correct word is called reincarnation of course but 'recycling' is a better word in many ways! One Time Traveller once said to his mum: 'We all get recycled!' So that was the great mysteries of Life and Death summed up in four words!

One small Time Traveller had some great ideas for the day his mum dies: *'When my mum dies I am going to make a mint-coke bomb and give her a good send off!'* (The mother concerned was very pleased at the prospect). I asked for the recipe. The reply was:

Mint Coke Bomb Recipe

You take a big bottle of coca cola and dissolve some mints in it. Then you put someone's ashes in it. Then you shake the bottle vigorously so the mixture comes exploding right out, up into the night sky. Then you look up to see the new star that has appeared in the night sky. That will be my mum looking down on me!

Teaching Notes

Preparation for the Field Trip to a Local Cemetery

Send out instructions about where to meet and what to bring, like a bottle of water and a snack.

Session

Open the group.

Talk about the Christian concept of Death, reflected by the tombs and architecture around the group. Then move into shamanic perspectives on Death and Dying.

What is Death? What is the purpose of Death?

I usually tell some indigenous tales about a time when Death didn't exist and what happened then. According to one African Asante myth, although people did not like the idea or experience of Death, they nevertheless embraced it when given the choice. There is one tale of an ancient people who, upon experiencing their first visitation of Death, pleaded with God to stop it. God granted this wish, and for three years there was no Death. But there were also no births during that time. Unwilling to endure this absence of children, the people beseeched God to return Death to them as long as they could have children again.[1]

Where do people go after Death? What is the role of a Psychopomp or Soul Conductor?

Explain what the role of the psychopomp is in shamanic

societies. Give some examples from all over the world.

Explain that shamans and shamanic practitioners do psychopomp work and why.

Walk around... Answer questions the children ask... Judge how much information they are willing and ready to absorb.

Where possible try to link this to what they are doing in school. Talk about their first experiences of Death. For example, grandparents or pets that have died.

Expect questions about this: do pets to go Heaven.

Explain that animal healers speaking of animals *crossing the rainbow bridge* when their time comes etc.

One of the most well-known stories about the Inuit is the strange practice that they have adopted when facing Death and old age. According to the popular conception, Inuit must work lead such a harsh life full of hardship that they simply cannot manage to support adults who are no longer contributing to the well-being of the group. Thus, when old-age strikes, rather than waiting around for Death and eating food their companions need to catch and clothing their companions struggle to make, the elderly Inuit are taken to sea and set adrift on an ice floe.[2]

You can weave in references to Halloween etc. My own group of children like playing morbid games such as lying on tombs and trying out how it feels to be dead. We have had one boy wandering off and getting lost and the cemetery closing for the night. This is a good opportunity to talk about vision quests and what it might be like to spend a night sitting out at a cemetery! This boy was swept out by the park keeper; in the end he spent the night in his own bed.

For us this is a fun and free-floating session where I will dance quite happily with whatever issues and observations the children themselves raise.

Close the group.

Notes

1. Taken from http://www.deathreference.com/Ho-Ka/How-Death-Came-into-the-World.html
2. From http://www.theinitialjourney.com/features/eskimos-old-age/

Session Plan 26: Digging to Australia: Introducing a Safe Way for Children to do Shamanic Healing Work

My 10-year-old son has been going the Imelda's Time Travellers group since it began over two years ago. The Spiritual Toolbox which he's cultivated in that time cannot be overestimated. He has a close relationship with his Power Animals, brilliant journeying skills and a firm grasp on several healing modalities amongst other shamanic talents. His sense of the sacredness of all beings and the spirit in all things is a joy to see. Not only does he have enormous fun in each session, but he also has an ever-growing confidence in his own spiritual connection and authority. I feel strongly that these shamanic teachings give him the best platform from which he can go out into the world with confidence and compassion. He has learned and is learning his own sacred place in the world. Our children truly are natural shamans and Imelda is such a brilliant teacher because she not only sees this so well, but because she also allows them to trust their own relationship with spirit, their connection to the universe and their absolute right to be who they are. I wish I'd had such a group as a child.

Marie Lloyd, London, UK

Preparation

This makes a good indoors session.

Please note that in Session Plan 1 I have already provided a session plan for using an egg to do safe extraction work. This session plan provides another safe way of working that poses no risks to the child.

Session

Open the group. Say:

How has everyone been since we last met?

Today we are going to do some healing work. Who remembers our egg healing session? Raise your hands please! Today we are going to do something different.

Let's talk about healing for a moment. What does the word mean again? Indeed, someone might be ill, or in pain and healing is about helping them get better. In some cases the healer may be able to reduce the pain or even take it away altogether.

What does the word healing literally mean, anyone? It means making whole, returning to a state of wholeness. The words 'whole', 'healthy' and 'healing' are all related when you look at the roots of those words. (And the science of studying word roots is called etymology, by the way).

Now let's talk about risk for a moment. Do you think it is possible for the healer to get hurt while doing healing work for other people – or perhaps for animals, like you have done in another session?

Most young people in our group are aware of this risk. So yes, if you are going to be pulling energy that is in the wrong place out of someone's body or energy field, you have to think very carefully about how you do this and what you are going to do with what is pulled out. [Mention the word extraction here.] *Like a dentist does tooth extraction, we are pulling something out.*

In this group everyone has a close relationship with their Power Animal. One safe way of doing a healing for someone is asking your Power Animal to go over to wherever in the world they are, they do not need you to be in the room with them, and perform a healing.

Be careful! One of my colleagues did this once, years ago. She told her PA to go somewhere but forgot to ask the PA to come back. So the PA stayed with her client. And what do you think happened to her? Indeed! She fell very ill! So don't do that. Tell your PA to come back!

Partner up with someone who is in the room. Talk for about five minutes. Ask them what issue they would like help with.

It is a good idea if you both lie down for this with both of you concentrating only on this! I will be drumming for all of you. Now send your Power Animal over, but track him or her. You lie there and observe what happens. Your client observes what happens. If anything changes. If they feel a bit better.

When everyone is clearly done, stop drumming and call sharing time.

Say:

How did people get on? What did you observe? Please share with the whole group.

Then turn around and repeat the exercise. Swap roles. If you were the one sending the Power Animal earlier, you are going to be the client this time.

Drum again. Then say:

Share again in the whole group!

Was it very different to receive the help from being the person organising the help?

Anything else you want to say about it?

Next I want to talk about transmutation[1] *to all of you. I know that many of you already know what this is.*

Can anyone explain? Thank you!

Talk some more about intrusions. What are toxic thoughts? How do they start leading their own life? Can they create the kinds of problems we have just asked our Power Animal to heal or pull out?

Now let's talk about spiritual hygiene.

Be honest: when was the last time you had a toxic thought? We all have them! Me too! Go back to that moment and observe how the thoughtform travels.

Now we do one journey:

J: Ask your Power Animal to show you a method for transmuting a toxic thought

After the journey, ask the children to share their experiences, then say:

So next time a toxic thought comes, do some work to help it shape-shift into a healthy thought, or even a blessing! If everyone did this, the world would be a cleaner and healthier place for everyone, on the energy level.

Well done, all of you! I really hope you will practise some of this at home and in school!

Answer questions and close the group.

Notes

1. *How to Heal Toxic Thoughts: Simple Tools for Personal Transformation* (Paperback) by Sandra Ingerman, Sterling, Reprint Edition, 2012

Session Plan 27: The Spirit of Music: Shamanic Jamming

Introduction

We have some keen young musicians in our group and the young people themselves have requested shamanic jamming sessions. Actually we once did a session on making power tools that shape-shifted into a musical session instead as they all picked up instruments we have around the house!

In our case this session was announced months in advance and took place on 11 January 2016, the day that David Bowie's death was announced and all over the news. David Bowie speaks more to the generation of parents (as his music was the soundtrack of their youth) than to the young people in my group. However, this session still became a tribute to David Bowie as all over the city other people too organised and attended impromptu tributes. It was beautiful to observe this 'Change of Guards': one generation leaving and a new generation of musicians taking over.

Preparation

Have shamanic drums and rattles ready for those who cannot bring a musical instrument. If you have access to a piano, this is helpful.

Session

Open the group. Say:

How has everyone been since we last met? Has anything come up that you would like to share with the group?

This session is going to be all about making music, as requested by some of you.

Let's just discuss very briefly: how might shamanic ways of making music be different from other bands or orchestras you play in? Yes. Shamanism is about allowing the spirits to create something through us, or guiding us to create something, so we are going to be open to spirit influences tonight.

Let's take a moment to invite the spirits of music!

All gather around the piano.

I know that we have several pianists here tonight and I suggest that you take turns and/or play double-handed.

Those who have brought musical instruments, please get them out and set them up!

(In our group we had two bass guitars!)

Who did not bring any instrument? I have a selection of drums and rattles for you to choose from. I also have some very unusual instruments from Africa and other countries you can try out if you want to produce some unusual sounds.

OK! Could the bass guitar gives us a base line… And everyone else can them come in and improvise.

If you really get stuck or need something, I will be here, but really I am mostly going to leave you to it and enjoy the music!

Provide assistance when and where needed. Experience tells me levels of musical competence will vary greatly and less accomplished musicians may be trying to play together in the wrong key etc.

At the end of session, ask:

Did you enjoy that?
Would you like to do this again?
What would make this session even better?
Would anyone like to start a band?
Any other questions or requests for future sessions?

Close the group.

Session Plan 28: The Hero's Journey: Creative Writing

Preparation

Lay paper and pens out in the room. Also have a selection of random, but peculiar, objects in the centre of the room, covered by a cloth.

Session

Open the group. Say:

> *How has everyone been since we last met? Has anything come up that you would like to share with the group?*
>
> *Some of you have requested a Time Travellers session where we do creative writing. You will all find papers and pens laid out in the room.*
>
> *Let's talk very briefly about the relationship between shamanism and creativity. Does anyone have any thoughts about this?*

This will generally flush out a discussion about whether all our creative efforts come from our own imagination or whether our imagination is a doorway to Other Worlds/forces and whether beings from those places come out to play with us. Say:

> *Next, I am going to ask all of you present to write just one word on a piece of paper. Then I am going to read out all of those words and invite you to write a very creative weird sentence in which all of these words appear. This sentence may sound very crazy indeed! We are not going to publish it so run wild!*

This will loosen the children up and get them in a mind frame of not worrying too much about the finished result or embarrassing themselves. There could be lots of laughter following the exercise. Say:

> *Great, that was fun!*
>
> *Now let's do a longer piece of writing. I have some objects here covered by a cloth. We are always practising our shaman's x-ray eyes and seeing with our eyes closed. So let's have a go at this: what is under this cloth?*

My group did pretty well here. All the objects mentioned several times by different children turned out to be under the cloth!

At this point I pull off the cloth and say:

> *I am going to give you all ten minutes to write a story that connects all of these objects in some way. And I would like to be it a Hero's Journey, if you can manage that.*

All children engage with this on different levels, but all finish the task. Ask the children read out to others what they have all written.

There are lots of hilarious moments, but it also demonstrates how some children have been more creative than others. I do not comment on this, but you see that other ones think: 'Ah, so that is how it is done...'

At this point most children want to either expand their story or rewrite it. We allow time for that and share the results with group.

In our session most children then also started drawing some pictures to illustrate their stories.

I close by briefly talking to the group about so-called writer's block. Most children agree that if you approach writing this way, as a fun task and no expectations about outcomes, it is not hard to get the creative juices flowing. You could write about literally anything. Therefore you could say that in shamanism, or in my own specialism: making and teaching sacred art, writer's block or artist's block does not exist. Discuss!

Ask if people would like to do another creative writing session another time.

Close the group.

Session Plan 29: Finding the Gift in Adversity

Preparation

If at all possible, be outside. Tell everyone to bundle up warm and have a large box of eggs ready.

Session

The Fire Keeper makes fire assisted by arriving children.

Open the group. Say:

How has everyone been? Is there anything you would like to share with the group?

Today we are going explore finding the gift in adversity. What is adversity? Yes, it is things happening to us that feel like really bad news at the time.

Let's go around the circle and share some of those things…

In our circle examples were: not gaining admission to the school of our choice, being rejected by someone you had hoped to be friends with, parents promising a holiday and then saying it was not going to happen after all.

Say:

So I think we all agree that those things didn't feel good at all at the time. But now some time has passed since they happened. I would really like to know two things:

How do you see these things some time later?

And might it be possible to find good things that have resulted from what felt like a bad thing at the time?

In our circle the young people rose to the challenge. Here are some examples:

I didn't get into the school I wanted, but I am really happy now at the school where I am and I have made friends I would never have met in the other school. So I wouldn't want to transfer to that school today!

For all of primary school I have tried so hard to fit in… And I never did. Somehow the other children always laughed at me and picked on me… I was dreading the move to secondary school… And wearing a school uniform… and a tie… But actually it has been brilliant, because no one has memories of me as a four-year-old in reception class saying stupid things, or talking about spirits... I have been able to do things differently and made really great friends! And because I know what it feels like not to be accepted, or even to be bullied, I am definitely reaching out to other children who are struggling with the move to a new school…

After the children have shared their stories, say:

So that is interesting then, to see that even bad things can bring good things more long term.

Is there anything anyone is struggling with today? Are you willing to share this with the group?

J1: Journey to Power Animals and ask to be shown the gifts in adversity in life?

All the children agreed that this is a good technique for getting a handle on things that are disappointing initially. They also agreed that holding this awareness of previous disappointments turning to gold can help us to keep our cool and stay calmer when something disappointing or highly annoying occurs.

Say:

Now I have another question for you: do you think adversity makes us stronger? Let's ask our spirit allies about this.

J2: Journey to Power Animals to ask: 'Does adversity make us stronger?'

And all children, guided by their Power Animals, agreed that it does and that we would all be weaker and more immature as human beings if we never suffered any disappointment or adversity.

All the young people also agreed that some things are terrible, no matter what way you look at them, or 'frame them' in contemporary language. A parent or grandparent dying is terrible, no matter how you look at it. Losing a pet is extremely sad too.

The group conclusion, therefore, was that it is important to not always say: 'It is all for the best,' to people who have just had a terrible experience. Sometimes we need to just listen to them and be there for them, in any way that helps them…

Close the group.

Session Plan 30: 'I Am Sorry, Please Forgive Me!' Hawaiian Ho'oponopono

Preparation

There are many excellent websites about Ho'oponopono and I have listed some of them in the footnotes to this session plan.

It is a good idea to prepare a small handout with both the longer prayer and the shorter one on it for young people to take home and keep at hand. Not 'homework' (teenagers don't like the sound of that!) but spiritual work you can choose to do at home.

Session

Open the group. Say:

How has everyone been since we last met? Is there anything anyone would like to share with this group?

What does the word forgiveness mean, anyone?

Forgive

1 *To give up resentment against or stop wanting to punish (someone) for an offense or fault; pardon.*
2. *To relent in being angry or in wishing to exact punishment for (an offense or fault).*
3. *To absolve from payment of (a debt, for example).*
v.intr.
To grant forgiveness[1]

When and why would we forgive people?

Do we know other words that have the same meaning?

I know that some young people here speak other languages than English. Can you tell me the word for forgiveness in another language? In the case of our family: 'vergeven' in Dutch and 'forlata' in Swedish.

I now invite all of you to close your eyes while I will rattle very lightly and speak those words. I would like you to feel the vibration of these words... If I keep saying them, what energy does it create? What does it feel like to be in the presence of this word?

J: Rattle journey or meditation while listening to the word 'forgiveness'

Say:

Has anyone here heard about Dr Masaru Emoto's work? Sadly he died in 2014. He said prayers for water and spoke words to water and then took photographs of the crystalline structure the water molecules took on, because he believed that the vibration of our thoughts and words change the structure of water. In other words: water responds to the vibration of those thought forms and emotions.

Here is a hand out. On it you will find some examples and images.

I have provided a website address so you can create your own handout.[2]

Dr Emoto claimed that human consciousness has an effect on the molecular structure of water. Emoto's conjecture evolved over the years, and his early work explored his belief that water could react to positive thoughts and words, and that polluted water could be cleaned through prayer and positive visualisation.

He charged water with words such as: 'You make me sick, I will kill you,' and: 'Thank you.' The molecular structure of water looked completely different. On his website you can also see pictures of the Fujiwara Dam before and after being blessed.

Dr Emoto explained the method he uses in the following words:

It was 1994 when the idea to freeze water and observe it with a microscope came upon me. With this method, I was convinced that I should be able to see something like snow crystals. After two months of trial and error, this idea bore fruit. The beautifully shining hexagonal crystals were created from the invisible world. My staff at the laboratory and I were absorbed in it and began to do many researches.

At first, we strenuously observed crystals of tap water, river water, and lake water. From the tap water we could not get any beautiful crystals. We could not get any beautiful ones from rivers and lakes near big cities, either. However, from the water from rivers and lakes where water is kept pristine from development, we could observe beautiful crystals with each one having its own uniqueness.[3]

The observation was done in various ways, including observing the crystals of frozen water after:

- Showing letters to water
- Showing pictures to water
- Playing music to water
- Praying to water[3]

Say to the group:

In shamanism we say that any water that is in the room while you do spiritual work actually becomes Holy Water!

Having loked at this interesting work done by Dr Emoto and having tuned into the vibration of the word forgiveness, I would now like to introduce you to a very short prayer that comes from Hawaii. In Hawaii they have a form of shamanism they call Ho'oponopono and they use this very simple yet very powerful prayer:

Thank you

I am sorry
Please forgive me
I love you

I have tried it myself and it works! I even used it to fix my camera in Canada this summer!

It means (in my own understanding of this prayer):

Thank you – for coming to awareness (so we can work on it)

I am sorry – I don't always need to understand exactly what has gone wrong or why, but I am willing take responsibility for the fact that it occurred and say sorry

Please forgive me

I love you

Those words are true magic. They call in great Divine cosmic powers we do not even understand. And they work!

Now think of something that bothers you right now. Something that is in your field of awareness. Ok! Now we are all going to say those words… ALOUD…

How does that feel?

In everyday reality you may have to say them for quite a long time or very often. But they will work. The situation will improve.

Are you willing to go home and try this on problems that occur? Examples could be:

- *An annoying brother*
- *A sister who steals your earrings*
- *When your mum is angry with you (even when you have not actually done anything wrong. Can you feel sorry that she is angry, and probably very tired too, and still be willing to forgive her?)*
- *Something that happens in school*
- *Worrying things that you read about in the newspaper*

And so forth.

Good luck! And please keep the group posted.

Close the group.

Notes

1. Found online at http://www.thefreedictionary.com/forgive
2. You can find photographs of Masaru Emoto's work here and create your own hand-out http://www.dowsers.com/dr-masaru-emotos-messages-from-water/
3. Taken from http://www.masaru-emoto.net/english/water-crystal.html

Session Plan 31: Peer Mediation and Conflict Resolution: Arriving at a Win-Win Outcome

Compassion is the radicalism of our time. Love and Compassion are the true religions to me. But to develop this, we do not need to believe in any religion.
Dalai Lama XIV

I remain convinced that most human conflicts can be solved through genuine dialogue conducted with a spirit of openness and reconciliation.
Dalai Lama, Speech before the European Parliament, 14 October 2001 [1]

Introduction

Earlier in this book I mentioned peer mediation as one of the things that can have a positive impact on the lives of children and young people. Judith Bogner introduced me and the Time Travellers to this work.

In December 2015 Judith Bogner and I did a presentation at Steiner House, in London, as part of our Inspiring Youth Talks, titled Mediation and Compassion. We were exploring how mediation can be used to arrive at compassion and how peer mediation has been successfully introduced in schools since the 1980s. A mediator will typically assist two parties in resolving a dispute or disagreement. The idea is to find a compromise or common ground, an outcome that both parties can live with. About 66% of mediation cases are resolved on the same day.

What is Mediation?

Participation is voluntary. The process is confidential and

without prejudice, meaning that there is no admission of guilt. Any agreement arrived at is binding.

Mediation is effective, much cheaper than most lawsuits, in the world of adults. It is creative and offers a wider scope of solutions than litigation and it has the potential to bring real closure on a human level. It brings compassion.

Session

Open the group

Ask if anyone present has ever experienced conflicts in school.

Ask if and how those conflicts were resolved. Did a teacher need to get involved or could they sort things out themselves?

Say: 'Today we are going to be practising something called peer mediation. This is a form of conflict resolution where one child helps two others arrive at a win-win solution.'

Show the group two short videos about peer mediation in schools.[2]

Discuss what the young people present think of this.

Practise Run in Conflict Resolution

Ask: 'Is there anyone here who has a conflict they wish to work on?'

If the other party in the conflict is not present, you can ask someone to stand in for them.

Set up three chairs. The people who have the conflict face each other and the mediator sits between them on the third chair.

Explain that in the adult world in very serious cases people may not be in the same room while mediation occurs. They may be in different rooms in the same building and the mediator walks between them to build bridges and seek common ground. Give the following example:

Louis and Brendan both want to decide what game is being played in the school playground today. Both are very angry with each other because the other person will not co-operate with their plan. Some other children stand around watching the argument.

What can be done here? As you saw, the mediator helped them agree that they could take turns deciding what game is played. At morning play today everyone plays Louis' game and at afternoon play the group plays Brendan's game. Tomorrow other children in the friendship group get to decide what game will be played.

This is a win-win situation because essentially both boys get what they want and they are also learning a lesson in co-operation and listening closely to what the other person is saying.

This is a pretty mild conflict. Adults often get into much bigger conflicts. Some of those conflicts can turn into wars between nations.

While working on this session I had just read that Britain had launched airstrikes on Syria.

It is always better when you can sort things out yourselves because children understand children best and grown-ups sometimes only make things worse when they try to play referee!

Run a few more demonstrations. Say:

Is this something you could use, not only in school, but also in other areas of life? Say when you run into a disagreement with your siblings or your parents?

Discuss!

I hope that all of you will take away some inspiration from this. Keep me posted!

Close the group

Notes

1. See http://www.goodreads.com/quotes/search?Q=Dalai+La

ma+compassion

2. In these video clips you see Year 5 students in a primary school in the UK practicing peer mediation http://www.bbc.co.uk/education/clips/z6stsbk and http://www.bbc.co.uk/education/clips/zvc3cdm

Session 32: Humpty Dumpty: A Toolkit for Transition

Preparation

You will need: masks, one egg and bowl, marshmallows and a prayer to the weather spirits.

Session

The Fire Keeper makes fire assisted by arriving children. Say:

Welcome group! How has everyone been since we last met?

Some of you have settled into new schools, secondary school. How is this going?

A new school year starts and after the summer we are all a little bit older.

Will any of us grow younger again?! (NO!)

So we are always in transition. Who can tell me what the word transition means?

Indeed, it means moving from one place to another, from one stage of Life to another or even from being a young person to being a slightly older person.

I am going to be very childish now and invite all of you to sing a nursery rhyme we all know: Humpty Dumpty.

The rhyme is one of the best known and most popular in the English language. The most common modern text is:

Humpty Dumpty sat on a wall,
Humpty Dumpty had a great fall.
All the king's horses and all the king's men
Couldn't put Humpty together again…

Who or what is Humpty Dumpty? A person, an animal or a tomato?

Most children know that he is an egg.

Now crack an egg open in this bowl…

Can we put Humpty Dumpty back together again?

Can we put this egg together again once we break it?

All the children present at my session loved having a go at reassembling the egg. It is a very messy process…lots of baby wipes and shrieking… Say:

No one put the egg back together again very convincingly…

Why not?

So what can we do?

We can allow the egg to shape-shift. As you know shape-shifting is a big theme in shamanism!

What other shape-shifting have we done?

So now let's talk about the new school year… The new class and the new teacher or teachers… How is this going for all of you? What is good and what is bad?

Can you behave exactly the same way as you did a year ago, or even before the summer? No! Why not?

Talk about growing up.

What happens as you grow older?

What are the good things?

And what are the bad things?

So yes...you need to grow and shape-shift… And if at all possible you need to enjoy doing it!

So let's practise some shape-shifting… Get out the masks...

What happens when you put on a mask?

Are you still yourself? Or is there a change?

Or are you two things at the same time?

Can other people recognise you easily?

Is there freedom or perhaps permission in being allowed to be something or someone else for a few hours sometimes?

Most children agree that you can run wild when you wear an animal mask.

So let's try this… Let's have a wild run around the garden wearing masks…or animal hats…

Now find some space and a partner and communicate with someone else both of you wearing masks…maybe you are barking or growling…how is this different from everyday conversations?

Our Alpha Wolf felt very powerful, but our Little Owl decided to fly off. And the wolf can't fly of course… So he was left behind…

Does anyone have a burning question on this? Or on anything that has come up in school?'

All journey on this and share…

Now let's try this with food. If we roast or toast a marshmallow over the fire, can we turn it back together to what it was before?

No? So what can we do with it? We can eat it and enjoy it!

Brainstorm on themes for future sessions and then close the group.

Part III

Rites of Passage

Section 1: Hosting Initiation Ceremonies

If the youth are not initiated, they will burn down the village
African saying

Nomadic societies could not allow members to act irresponsibly and antisocially lest the fragile social ecology be ruptured. As an Aboriginal Elder once told me: 'For us adolescence lasts five days – the length of the initiation. Before initiation he is a child, after initiation he is an adult.'
David Tacey in *God and Diseases: Making Sense of our Physical and Mental Wellbeing*[1]

Crying for a Vision

Before I present suggestions for ceremonies and Rites of Passage that can be performed with young people and their families, there is one more concept I wish to discuss. I already touched upon it in Part I.

In our Western culture today we are over-protective of our children and we try to keep them out of harm's way. Native American peoples always had (and many still have) a radically different approach. By the time a young person reaches puberty the teenager is sent on a vision quest out in nature by him or herself. They are expected to spend a night out alone on a hill, or in the forest, in the hope that their helping spirits will show themselves and give them pointers for their spiritual calling, for their future life path. Sometimes they literally 'cry for a vision'[2] for a sacred dream to guide them in their lives.

Where Have Our Initiators Gone?

Earlier on in this book I have already talked about the importance of Rites of Passage and Initiation. I have said that if young people are not offered appropriate Rites of Passage, involving a symbolic death and rebirth, they may freeze developmentally and get stuck at an earlier stage of functioning. The Latin phrase for this is 'puer aeternus' (literally 'eternal boy', more loosely I would translate this as 'forever child'. As for a girl, the phrase would be 'puella aeterna', but psychoanalysts more commonly use the Greek word 'kore' meaning 'maiden' for this stage of development in girls).

Alternatively young people will create their own Rites of Passage through thrill-seeking (drugs, street gangs, joy driving, alcohol abuse, sexual acting out). Bungee jumping is extremely popular just now. It combines the elements of a free fall and rebound – but people are clipped onto a safety harness. In shamanism this makes perfect sense: we all have an innate soul desire to 'get over ourselves and move beyond our own ego'. To do this we need to 'drop into trust'. We need to drop into the arms of our helping spirits. We need to give up our compulsion to know and control everything and learn to trust that Spirit will take us to the right place, at the right time. So you could say that Spirit provides our safety harness. We need to clip our lifeline onto Spirit if we are to reach our full human and spiritual potential.

Another thing we observe in our society is that many young people are slow to grow up and take on the full set of responsibilities of adult life. We see eternal students, mother's boys, 'ladettes'. Unavailable men have become a cliche and the bane of their lives for many modern women who want to settle down, have children and provide a secure base for those children on all levels: materially, emotionally and spiritually.

What is Going On With Our Young People?

The fault of the nuclear family today isn't so much that it's crazy and full of double binds (that's true in communes and corporate offices too – in fact in any group). The fault is that the old men

> *outside the nuclear family no longer offer an effective way for the son to break his link with his parents without doing harm to himself.*
> Robert Bly in *Iron John*[3]

> *Initiation is equivalent to basic change in the existential condition; the novice emerges from his ordeal endowed with a totally different being from that which he possessed before initiation; he has become another.*
> Mircea Eliade, quoted by Edward Tick in his book *War and the Soul*[4]

One of my students commented just the week before I wrote this section, how we lost our last Rite of Passage for boys when military service was abolished in the UK. As a Rite of Passage it was far from perfect, but it was something. (And my very pacifist younger self would not believe I'd ever say that).

On the level of soul we all crave to be touched by The Divine, to experience the realm of the sacred, that which is set aside from the everyday. Myth allows us to enter that realm where The Divine intersects everyday reality: sacred space, power objects, ceremony, ritual, ancient stories that contain powerful teachings about the human condition and human dilemmas. Tick says that myths are the master templates for the patterns of our lives. Therefore all religion has its roots in myth. When our experiences of love, danger, challenge, quest, loss, calling or adventure captivate us, we find ourselves in the realm of myth. Myth also underlies all rituals and Rites of Passage. Mythology can be a great guide, for myth always takes place in the landscape of the psyche and it reveals the journey from the human soul's perspective. In Tick's own words:

> *When any country goes to war, it does so in the name of what it holds most sacred. And when any country claims victory, it does so in the name of that holy cause and as proof that it represents*

the truth.

Elsewhere in this book I already mentioned the oxymoron of Holy Wars and now we arrive at the explanation. In tribal societies training young men as warriors was a tried and tested path of Initiation. Young men toughened up and proved themselves in battles. The community provided spiritual support by sending them off ceremonially and welcoming them home with great pomp and circumstance. Often warriors received a new name and new status too, reflecting the great life change that had occurred.

However, today warfare has become so large-scale and lethal (think of chemical warfare and weapons of mass destruction) that war is no longer a realistic Rite of Passage. (So I remain very glad that military service has been abolished in the UK, after all I have three teenage sons!)

One core element that needs making explicit here is that being an adult means defending loved ones, young children, the elderly and cherished moral values when they come under attack. This is one element of war as a Rite of Passage we actually need to preserve and keep alive. We once again need to teach our young people about their sacred duty to the larger community. A keen observer might remember that this issue did indeed come up in our youth seminar exploring violence.

Millennials

In this context my friend Judith Bogner has brought Millennials to my awareness. The Millennials (also known as the Millennial Generation or Generation Y) follow in the footsteps of Generation X. Most researchers and social commentators say these were born sometime between the early 1980s and the early 2000s. My own sons might thus be Millennials (all born between 2000 and 2004) or they may be part of Generation Z (Generation Zhaman perhaps? I couldn't resist making the pun!)

As goes for all things and all people, it seems that Millennials have both a light side and shadow side as a collective. One the hand I am hearing that they have community spirit, that they are not very materialistic (some in San Francisco live in converted containers and the same phenomenon has now arrived in London). They prioritise *having a life* over *having a career*. On the other hand I hear that they show a lack of stick-ability (driving human resources departments hiring young people for mainstream companies mad) and that they just cannot take the values of people aged 25-plus very seriously.

For me this poses an interesting question: do we ever change the world or does the world change as young people with a different level of consciousness are born? And if this is so, do we perhaps only ever pave the way? That is what I like to think I am doing with this work, paving the way, offering a road map (a bit outdated perhaps, but a map nevertheless), opening sacred space and witnessing the ways of the future being born.

This is connected to my next question.

Is it the Job of Elders, Youth Leaders, Shamanic Teachers and Practitioners to Host Initiation?

In the shamanic teacher community I myself have participated in debates about this.

Some say that for our culture to be healthy and for young people, and people of all ages, to complete certain lifecycles spiritually speaking, we need to arrive at an understanding of symbolic death and rebirth or dark nights of the soul (to use a Christian phrase that may be more familiar). We need to actively teach young people how to embrace such ordeals and extract spiritual insights, wisdom and personal strength from them.

Some shamanic teachers, like me, do see it as their responsibility to provide experiences of Initiation for students. When I started my own shamanic practitioner training I experienced a life burial.[4] I was asked to dig my own grave for four days. It was the hardest physical work I have ever done. Every stone and clod of clay represented my own ego I was chipping away at. I will always be extremely grateful for this Initiation. It shaped me. It also shaped my ideas about what needs to be included in the training of a shamanic practitioner.

Another school of thought says that we do not need to initiate shamanic practitioners because if we do not, Life will. The very fact of leading a life in a human body on Earth means we move through Initiations and many small symbolic deaths ultimately prepare us for our final death and rebirth in the world of spirit. This is certainly true on one level, but it is my personal belief that human beings need human initiators who have been initiated themselves. A lineage of initiators thus passes on the gifts, wisdom and traditions of many generations. A related phenomenon I observe, working with both teenagers and adult students, is that it is often kinder to initiate people, because Elder-led Initiation builds in the support and sacred space that those being initiated need so badly. Not doing so just means that Life will come down with a sledgehammer at some later time and do the job more harshly. There is a fine line between finding strength through Initiation and being traumatised for the rest of your life.

This is one of the many reasons why the devaluing of old people in our society wounds and deprives our whole culture. When we lose our Elders and initiators, we fail to grow up fully. If a population remains stuck in immature consciousness, their leaders will make short-term decisions, decisions without long-term vision. Everyone suffers. The planet suffers. Future generations suffer and are short-changed before they are even born.

I will again mention the Seven Generations concept in this context: the Seventh Generation principle is based on the Iroquois cosmology. Every decision we make today should contribute to a sustainable world and so every decision needs to stretch Seven Generations into the future. Today this principle is often quoted, in our culture, in discussions about fossil resources, pollution, the state of drinking water, deforestation and so forth. However, the Iroquois people themselves would emphasise that this principle ought to apply to *all and any* significant decision *anyone* makes.

The Wound in Vulnerability

Earlier in this book I have spoken about vulnerability. We develop many behaviours that allow us to hide and run from vulnerability: anger, blaming, shaming, addiction, numbing, escapism… Yet, as Brene Brown's research[6] shows, vulnerability is at the heart of leading an authentic life, a life of integrity, where our sacred wholeness shines through the 'cracks' that the School of Earth Life inflicts. One of the (no longer understood in our culture) purposes of Initiation is to inflict a wound under relatively safe and controlled circumstances, so 'it is done at the right time in a human lifespan', from a great cosmic point of view, and a larger wound inflicted by Fate under far less safe circumstances is avoided. And I think many of us are familiar with C.G. Jung's famous words: 'When an inner situation is not made conscious, it appears outside as fate.'

Bly too words it perfectly:

> *Ancient initiation practices would affect all these responses (examples: paralysis, robot behaviour, seriously pursued numbness IA) since it gives a new wound, or gives a calculated wound sufficiently pungent and vivid – though minor – so that the young man remembers his inner wounds. The initiation then tells the young man what to do with his wounds, the new and the old.*

For me the concepts Initiation and vulnerability are close relatives. Initiation imposes ordeals and wounds, but ultimately those wounds are the cracks that allow our soul light to shine. Here the image of a carved Halloween pumpkin comes to my mind and I used this metaphor with my shamanic practitioner students last week. If we didn't carve the pumpkin, it would never have a face and individuality. It would never shape-shift into a lantern. It remains just a pumpkin. The inside of such a pumpkin is quite dense, with a lot of fleshy hairy material. If we try to put a candle inside such an un-carved pumpkin, any flame would perish for lack of oxygen (if we could squeeze it in at all).

Cycling back to Mircea Eliade[5] for a moment: Initiation is about arriving at *something other*, we are no longer the person we were before, we return changed, as *someone other* and our society needs to honour and celebrate this.

Another way of saying this is that all human beings need a healthy sense of self to live an independent life and make wise choices. But the human ego can get in the way, become very limiting, keeping us in the comfort zone, keeping us overly focussed on our own needs. (Writing this in September 2015, just see the responses refugees from Syria invoke in many people all over Europe. 'Please don't come and upset the established order and our comfortable lives!') There needs to be what we call in shamanism a shattering of the egoic container if we are to become containers for Divine Light to shine through. There even needs to be a shattering of the larger egoic containers of whole societies and cultures.

Societies too have both egoic structures and a Shadow. Returning to the image of the Jack-o-lantern: only a pumpkin that has been carved in many places can become a true lantern or even beacon, radiating Divine light (soul light if you like) in all directions. Only a lantern that is lit can show others the way in darkness. If a large group of people perceives egoic and self-serving thinking as 'truth', collectively we can be sucked into disputes and even wars. Staying in close communication with our spirit allies can help us avoid that sadly very common state of affairs.

Mothers and Sons, Fathers and Daughters

I am a mother of three sons and they are all shape-shifting teenagers at the time of writing. When our own sons hit certain stages of development, a spiritual intervention was called for – and the children themselves agreed. This was decided in communication *with* them, not *for* them and I have called on my colleague and friend Nick Taylor. He has taken them out on the land and done mysterious things with them. It is not for me to know exactly what happened there. The spiritual task of any teenage boy is pull away from his parents and the domain of the mother, the opposite-sex parent, in particular and stand on his own feet, surrounded by peers and other role models. Yet a shamanic teacher colleague was telling me the other day that her children have grown up absorbing everything she embodies and they now feel perfectly ready to create their own Rites of Passage. As she says: 'Ceremony is innate in us. We do not always need others to host or facilitate this for us.' This is a fair comment. The artist in me wishes to paint the full rainbow of possibilities, use all options on the great palette of creation.

It certainly raises the following question: what spiritual wisdom do the parents embody? Many parents have ditched the religion of their childhood, because it feels like a can of worms, and left their children without a spirit canoe on the tempestuous waters of life. Other parents teach and embody forms of spirituality that their children reject. I was raised as a Roman Catholic and as soon as I left home, I moved on with gratitude for what I had received but a deep inner knowing that this was not the path for me.

So what options are out there for young people? What is on offer? Can we respect them enough to give them the space to express their innate soul connection to The Divine, in whatever form that takes for them? Shamanism is not for everyone, I am well aware of that and I will never try to convert anyone. There is no True Faith (to use a catch-phrase from my own childhood).

However, to stay sane and healthy on the level of soul we all need a spiritual orientation and cosmology, in the sense of our own understanding of the cosmos or universe.

Working with teenagers I feel most at ease working with teenage girls. When people ask me to work with 14 to 16-year-old boys, I will always tell them about Nick. I ask the parent to ask the young man: 'Would they perhaps prefer to work with a person of the same sex?' I cannot claim to know the world of teenage boys, other than having a house full of them! I have no first-hand experience of being a teenage boy. To be a safe and trustworthy practitioner I need to know my limits. For me that means sometimes pointing out to people that there are other choices than working with me and promoting other people's work. No two practitioners have exactly the same strengths or blind spots. That is why community is so important. Nick takes groups of young people out on his ancestral land, in Wales. I live in London. I take people to Nunhead Cemetery if I need a wild place on my doorstep! It is lovely but not quite the same as the wilds of Wales.

Our work is spirit-led and child-led. The needs of any particular child/youngster at any given time are going to be a mandala (sacred circle) in which location, the interests and lifestyle of their parents, the kind of school they attend and the friends they have are all going to be shaping forces. The soul of the child and the spirit allies (both yours and theirs) will always tell you what needs to be done. If you can polish your mirror and push your own preconceptions out of the way, that is.

I find myself telling people proudly about the work Nick is doing in Wales and the work we have done there together. People will say: 'Oh I see, you take them camping!' And I feel a bit defensive: 'Well, hang on… Nick does a lot more than just taking them camping…' However, on reflection, maybe families that go camping naturally build in experiences of Initiation? Children climbing trees (and maybe falling out of a tree or getting stuck up there), getting lost in the forest and finding their way home again, eating mushrooms or berries in the forest and maybe learning that not all such things are edible... Maybe my mind insists on a dividing line that does not always need to be there?

I am not a camping kind of person myself, but our family has sailed all around the Caribbean and up the coast of Central America. We have certainly seen our children move through Initiations in those sailing years (swimming with sharks, being bitten by a wild dog, being pestered by monkeys on a beach in Honduras, our eldest son being taken by the current out to open sea and being rescued by a dive boat due to Divine intervention).

To cut a long story short, your own helping spirits and the children/young people themselves will tell you if 'organised Initiation' is on the menu – or not. Practitioners, always make a point of checking for Initiations that have already occurred naturally. Initiations are always on the curriculum in the School of Life.

I will finish this chapter by stating my firm opinion: the world needs the return of Elders and Initiators. And our culture pays an immense price for having made both redundant. This imbalance, this failure to grow up spiritually speaking, is affecting all sentient beings, the way we take care of our planet, the relationships between men and women – and ultimately our relationship with ourselves.

Notes

1. *Gods and Diseases, Making Sense of our Physical and Mental Wellbeing* by David Tacey, Routledge, Reprint edition, 2012
2. I thank shamanic teacher Simon Buxton for introducing me to the concepts of Crying for a Vision and Life Burial
3. *Iron John: A Book About Men* by Robert Bly, Rider, New Ed edition, 2001
4. *War and the Soul, Healing Our Nations Veterans from Post-*

traumatic Stress Disorder by Edward Tick, Quest Books, U.S., 1st Quested Ed Edition, 2005

5. *The Sacred and the Profane: The Nature of Religion* by Mircea Eliade, Harcourt Australia, Underlining/Highlighting edition, 1959
6. *Daring Greatly: How the Courage to Be Vulnerable Transforms the Way We Live, Love, Parent and Lead* by Brene Brown, Penguin Life, 2015

Section 2: Vision Quest and Wilding Young People in Nature

In many areas of the world, an animal or spirit that appears in a dream or vision quest chooses a shaman. Among my grandmother's people, the Ojibwe of Canada, for example, young children are sent into the woods to encounter spirits. They sit all alone 'singing in their hearts', humming silently to the spirits to contact them and call them forth. If they are successful, a bird, deer or other spirit may notice them and teach them natural wisdom, including sacred healing. Eventually tribal elders take these children on as apprentices and share the knowledge they themselves have gathered during a lifetime of careful observations.

Barbara Tedlock in *The Woman in the Shaman's Body*

A Night of Sitting Out

Part III of this book does not offer session plans, it aims larger. It is about taking young people away from cities and screens altogether, for extended periods of time, to allow them to reconnect to Mother Earth and to Nature herself as a great source of healing.

My colleague and close friend Nick Taylor helped me start the Time Travellers group in 2012. After we had run sessions for maybe half a year, the children themselves asked for a longer immersion. Their collective dream was to sit around a fire all night and not even go to bed! At that point Nick organised one night of sitting out at a place called Druid's Grove, just outside London. This was summer 2013. We decided to take sleeping bags, just in case. The children discovered that it takes a lot of wood-gathering to feed a fire for one whole night.

My eldest son Quinn had reached the age of 13½ and guidance received from Spirit was that he needed an experience of Initiation. This was explained to him and he agreed to 'have this great encounter with The Unknown'. It is not appropriate for a mother to initiate her teenage son, so I handed the responsibility over to Nick. What I do know is that, as it got dark, Quinn was led away from the fire and put through a series of experiences and challenges on the land.

This is something you can organise for young people in your care, in dialogue with Spirit. Maybe your group is larger and you will have several teenagers sitting out on the land at the same time. The younger people can hold space by the fire. By being part of this they will digest the fact that their moment will come. Energetically speaking a template is set, a deep inner knowing receives confirmation: *As someone holds space for me, one day I myself will hold space for others.* That was always the way in tribal or indigenous societies.

Personally, I also felt very strongly that the land needed to receive a message about this type of work returning and the spirits of the land being invaluable allies for this. Nature welcomes us home, when we return to Nature in our work.

Seidr and Uteseita

I have chosen a quote by Barbara Tedlock to go with this section, but I would just like to mention that in Norse Shamanism, or Seidr, the concept of *uteseita* (literally: sitting out) goes strong even today. Adults will sit out on the land at night to receive visions and dreams from Spirit. A family friend owns forest land in Sweden and whenever we visit him I take the opportunity to sit out in the forest by a lake. I have received some of my most profound revelations and gifts from the Norse gods there, sitting out in the snow under a starry sky, with wolves howling in the distance.

I highly recommend that anyone, no matter their age or stage in life, undertakes a vision quest or night of sitting out.

Wilding Young People: Unplugged in Nature for Longer Periods

I also want to emphasise the importance of extended retreats in Nature that reset the body clock and rhythms, overturn personal habits and activate the dark-adapted eye of the Natural Born Shaman.

Our one night of sitting out with the Time Travellers at Druid's Grove was a success. The children and families involved immediately asked for more, for a longer time out in Nature, away from the city. For my colleague Nick Taylor this coincided with his own decision to spend more time on his ancestral land in Wales, working closely with his local community there. Nick is committed to 'exploring the extraordinary', to use his own words. In the summer of 2014 he organised a wilderness retreat called Wild Ways at Tir Ysbrydol, in Wales. Tir Ysbrydol is a Mystery School visioned and created by Emma Orbach. As guardian of the land, she holds very dear the many animal, plant, tree and elemental energies that abound in this magical place. During their time in Wales the young people explored ancient woodlands, played games of hide-and-seek with the Tylwyth Teg (or fair folk), they did wood carving, they waded in rivers, they made an art installation on the beach led by artist Marc Treanor. They made their own bows and arrows. They also went foraging, tracked animals and sat around the fire telling and hearing stories. This was a chance for young people aged nine to 16 to leave behind the abundance of material possessions and confusion of wires, to plug into a very different sort of energy. Jim (James Stuart Gourlay), a survivalist who knows all about surviving in the bush taught our young people some valuable survival skills such as ways of making fire without matches.

This is all a work in progress and our visions grow as the children continue to grow and their needs and dreams change. I am aware that there are specialist organisations that offer wilderness experiences for children. They are easily found on the internet. As a city-dwelling shamanic teacher I freely admit that I am no expert on this – but passionate enough about this work to mention it in this book!

Note of Gratitude

I would like to thank Nick Taylor for being Founder Father of the Time Travellers and for helping me to get the group off the ground in 2012. Thank you for all the spirit-led visioning and pioneering work we have done together over the years! Our adventures continue!

I would also like to thank my shamanic teacher colleague John Brennan in the USA for reminding me at regular intervals that Nature herself is the Great Healing Spirit.

Section 3: Personalised Ceremonies for Times of Transition

Rites of Passage

Rites of Passage is a phrase often found in anthropology books. I like to think that awareness of the need for such rites and personalised ceremonies is now returning to our culture. I can see this might be the case just from the increasing volume of emails I myself receive about this topic. For example, I have been contacted by couples expecting a child, who do not want a regular christening or baptism but a personalised ceremony for welcoming their child in to the world. The beauty of shamanic work is that the soul of an unborn baby can be consulted and so the child can help co-create this ceremony even before birth. Some people choose to have a naming ceremony instead and they consult the soul of the child before birth about the right name. At the other end of the spectrum I have been contacted by parents of teenagers asking me to consult Spirit on issues around self-harming, bullying, self-esteem, dealing with trauma and loss etc. The possibilities are endless.

Examples of Occasions that Deserve to be Marked with a Special Ceremony

- Ceremony following a miscarriage to mark and honour the passing of a small life and giving this event a place in our hearts and life
- Ceremony following an abortion
- Naming Ceremony or ceremony to welcome a new baby and family member
- Healing Rebirth Ceremony (as described in Chapter 9)
- Menarche: Ceremony marking the first menstruation
- Initiation for boys reaching puberty (generally around the

age of 13 to 14), an Initiation that tests their mettle, gives them a vision of their calling in life and allows them to return to the community as young men ready to shoulder responsibilities in the community

- Mother Blessing for a pregnant woman
- Blessing for blending families
- Marriage. One thing that does remain in our culture is hen nights and stag nights, but they are often more raucous than spiritually uplifting!
- Pagans already celebrate hand-fasting rites
- Marrying yourself
- Divorce: a respectful rite to honour what was, express gratitude for all the blessings and good things that came out of this partnership, cutting cords to what serves no more and telling the world that this partnership served its time and has now been dissolved
- Rites for Crowning the Crone: so older women become esteemed Elders of the community, true Wise Women, who stay involved with younger generations, imparting knowledge, wisdom and traditions
- Death and ceremonies preparing for the final transition: saying goodbye to loved ones, tying up any unfinished business, being involved in the planning of your own funeral or memorial service, celebrating a human life, the gifts this person bestowed. And them still being around to enjoy this! Obviously this only works if there is notice or warning that death is on the horizon.

We can be as creative as we like. The possibilities are endless!

Blessing for Blending Families

We can do ceremonies and draw down blessings for blending families, where two people, both with children from previous partnerships, come together and children acquire a new set of siblings overnight.

Marrying Yourself

In my shamanic healing work I have performed ceremonies where people married themselves because they had realised that to function fully in the world, they needed to love and cherish themselves first of all. I have also seen people do this all by themselves: buying a wedding ring and making a sacred commitment to themself. Only if we love and cherish ourselves, can we truly love and cherish others.

Miscarriage

One very sore point in our society, as discussed in Chapter 5, is when a miscarriage occurs and the soul of a child returns to the spirit world. Our society has no way of marking this occasion. Often there is awkwardness as well. What do you say when you next meet the person? It is appropriate to say something? Is it better to stay quiet?

The parents could consider doing a small ceremony with friends or family to honour the passing of that child. They could then also indicate to those around them if they want others to refer to this child in the future or if they wish to close a door and make this a very private life event. I know women who have given a name to a child lost in early pregnancy and still refer to those spirit children fondly. They feel they receive an occasional visit from a spirit child checking in with the family. On a similar note I have advised women who were about to have a termination on performing a small ceremony to honour the life that passed through them and to say goodbye. This serves the soul of the baby as much as the souls of the parents.

Menarche/First Menstruation

Menarche is the occasion where a girl menstruates for the first time. In our culture this is generally around the age of 12 to 13.

The guidance from Spirit I myself received about this is that it is beautiful to give some of that first blood back to the land, as a Daughter of the Earth. I do not have a daughter myself, but I have heard of families where women keep a box with stories and sacred objects that is passed on to the next young generation.

Important elements are:

- Making a girl feel part of larger community of women so she doesn't feel alone
- Celebrating this and not going with the current trend of seeing menstruation as 'the curse' or something shameful

Anita Diamant's book *The Red Tent*[1] is a helpful text here. It is a novel, but I know many women have found inspiration in it.

Usually only women are present for this. The younger girls get to observe and look forward to their own Big Day. There is no prescription or set ritual for this. Ask around. Are there family traditions around this? Did your mother/aunts/sisters do anything for you? Did that feel positive? Then link back to that and preserve this as family tradition for future generations. Talk to grandmothers and elderly aunts if you can. Often things skip one generation because one generation comes under cultural pressure or tries to move with the times. So dig a little deeper and see if there are any threads you can pull up from Beyond the Mists of Time! When I started my period (at a younger age than most of my contemporaries, I think I was about 11) there was no celebration. My dad did say something like: 'Your mum tells me that you are a woman now' – which is something, I suppose... I was given a big pack of sanitary bandages. Then I was told off for disposing of those in the regular bathroom bin. I had two younger brothers who might, apparently, be traumatised by seeing bloody bandages appear in the bin. After that I learned to wrap those bandages until they looked pristinely white and inoffensive. I remember feeling resentful about being asked to menstruate secretly, shielding my brothers from the facts of life. After all I was not shielded from their stinky football socks and other messes in the bathroom!

Ceremony 1: Ceremony after a Miscarriage: Honouring a Small Life that Passed Through Us

Undertake a shamanic journey to the soul of the baby and explain that you want to say goodbye properly and ceremonially. If you cannot journey yourself, or if you feel too emotional to do this yourself, request help from an experienced shamanic practitioner.

In that soul-to-soul conversation, address questions like: why did the soul return? (Some souls only wish to taste life briefly before moving on again).

Ask:

Is there any unfinished business?
Is there any information to be passed between parents and child?

Then put together the wishes of child and mother or both parents and perform a small ceremony. For instance, step out in your own garden or go to another secluded place in nature, speak the words you need to speak ('thank you for passing through', 'thank you for touching our lives, you have a place in our hearts, we will always remember you') and then symbolically release the soul of the baby back to the Universe and the great Guardian Spirits of Unborn Children in the Other World.

This could be done by lighting a sparkler or by casting a handful of rose petals in the air, or anything you are guided to do. If you do this sincerely, with an open heart, Nature will align with you and send you confirmation, for example a bird flying off, a cloud with a very specific shape passing over, the sighting of a special animal playing their part perfectly and so forth.

When it is done, it is done. It is time to give this a place in your heart and move on.

Ceremony 2: Ceremony after an Abortion

This ceremony is similar to the one I just described (please read the previous ceremony), but the woman or couple concerned will have had their reasons for making this decision.

Thank this human soul for passing through you and touching your life. Explain to the small soul why you made this decision and how it made you feel sad (assuming this is so, always be sincere).

Some people I know have added words along the lines of: 'Now is not the time for you to be born because I am not able to care for you the way you deserve but I invite you to return at a later time in my own life.'

If there were medical reasons for the abortion, explain this.

Perform this ceremony outside – in a garden, countryside, woodland for example – with an open heart and pay attention to the coincidences, synchronicities, signs from Nature. Generally you will find that you receive confirmation in some way or form that the human soul has received your message and now feels free to move on, freeing you to carry on with your own life.

A ceremony like this can have a very freeing effect: unfinished business is taken care of and healing words of release are spoken, a great burden lifts. Sadness is likely to remain for some time. You will need to grieve this event in the same way as other losses (such as the death of a loved one) require grief work.

Ceremony 3: Naming Ceremony for a New Baby

Make a shamanic journey to the soul of the baby during pregnancy. Alternatively do this a meditation on the same questions. You can ask a shamanic practitioner to do this for you, but you could also attend an introduction class in shamanic journeying and learn how to do this yourself

Journey Intention 1

To undertake a shamanic journey to meet the soul of this baby, ask for guidance in choosing the right name for this child.

Journey Intention 2

Undertake another journey and ask the soul of the baby what naming ceremony it would like. In an ideal world both mother and father would journey and receive complementary information.

Then start putting the ceremony together. Consider:

- Location
- Who is present? (Any godparents or other special people who promise to be involved in the life of the baby)
- What to bring?
- Food/drink/celebration/picnic afterwards
- Flowers
- Ceremonial items
- A rattle, drum or musical instrument(s)
- Any ceremonial words to be spoken?
- Rehearsals

Organise it and enjoy it!

Take some photographs or make a small film to show the child once he/she is older.

I vividly remember one couple in my practice receiving guidance to stand on a hilltop here in the UK just before sunrise and name the child as the sun rose over the horizon and another day started.

The possibilities are endless. No two ceremonies are the same.

Ceremony 4: Rebirth

You will find a Healing Rebirth Ceremony is described in Chapter 9.

Ceremony 5: Menarche: Ceremony Marking the First Menstruation

Today menstruation seems to happen earlier and earlier for large numbers of girls. Some people think this is related to the hormones and toxins in our food.

A young woman comes of age. She is no longer a child because she has (biologically speaking, not necessarily emotionally or spiritually speaking) reached the age where she becomes physically able to give birth herself.

I just did some research and discovered that girls usually start to move through puberty somewhere between the ages of eight and 13. Their bodies change. Their minds and interests change too. Hormones kick in and they start to develop breasts.

What would have been of great help to me and what I have observed close friends do for their daughters is a ceremony along the following lines.

Keep a special ceremonial box where all women in the family contribute something: a story, an object, a song, a poem etc. Those objects can be taken out and used/read during the ceremony.

In close discussion with the young woman concerned, put together a ceremony that is partly a rite of passage and partly a super fun party. Invite family and the girl's friends, but perhaps make this an all-girl or all-women event.

Explain that as well as a human mother we all have another mother too and that is Mother Earth. The physical components for our body all come from Mother Earth.

At this time it is a beautiful gesture to give something back to the Ultimate Mother of all physical life forms: pour a small amount of menstrual blood out on the land, if the girl is OK with this. Make the connection to Mother Earth. Say thank you for this human body, for the great gift of a life on Earth.

You could choose to talk a bit about women's mysteries and how there has always been a feminine path in traditional societies where girls learned about healing, delivering babies and preparing the dead for burial or cremation. Judge how much the girl is ready for, which will depend on the upbringing she had and the significant women in her life.

Pay attention to the following things:

- Location/venue? Indoors/outdoors? (Garden, countryside, woodland, beach)
- Who is invited? Girls and women only or boys too?
- Food and treats
- Consider making a fire and telling stories around a fire. All young people I know love this!
- Build great memories for all!

Afterwards, in the weeks or months that follow, ask the girl if she is now willing to write something for the ceremonial box for her sisters/cousins or other girls in the family to open and find when their day comes.

Ceremony 6: Boys Reaching Puberty

As a mother of three boys I have chosen do things differently, as described in the previous chapters about Initiation and Wilding Children.

Ceremony 7: Mother Blessing for a Pregnant Woman

The Mother Blessing is an old and beautiful Navajo tradition. My colleague and close friend Sony Baron performed one on the week of writing this and I have asked her to describe it. She has given permission for me to share but says any and all credit needs to go to the Navajo People, not to her!

> *Mother Blessing is a tradition inspired by the Navajo ceremony called The Blessing Way. I don't know much about how the Navajo did it, but the focus is on the mother rather than the baby. It is to*

prepare the mother for the journey of giving birth and mothering. It is a ceremony for women only.

We created an altar with a candle, and flowers around the candle placed in a circle. We each brought a flower for the altar (I blessed mine).

We each introduced ourselves very much in the native tradition of, 'My name is... I am the daughter of...and the granddaughter of...' We mentioned only the women's names (mother, grandmother).

The mother of the woman (soon to be grandmother!) spoke about her giving birth to the expectant mom and her experience and significant stages in her daughter's life. Her sister spoke, and then each one of us spoke of her strengths and attributes and our relationship to her as her supporting community of friends.

Those who already have children shared wisdom.

We each wrote a quality of the mother-to-be on a river stone for the altar. Each of those qualities will help her in her mothering.

We each brought her a card with personalised message, and we also wrote a short poem or message in a special 'Mother' book.

Two women read out short poems.

There was food to share of course!

I brought a cake that said 'Blessings to Mother', that was added to the altar at the end of the ceremony, and we all shared the cake as a conclusion.

That's about it. It was moving and beautiful, and I can't think of a nicer way to show love and community spirit for the mother-to-be!

Ceremony 8: Blessing Ceremony for Blending Families

When two families come together (maybe because two people who both have children from previous relationships decide to share a house and their lives), I highly recommend asking a shamanic practitioner to do some work on this for you.

Check for unresolved issues and any cords that need cutting. Going into a new relationship without fully releasing the partners that came before stores up serious trouble and turbulence for the future.

Check on ancestral issues as well. What is present on both sides and how can this be healed and/or transmuted to give this new couple a fresh start in life?

Spiritually speaking run a check on all children involved in this. Is there anything that needs completing, explaining or resolving for them to arrive at a positive attitude regarding this new partnership of a parent?

When all of those things have been addressed I would organise a brief but joyful ceremony.

Journey on this yourself, or the shamanic practitioner can do this.

Think about how to symbolise the coming together.

How will you draw down blessings on this new partnership? Acknowledge that any children of this couple have also been presented with a new alliance and new partnerships.

You could use words like: 'I honour the partner I had before and the children we have together, but I choose you now.'

Some suggestions:

- Symbolically pull stardust down from the night sky
- Bless rose petals and throw them over the couple

Anything sincere goes. You may then want to cut a cake and all eat it together to celebrate. Or have a great party where everyone is invited to join in celebrating your new partnership.

Ceremony 9: Marriage or Hand-fasting

This is one ceremony our society does provide a script for and Pagans already celebrate hand-fasting rites.

Ceremony 10: Ceremony for Marrying Yourself

It has been said that we can love others only as much as we love ourselves. It can also been said that before we can commit to someone else, we first need to make a wholehearted and sacred commitment to ourselves.

In healing sessions there have been occasions where I was told, in no uncertain terms, that this person needs to marry themselves and make a sacred vow to be in loving relationship with themselves. So I have found a ring, or asked them to bring a ring, and researched the wedding vows as used in the Anglican Church here in the UK (the church where I married myself 20 year ago). Sometimes people have brought a friend for moral and spiritual support and the friend has played his or her role to perfection. (Anyone who attends a shamanic healing session with me is put to work!)

So here is a very basic script for marriage to yourself as a healing ceremony:

- Prepare the room
- Think about fresh flowers, maybe even a cake, other personal touches that personalise the space for this particular person. This is their Big Day!
- Are there any words that the bride or groom need to speak or read out during the ceremony? (Consult spirit about this!)
- Have a ring ready
- Agree on what vows to speak and personalise/amend them if required

Here is the Church of England version:

Church Wedding Vows from The 2001 Marriage Service[2]

I, <Groom's name>, take you, <Bride's name> , to be my wife/husband.
To have and to hold from this day forward; for better, for worse, for richer, for poorer, in sickness and in health, to

love and to cherish, till death us do part, according to God's holy law.
In the presence of God I make this vow.

OR

I, <Groom's name>, take thee, <Bride's name>, to my wedded wife.
To have and to hold from this day forward; for better for worse,
for richer for poorer, in sickness and in health.

Groom: To love and to cherish, till Death us do part.
Bride: To love, cherish, and obey, till Death us do part.

According to God's holy ordinance, and thereto I plight thee my troth.

By means of an example, one version I have arrived at ran like this:

I (person's name) take myself (repeat person's name) to be my wife/husband (as appropriate),
To have and to hold from this day forward; for better, for worse,
for richer, for poorer, in sickness and in health,
to love and to cherish, till death us do part, according to the sacred law of Spirit.
In the presence of Great Spirit I make this vow.

Choose your words to reflect the spiritual orientation of the person. Some are happy with God while others prefer Goddess, Great Spirit, Universal Love, Buddha Mind…and so forth.

As the ceremonialist, I have been known to give people the ring and then pass them a mirror saying 'you may now kiss the bride!' (And sometimes people have kissed their own hand!)

I have also made sure to send a bouquet of flowers home with the person.

Be as creative as you like! There are no limits! Witnesses and props all help cement the message that a sacred act occurred and was witnessed. This means that things are going to be different from this point onwards.

The person is now in a sacred committed relationship with themselves!

Ceremony 11: Marking a Divorce

Not everyone will be up for doing this publically, but it is a very good idea to perform a ritual by yourself or assisted by a shamanic practitioner to:

- Deal with unfinished business
- Cut cords and connections to the family karma and issues of the family you are leaving. Respectfully hand it back to them, explain to the family ancestors that the time has come for you to make a new start.
- If there are children involved, book an ancestral healing session to clear ancestral imprints and spare them unnecessary burdens
- Deal with memories and energetic patterns that could affect your new relationship
- Do forgiveness and transfiguration work on this to create the best possible constellation for a fresh start

Basically set right anything that needs tending to and create space in your life for new things and new people to come in.

Formulate a strong vision and set strong healthy intentions around what is going to come in and what you are no longer willing to let in or tolerate.

Then let go (maybe blow bubbles to release the old) and walk through a symbolic doorway.

Ceremony 12: Rites for Crowning the Crone

This ceremony allows older women to step into the role of Wise Women and Elders of the Community as discussed in previous chapters of this book.

For inspiration you may want to look at the website of the Council of Thirteen Indigenous Grandmothers.[3]

I can't really provide a script for a ceremony like this. However, I can give some guidelines:

- This needs to be done by a community on behalf of members of that community
- Honouring the Ancestors and Wise Ones in Spirit is an important part of this
- Working closely with the Spirits of the Land is another crucial element of this
- Weaving history and future together is important. Do your research: what has been done locally? What did older generations, or other people who lived on the land where you live now, do to honour and inaugurate their Elders in some way? Link back to this, if possible, and derive inspiration from this.
- As a community what do you need from your Elders?
- Elders, what you willing and able to provide?
- What support do the Elders need from the larger community to take on this most sacred task?

Then organise this event the same way you would organise an important wedding or harvest festival or other ceremonial event.

Pay attention to the location/venue, who is invited, who carries out a special task, what ceremonial objects are involved, food and drink and so forth.

Ceremony 13: Preparing for Death and the Final Transition

For many people this will be a very private event.

If you receive advance warning of death (say because you are diagnosed with a terminal illness) it could be said that you are granted the gift of a window of time to put your affairs in order.

During this process, here are some issues you may want to look at:

- Unfinished business: is there any forgiveness work to be done?
- Are there amends to be made?
- Attempts at reconciliation?
- Words that need to be spoken before going?

Make a (private!) list of people you need to contact, or a trusted person will be asked to contact on your behalf, and prepare the message you wish to send.

You may want to have a quick look at Session Plan 30 on Hawaiian H'oponopono at this point.

Thank you (for being in my life, for the good moments we shared, for the things you taught me etc.)

Remember we all have informal human teachers who show us how to do things, and how NOT to do things. Both forms of teaching tend to be powerful!

I am sorry! (I am genuinely sorry for my part in this and for the fact that difficult things happened between us etc.)

Please forgive me (For my part in this, even for the harmful things I said or did that I am not even aware of!)

Perhaps:

I would like to see you one more time before I die (if time, health and energy levels permit).

And so forth.

Practical Considerations

Have you made your will and appointed an executor? Have you discussed with family what is to happen with houses/possessions/land/animals and so forth?

Are there any projects that need completing? For example, do you need to appoint someone to finish writing a book, or finish composing a piece of music you have started? Or someone to be the guardian for a community garden or a special piece of land close to your heart?

Plan your own funeral or memorial service – this is the only way your wishes are going to be honoured.

As a final but important note on forgiveness work: *asking for forgiveness is not always the right course of action. If the other person is not open to this, or if they have moved on and settled with a new partner, the 'blast from the past' could actually do more harm than good. Tread with care and if necessary work closely with a shamanic practitioner on this, always seeking and following spirit guidance.*

Transition Preparation

Most importantly I would work with a shamanic practitioner on preparing for the great transition. There are ways of accessing the spirit world and connecting to what awaits you there.

In my experience it helps greatly not to feel like you are 'falling into a black hole' so to speak. You may remember me describing earlier in this book how my middle son remembers where he was before he was born and how he visits this place in his dreams and looks after it, so it will be waiting for him the day he dies.

It is also my experience that as you start moving closer to

death, loved ones on the other side start appearing to welcome you. The Veil between Worlds starts thinning and for some time you may be walking between worlds like a shaman. And a shaman (shamanic practitioner) can walk with you at this point.

In the next (and final) section I describe a NDE (Near Death Experience) I had myself in 2012.

Notes

1. *The Red Tent* by Anita Diamant, Pan, Reprints Edition, 2002
2. Taken from http://www.weddingsday.co.uk/church-wedding-vows/
3. http://www.grandmotherscouncil.org/

Note of gratitude for the Mother Blessing to Sony Baron MA, MA, RCC, Baron Counselling Teaching Winds in Victoria, Canada

Section 4: Ourobouros: The Serpent Bites Her Own Tail

Ourobouros

We have come full circle. All that remains for me to do is to sum up and sketch some things I see shaping up in the future.

This book is about a spiritual toolkit for young people. It addresses the innate need of all human beings to have a vital lifeline to Spirit, no matter whatever external expression that lifeline takes.

I am grateful to be alive at this time in world history because life is exciting and full of possibilities unheard of just a few decades ago. My intention is to lead my own life well and by this I mean leading a life that expresses my unique talents in the world. A life in which I accomplish what I envisioned when I asked to be born on Earth this time.

Then my sacred task will be to prepare for my own death so hopefully it will be a good death (in the shamanic sense), which teaches my children and students about death. Death is a great ally, as even the Time Travellers have discovered over the years. It remains one of our favourite sessions.

Near Death Experience (NDE)

In the year 2012 I had a Near Death Experience (NDE) on an airplane from London to New York City. Exactly mid-Atlantic Ocean I keeled over (waiting for a bathroom to be free) and lost consciousness. The flight crew eventually managed to bring me back, guided by a medical doctor in NYC.

While I was 'gone', I was taken to the most beautiful place I have ever been to, where everything was made of light and there was no pain, just unconditional love and beauty. It was a place where everything exists in its divine perfection and radiance. I did not want to return. In fact I had decided to stay, until I remembered I had young children waiting for me on Earth. The spirits said: 'This time we will give you the choice: you can return, or you can stay. But next time you will not have that choice. We will come and take you home.'

I returned. The flight crew was relieved! They had paramedics and officers of the New York Police Department waiting for me as I was carried off the plane.

For about three or four months, I felt gutted that I had decided to leave that blissful place. While my children were in school I allowed myself half an hour at lunchtime to cry and grieve over the fact that I was not dead. But it was the right decision, there is much to do before I make my final exit. Most importantly there is parenting to be done.

The Shape of Things to Come

Based on four years of intense shamanic work with children, I will end with a shamanic weather forecast.

Shamanic Weather Forecast

The Future is something all of us co-create through our thoughts, actions, inter-actions with others, dreams and decisions. The future is what we make it, not some inevitable force that blindly washes over us. It is imperative that we all take our own piece of responsibility and accountability in this process.

I see the young people of the future reclaiming the art of being in constant communication with Spirit. I don't think they will be using blankets, cushions and drums to journey core-shamanism style, but they will sharpen their intuition and connect with Spirit in all life forms and all its manifestations. They will do everything much faster than we do things now.

Children who spend time in Nature and are at one with Nature grow into adults who value Nature and protect Nature, who will take their own children out in Nature.

Children who communicate with animals will not tolerate

animal abuse as adults or choose to eat meat sourced from ill-treated animals. I have visions of young people working towards dissolving the separation and hierarchy that exists between humans and animals today, between what we consider animate and inanimate beings. That work of dismantling the biblical concept that God gave humanity dominion over animals has already started in my Time Travellers group. I even hope and pray that our children, once they grow up, will know to make amends to all animal species that have been abused and wounded by human beings over many centuries.

I think that young people will lead far more multi-dimensional lives than we adults do today (even if we think we are *with it*). The virtual world they inhabit so effortlessly has already prepared them for this. I think that they will connect with their selves outside space and time and truly explore the cosmos. The words imagination and myth will take on completely new meanings.

One informed guess is that they will revive the ancient art of time travel but, unlike us, they will know to leave their bodies behind as they travel, to save on fossil fuel consumption and air miles. Time travel done the shamanic way carries no carbon footprint!

Children in whom the Natural Born Shaman goes strong will encourage and support the Natural Born Shaman in all children and their own children one day. Collectively they will reclaim magic and healing as our birthright.

Children in whom the Natural Born Shaman lives on will reclaim the human right to live an unique sacred dream, rather than living out a life circumscribed by expectations and parameters set by our society, or older generations (e.g. us!)

I hope that young people will solve the conundrum of 'waging war on war' and lead all of us out of polarised thinking into holistic multi-dimensional thinking where difference is celebrated and the human ego is kept in check. I trust that they will learn to embody the archetype of the spiritual warrior: standing up for the vulnerable, the rain forests, endangered animals, fragile eco-systems, political prisoners and so forth.

One Time Travellers session in early 2016 is set to be titled 'Back to Atlantis'. Many people today say that Atlantis is a myth or a figment of our imagination. However, Plato said that a continent called Atlantis used to exist, near the Strait of Gibraltar, and that an earthquake swept it to the bottom of the sea after the people of Atlantis became greedy, decadent and corrupt. They over-reached themselves by waging war on Greece and that was the beginning of the end. Whatever you personally believe about the existence of Atlantis, this can be read as a cautionary tale for our times. The Time Travellers will undertake a shamanic journey and I am very curious to hear what they report. The story of Atlantis is explored in a small film I made in 2015, called The White Land Beneath The Bear.[1]

Our worldview shape-shifts as we grow older. Shamanism shape-shifts too. In world history it has never been a unified practice and it is unlikely to become that in the future. This book is a snapshot taken at a specific point on the time-space continuum. I know that today's young people will become older people. They will be the Earth Keepers and shapers of spiritual traditions. They may create spiritual traditions beyond our comprehension just now. I know they will and I look forward to this. I will observe this from this world for as long as I can and then continue to observe from my home in the spirit world once I die!

This book is not a definite take on anything. It is a very personal account of a great Labour of Love! I hope some it is helpful for others

Imelda Almqvist,
January 2016

Notes

1. The White Land Beneath The Bear: www.youtube.com/watch?v=auJNPF8Bruc

Open Letter to Paediatricians

Dear Paediatrician,

This is an open letter from a shamanic practitioner, painter and teacher who receives correspondence from all over the world about challenged and misunderstood children.

The occasions when my husband and I have consulted a paediatrician about our own three children have given me insights into your world and your work. I am very grateful that talented medical doctors choose this specialism, as our children are very literally our future.

On a professional level I can only say that parenting my own three children has changed me and my outlook on life. Their births and innate spirituality and wisdom have challenged every belief I hold dear.

What I have discovered and observed closely along this journey is that there is a growing group of children that defies labels and diagnoses. Tribal or indigenous (first nations) peoples have always known this. These special children were seen as having the energy signature of a shaman. At an early age they were spotted and given support and training in developing their abilities. It was understood that some of those children would one day become the spiritual healers and leaders of their communities.

Not infrequently they had disabilities or behaved 'oddly' compared to their peers. This is because they are plugged into another world, the spirit world. They talk to animals, nature spirits and invisible spirit helpers. They intuitively know where other people hold pain in their bodies.

When our society prioritised the 'linear scientific' way of thinking over the poetic/intuitive/psychic mode (that inspired such wonderful art and music and mythology in all cultures over many centuries) we lost some precious things as a collective.

This growing group of gifted individuals holds the potential to restore our collective ability to live our lives in more holistic, creative and meaningful ways. However, as we have no diagnosis for such children and no structures in our society to help them develop their gifts, often their talents go wasted (undiscovered) or seek expression in negative ways (through addiction, mental health issues or even aggression).

The verb diagnose is derived from classical Greek and literally means 'to know thoroughly' to 'to learn through taking apart'.

This open letter is to urge you to re-discover this ancient phenomenon, that of Natural Born Shamans. Of children born to be the shamans, the healers, seers and visionaries for their communities. I invite you to read this book and think of all children you have ever met, personally or professionally. Do some of them fit the patterns and profile I am describing here? If they did, it is my greatest hope that you will rethink and adapt existing labels to reclaim this ancient wisdom.

In tribal societies shamans are awarded immense respect. The title 'shaman' is never bestowed lightly. In Western society we call these people 'shamanic practitioners' to honour the great indigenous shamans who face great trials and tribulations as they embrace their calling.

I urge you to focus on the unique gifts and perspectives these children are attempting to bring to a world that faces many grave global problems such as pollution, global warming, weapons of mass destruction and overpopulation – to mention but a few.

I urge you to call for structures that reassure and support the parents and families of such children.

The last thing I want to say, as a shamanic practitioner, is that all children alive have a natural born shaman somewhere within them. Even if it was only a magical phase they passed through briefly. And all of us adults were children once. These unique gifts are our birth right and serve an important function in a spiritually healthy collective.

Children whose innate spirituality is fed make healthy choices that honour Life and all sentient beings.

Yours sincerely,
Imelda Almqvist,
January 2016
Shamanic practitioner, painter and teacher
London, UK

Acknowledgments

I would like to thank all shamanic teachers I have had the privilege of training with and learning from both formally and more informally: Simon Buxton, Naomi Lewis, Kate Shela, Betsy Bergstrom, Anna Kjellin, Chetna Lawless, Ruth Aber, Karmit Evenzur, Carol Day, Sony Baron and last but not least Sandra Ingerman.

Thank you Jill Hunter for joining my shamanic practice and sharing the caseload, for being my assistant teacher on many courses I teach and for teaching the Time Travellers about animal healing work. Nick Taylor for being the founder father of the Time Travellers group and for anchoring the energy of the healthy sacred masculine in a group with so many boys! Sony Baron for the steady supply of inspiration and peer supervision. I would also like to thank Sony Baron and David Crumpton for offering me an artist's residency at Bear Hollow on Vancouver Island when I badly needed to leave London for a while and spend time in a place where the forest meets the sea! Carol Day, you never fail to inspire me – thank you for being my roomie in Santa Fe. Those were some of the best shamanic seminars I ever attended! Thank you Judith Bogner for being my shaman sister on many adventures and for teaching the Time Travellers about public speaking, conflict resolution and exploring media violence. Thank you Simon Cook for being a wonderful Fire Keeper for the Time Travellers and for sharing your pyrography skills with the kids. Thank you Karmit Evenzur for widening my windows of perception and teaching me so much about geomancy and shamanic work with the land. Janet Gale, my polar bear sister: thank you for the encouragement and help with editing! I would like to thank Sandra Ingerman for writing the foreword for this book, for her unstinting support and encouragement as I stepped ever deeper onto the path of teaching shamanism. I would also like to thank Sandra Ingerman's network of the global shamanic teachers for all the inspiration, feedback and wonderful support over the years. Thank you for encouraging me to find my writer's voice! Todd Wiggins, thank you for invaluable advice on British versus American spellings and idioms for a first time author. I can't thank Hannah Beadman enough for her brilliance and generosity in making a beautiful film about the 'Time Travellers and a Shamanic Toolkit for Bullying'. I would also like to thank all the authors, dead or alive, of the countless life-changing books I have read in my 48 years on this planet. My house is a library in honour to all of you! And I thank the ancestors on both sides for passing on some cool genes and talents. I honour you by seeking full expression of those gifts!

Most of I all I thank Quinn, Elliott and Brendan for putting up with a full time weird mother! (I know that other young people ask you on occasion if your mum keeps her broomstick by the door. Yes she does!) Ulric Almqvist for giving me the space to find my spiritual feet and teach so many courses, often in our family home and garden.

For being my greatest shamanic teachers ever I thank the Time Travellers of Past, Present and Future! Quinn, Elliott, Brendan, Louis, Molly, Bert, Ali, Ruby, Vasco, Thibault, Margot, Roxanne, Sam, Sam, Janek, Wojtek and others.

From Imelda Almqvist

Thank you for purchasing *Natural Born Shamans: A Spiritual Toolkit for Life!*

I hope that you found the information you were looking for and that this book inspired you, just as working with children never fails to revitalise and inspire me.

I invite you to post your review of this book at Amazon, thank you!

If you would like to connect with other books that I have in the pipeline, please visit my website and request to be added to my mailing list. You will receive updates and some soul food from me about eight times a year.

Please note that by December 2016 you will find a listing on my website of shamanic practitioners trained by me personally. I also intend to offer specialist seminars open to all shamanic practitioners in working with children and teenagers as the need for this specialism has become very clear while writing this book.

I always love hearing from and connecting with colleagues and people doing innovative healing work with children in other ways. I invite you to contact me and to join our Alliance for Childhood project Inspiring Youth – Feeding Spirit, Finding Self to connect with people who are equally passionate about the spiritual needs of young people.

Thank you for reading this book and reaching out to young people!

Imelda Almqvist,

January 2016

www.shaman-healer-painter.co.uk

www.imelda-almqvist-art.com

https://imeldaalmqvist.wordpress.com/

www.facebook.com/groups/InspiringYouthAfC/?fref=ts

Contact Details and Other Creations from this Author

You can contact me through either of my websites:
www.imelda-almqvist-art.com
www.shaman-healer-painter.co.uk
or through Wordpress:
https://imeldaalmqvist.wordpress.com/
Make sure you watch Hannah Beadman's brilliant film about the Time Travellers:
https://vimeo.com/138086974
To hear me speak about my work: Life Force TV interview: Barbara Grammeniati interviews Imelda Almqvist about Shamanism, Sacred Art and Soul Retrieval
www.youtube.com/watch?v=kZb8ijDBdZw
The book about shamanism my son Brendan wrote when he was nine years old is titled *The Love Hall, Brendan's Travel Guide to the Best Places in the Spirit World* and is available through
www.shaman-healer-painter.co.uk
You can also find some small films I made myself on Youtube, here are links for the six most popular ones:
Spirit Children: www.youtube.com/watch?v=GpSLQLHN2B4
Seal Mother of Souls:
www.youtube.com/watch?v=5t5VP0Me24Q
Gnosis of the Earth (Rock Art Seminar in Andalucia):
www.youtube.com/watch?v=wz9n5SwcjsI
The White Land Beneath The Bear:
www.youtube.com/watch?v=auJNPF8Bruc
Raven Man and Killer Whale Woman:
www.youtube.com/watch?v=mf39UHN2-mU
Seven Desert Maidens:
www.youtube.com/watch?v=NlPVEVdw5d0

MOON BOOKS

Moon Books invites you to begin or deepen your encounter with Paganism, in all its rich, creative, flourishing forms.

9781785353680.